5110

GOVERNMENTALITY

GOVERNMENTALITY

Power and Rule in
Modern Society

Mitchell Dean

SAGE Publications
London • Thousand Oaks • New Delhi

First published 1999
Reprinted 2001

 SAGE Publications Ltd
6 Bonhill Street
London EC2A 4PU

SAGE Publications Inc
2455 Teller Road
Thousand Oaks, California 91320

SAGE Publications India Pvt Ltd
32, M-Block Market
Greater Kailash – I
New Delhi 110 048

British Library Cataloguing in Publication data

A catalogue record for this book is
available from the British Library

ISBN 0 8039 7588 0
ISBN 0 8039 7589 9 (pbk)

Library of Congress catalog record available

Typeset by M Rules
Printed in Great Britain by Biddles Ltd, *www.biddles.co.uk*

CONTENTS

Acknowledgements   vii
Introduction   1

1   **Basic Concepts and Themes**   9
    Government and governmentality
    An analytics of government
    Analysing regimes of government

2   **Genealogy and Governmentality**   40
    Genealogy and government
    Liberalism, critique and 'the social'
    Neo-liberalism and Foucault

3   **Dependency and Empowerment: Two Case Studies**   60
    Dependency
    Empowerment
    Conclusion

4   **Pastoral Power, Police and Reason of State**   73
    Pastoral power
    Reason of state and police
    Conclusion

5   **Bio-Politics and Sovereignty**   98
    Bio-politics
    Sovereignty and the governmentalization of the state

6 Liberalism   113
Economy
Security
Law and norm
Society and social government

7 Authoritarian Governmentality   131
The illiberality of liberal government
Bio-politics, race and non-liberal rule

8 Neo-Liberalism and Advanced Liberal Government   149
Society, freedom and reform
Advanced liberal government
A post-welfarist regime of the social

9 Risk and Reflexive Government   176
Two approaches to risk
Risk and reflexive modernization
Insurance and government
Reflexive government

Conclusion: 'Not Bad . . .but Dangerous'   198

Glossary   209
References   213
Index   215

ACKNOWLEDGEMENTS

This book began life as a series of lectures delivered at Macquarie University during the years 1994–6. Its first audience was my third-year undergraduate and master's students in those years. I thank them for perceptive engagement and criticism. It has taken somewhat longer to transform these lectures into a book than I had originally foreseen. I offer my sincere gratitude to my publisher and editor for their patience and support during this time. A number of people have contributed to the book in different ways by encouragement, critical discussion, and the reading of parts or all of the manuscript. James Tully commented on an early draft of the Introduction and five chapters of this book and offered assistance when it was much needed. David Owen, Giovanna Procacci and Mariana Valverde read and critically commented on the penultimate version of the whole book. Without their support and input, I doubt I would have had the confidence to finalize this work. The manuscript was moved considerably towards completion by a Visiting Fellowship at the Department of Political Science, Research School of Social Sciences, during the spring semester at the Australian National University in 1997. My warm appreciation goes to Barry Hindess for making that visit possible and to all members of his department for making my time there memorable and valuable. I must also pay tribute to Niamh Stephenson for her subediting work on early drafts of many of the chapters. Finally, I cannot neglect to mention the tolerance and patience shown to me by Sharon Gaby during the finalization of the manuscript, and her willingness, beyond the duty of any 'significant other', to assist with the labours of its preparation.

This book comprises substantially unpublished material. All of the Introduction and Conclusion, the Glossary, Chapters 1, 2, 3, 5, 6 and 7, and most of Chapter 4 have been previously unpublished. However, the section in Chapter 4 on 'Pastoral power' draws upon a 1994 paper, 'The genealogy of the gift in Antiquity', published in the *Australian Journal of Anthropology* 5 (3): 320–9. The second half of Chapter 8 draws upon 'Sociology after society' in David Owen (ed.), *Sociology after Postmodernism*, London: Sage, 1997. A version of Chapter 9 was published in 1998 in English in the journal *Soziale Welt: Zeitschrift für sozialwissenschaftliche Forschung und Praxis* 49: 25–42.

INTRODUCTION

One of the more startling developments in the social and political sciences in recent years has been the rethinking of the notion of government that followed a lecture delivered by Michel Foucault, 'Governmentality'. The lecture was delivered at the Collège de France in February 1978, and, via a somewhat circuitous route, was first published in the independent English journal *Ideology and Consciousness* (or *I&C*) in 1979.[1] The influence of this English translation seems to have been narrow but deep although, for quite a long time, it was rarely visible in published forms. By the early 1990s a number of major studies had been published that betrayed some debt to the lecture and employed the term 'governmentality' itself. More significantly, perhaps, the lecture was republished in a volume which placed it against the background of Foucault's own work on government and liberalism at the Collège de France in the late 1970s and which also made available, some for the first time in English, a host of important cognate studies (Burchell et al., 1991). This republication no doubt accounts for a certain amount of the current popularity of the concept. However, there are also other important factors at work, some of which I will mention in a moment and expand on further in the body of the present volume. By the late 1990s it would seem that 'governmentality' was a concept whose time had arrived. One suspects, however, that this diffusion of the term risks a certain dilution of the conceptual focus and analytic force it helped make possible. A part of the inspiration for the present volume is to retain some clarity about these studies in governmentality and to provide a framework and perspective for their use.

While the term itself might suggest yet another fashionable neologism characteristic of much of twentieth-century social and political theory, the types of analysis it has helped to guide evince a seriousness of purpose, a depth of scholarship and – dare one say – a certain untimely timeliness in the issues and problems they cast new light upon. Perhaps the rise to prominence of these studies of governmentality is more than intellectual fashion. Perhaps at some point in the future they will be viewed as part of the most vital and concrete engagements with the exercise of authority and how we think about that exercise. In this sense the study of governmentality can be placed among myriad forms of analysis that have arisen in a rather uncertain present. This present is marked by at least three major phenomena: the long-term recession of the ideal of a welfare state and the revitalization of the claims of a form of economic liberalism in liberal democracies; the collapse of really existing socialism, often with catastrophic and tragic consequences, in Eastern Europe; and the erosion of the claims of the liberal constitutional state by movements for indigenous rights and cultural recognition and by the exposure of its colonial legacy. At a minimum, the study of governmentality seems to respond to such a context without the nostalgia current on much of the Left or the complacency of the 'end of history' thesis. In hindsight, we can say that the name 'Foucault' might mark the earliest attempt to understand this new political constellation among the intelligentsia in those societies that still consider themselves Western. While recognizing the debt we consequently owe to him, this volume is not a simple exposition of Foucauldian concepts. Indeed, it is clear that others have made great contributions to the study of governmentality, both empirically and in the development of its conceptual apparatus. A field of study like that of governmentality is of necessity a collective project, conducted in many places and from many perspectives.

Foucault's own work on governmentality responded most explicitly to the first of the three movements I have just mentioned, i.e. to the changing status of liberal government and the recession of the welfare state ideal. Owing to my own interests, I have retained this focus in the current volume. However, there are clear indications in Foucault's lectures and what might be called his political journalism, not to mention his own political activities, that the theme of the genealogy of social government cannot be disconnected from either the rise and fall of state socialism in Europe or the relation between the development of European and American constitutional nation-states and colonial and anti-colonial forces and the subjugation of indigenous populations. I hope the reader will allow me the luxury of indulging my own concerns to exemplify the strengths of the study of governmentality in the present volume. This should not be taken to preclude a redescription of the genealogy of government from these other no less significant perspectives.[2]

The term *governmentality* seeks to distinguish the particular mentalities, arts and regimes of government and administration that have emerged since 'early modern' Europe, while the term *government* is used as a more general term for any calculated direction of human conduct. Typical of his flair for a catchy and perspicacious phrase, Foucault redefined 'government' in a fashion compatible with its sixteenth- and seventeenth-century uses as the 'conduct of conduct', i.e. as any more or less calculated means of the direction of how we behave and act. This development is startling in several ways.

First, the work it has produced could be regarded as forming a new subdiscipline within the social sciences and humanities (Gane and Johnson, 1993), one concerned with the manner in which we govern, or what is sometimes referred to as the 'how' of governing. It asks questions concerned with how we govern and how we are governed, and with the relation between the government of ourselves, the government of others, and the government of the state. It thus resumes older and broader meanings of government and governing that are not necessarily tied to the nation-state and, in some ways, have become obscured by the rise of the liberal constitutional national state and its identification of government with *the* government, i.e. with the body that claims supreme authority within a given territory and its various apparatuses. It gives particular emphasis to issues of the government of human conduct in all contexts, by various authorities and agencies, invoking particular forms of truth, and using definite resources, means and techniques. This sub-discipline, however, is also interdisciplinary: the 'take-up' of the question of governmentality already has had a profound influence on new work in and across disciplines as diverse as politics, sociology, economics, accounting, law, philosophy, the history of ideas, education and the history of the human sciences.

Second, this work is characterized by its concreteness. If studies of governmentality form a new sub-discipline across the human sciences, it is not as a theory-based one. Its concerns are problem-centred and present-oriented. Thus the work already produced with some central reference to the rubric of governmentality concerns problems in a range of domains. These include: psychology and the 'psy' disciplines (Rose, 1985; 1989; 1996c; Castel, 1989); education (Hunter, 1988; 1994); poverty and welfare (Donzelot, 1979; 1984; Dean, 1991; Procacci, 1993); social insurance and risk (Ewald, 1986); ethics and sexual politics (Minson, 1985; 1993); economics and accounting (Hopwood and Miller, 1994); political theory (Hindess, 1996; Tully, 1993); space and architecture (Rabinow, 1989); and law (Hunt and Wickham, 1994).[3] There have been several collections in English (Barry et al., 1996; Burchell et al., 1991; Dean and Hindess, 1998; Hänninen, 1998) and at least one in Finnish (Hänninen and Karjalainen, 1997). It has, further, been 'applied' in areas ranging from issues arising from 'self-identity' (Dean, 1994c; Rose, 1995), 'false memory syndrome' (Hacking, 1994) and criminality (O'Malley, 1992; Stenson, 1993) to the government of the firm (Miller and O'Leary, 1993) and national and international economies (Miller and Rose, 1990; Hindess, 1998b). Another interesting intersection is the employment of the themes and analyses of governmentality to address various issues raised by feminist concerns and studies, including the regulation of pregnancy (Weir, 1996), programmes of self-esteem and empowerment (Cruikshank, 1993; 1994), childhood, law and sexual abuse (Bell, 1993; Ashenden, 1996), and sexual harassment (Minson, 1993; Smith, 1998). The fecundity of empirical work has given rise to preliminary attempts to codify and generalize its results (e.g. Rose, 1993; 1996b) and to organize a loose chronology of forms of government, but the substantive nature of the work makes this difficult, contested and, at best, a second-order and somewhat tentative activity.

Third, these studies have had a profound influence, even if it is one that is less visible than debates over the normative grounds of theory (including the 'Foucault–Habermas' debate, Ashenden and Owen, 1999; Kelly, 1994) or over modernity and postmodernity. Its presence is of a truly 'rhizomatic' character, to use Deleuze and Guattari's (1981) famous metaphor, starting in local centres, forming networks, and appearing in and connecting unlikely places. The influence of such studies, despite their evident scholarship, has

been due to their present relevance (Dean, 1994a). Outside Foucault's immediate circle, England and Australia appear to have been the major centres,
with a growing body of work appearing in North America, particularly
Canada. International research networks, electronic mailing lists, workshops,
etc. complete the picture of a growing and fertile collective intellectual
endeavour. The work among current postgraduate students and junior academics in this area is enormous. National conferences in various disciplines –
e.g. sociology and law – have had sections devoted to this style of research. A
major concern at recent explorations of the 'legacy of Foucault' has been the
place of the theme of governmentality in his writings and its relations to
techniques and concerns for self-government (O'Farrell, 1997). Moreover,
an examination of a journal such as *Economy and Society*, as well as mainstream social science and humanities journals, would confirm the impression
that the already published work in this area is but a very small proportion of
that which will surface well into the twenty-first century.

For those of us who are teachers, as well as researchers, there have
emerged some difficulties involved in the further communication of this
field and its literature. I have already said that there have been limited
attempts at overview and codification. However, these do not go uncontested. Given its empirical basis, such accounts will remain open to revision.
Many of the researchers 'enlisted' above would probably find it difficult to
recognize themselves as part of a more general intellectual movement. There
is no one governmentality paradigm. There is no one common way of using
the intellectual tools being produced by workers in this area. There are no
prescribed limits to the intellectual formations of which studies of governmentality can be a part or to the empirical areas in which they can be
developed. There are also the problems of accessibility facing any cutting-
edge research domain. Some excellent work will be concerned with the
necessity of accurate dissemination of already established analytical frameworks (e.g. Burchell et al., 1991). Others will be concerned with the scholarly
presentation of their own arguments or research findings (e.g. Barry et al.,
1996; Dean and Hindess, 1998). At the same time, many of the major conceptual innovations in the field will be found amidst this detailed and
meticulous work. In short, there is no single volume that surveys this literature, presenting its major concepts, providing an overview of its historical
perspectives, or making intelligible its contribution to the analysis of present
styles of government.

As it was initially conceived, this book would try to play the role of such
a text. Its primary aim would be a modest, if difficult, one: to provide a general, clear, concise, legible overview of this literature that is accessible to
research students and their teachers, across the humanities, social and political sciences, public policy and law, as well as for interested learned publics
more broadly. While the execution of this task has inevitably strayed from this
conception and aim, I still hope that the book will be used by those interested
in a way of approaching the issues and concerns I have mentioned, or those
who would like fresh tools to address new domains. I noted above that gov-

ernmentality tools have already been used in areas of feminist concern; they may also be of use in such fields as development studies (Philpott, 1997), international relations (Dillon, 1995; Hindess, 1998a; Lui-Bright, 1997) and colonial and post-colonial studies (Gupta, 1998).

The reader should note that what is presented here is not a straightforward 'Foucauldian' text, whatever that might mean. While I have tried to offer fair and clear readings of Foucault's somewhat fragmentary legacy on the problem of government, I have sought, as far as possible, to extend, text and criticize particular propositions with the help of alternative or complementary accounts, drawing mainly upon the work of historians. Thus the problem of the genealogy of economic thought is complemented by the work of Keith Tribe (1978; 1995), the question of pastoral power in antiquity by the work of Peter Brown (1987; 1992; 1995) and Paul Veyne (1987; 1990), the problem of the formation of conceptions of reason of state by the work of Quentin Skinner (1978; 1989), Gerhard Oestreich (1982) and Reinhardt Kosellek (1989), and of police, population and political economy by numerous scholars I have drawn upon in earlier work (Dean, 1991; 1992). My reading of Foucault's methodological precepts is most influenced by its perspicacious representations by Gilles Deleuze (1988; 1991) and Paul Veyne (1982; 1992; 1997).

There are a number of senses in which I have stayed faithful to the initial conception and aim of this book as an introduction to the field. This conception requires some attempt at codification of the conceptual and theoretical bases and innovations undertaken by this work and some typification of the historically different styles of government. Yet, in keeping with the present relevance of this research, it also addresses concerns of contemporary social and political life and focuses on present forms of governmentality and present problems. Finally, in keeping with the intensely historical nature of much of Foucault's work and those who have taken up this study of the practices, mentalities and techniques of government, this work endeavours to illustrate some of the historical richness of its 'genealogy' of government.

In fulfilling this role as introductory text, this book would thus need to strike a balance between current problems, conceptual and analytical foundations, and the critical historical dimension of these studies. On completion, I find that these three concerns are reflected in the organization of the text. The first three chapters address issues of the conceptual and analytical foundations of the literature on governmentality. They do this by providing a basic statement of method and concepts (Chapter 1), by contextualizing the emergence of an 'analytics of government' in France in the late 1970s (Chapter 2), and by comparing two recent illustrative studies (Chapter 3). The next four chapters try to reflect the historical dimension of the study of governmentality as a feature of a style of work sometimes characterized as 'genealogy'. There I address a number of historically specific rationalities and forms of rule crucial to our contemporary views of government (Chapter 4), reflect on Foucault's own accounts of bio-politics, sovereignty and the 'governmentalization of the state' (Chapter 5), provide an outline of liberalism and the emergence of social government (Chapter 6), and begin to redress the relative neglect of various forms of non-liberal rule or 'authoritarian governmentality' (Chapter 7).

In so far as the analysis of authoritarian governmentality alerts us to the continuities between liberal and non-liberal forms of rule and the dangers inherent in bio-political governmental imperatives it begins to offer a diagnostics of our present. This task is more directly undertaken, however, in Chapters 8 and 9. In the first, I address the relation between neo-liberalism as a general rationality of government and advanced liberalism as an assemblage of particular elements. In Chapter 9, I tackle the diagnostic task from another viewpoint: that provided by risk, especially by examining the relation between Ulrich Beck's influential work on risk society and reflexive modernization, and a governmental account of practices concerned with the societal management of risk. Borrowing from Beck, and drawing on a concept first used by Ashenden (1996), I introduce the idea of 'reflexive government', of which neo-liberalism and advanced liberal government are but initial points in a series yet to be completed.

The critical historical studies chart what might be called after Foucault 'the governmentalization of the state'; the diagnostic studies of the final two chapters, 'the governmentalization of government'. These phrases indicate something of a very broad diagram for understanding historical trajectories of forms of government that emerged in the course of the writing of this book. This diagram follows Foucault's own narrative by suggesting that government first emerges as 'the right disposition of things arranged to a convenient end' (La Perrière), a phrase we shall take some pains to explore. It was as such that government gained some autonomy from the problem of sovereignty and then proceeded to transform the way sovereignty was exercised. The governmentalization of the state tracks the trajectory by which the 'dispositional' and 'householding' conception of government, manifest in cameralist notions of police and in mercantilism, comes to be modified by a form of government concerned with the government through certain processes – whether economic, psychological, biological, demographic or social. The governmentalization of government identifies a new trajectory in which the government of the state is today being augmented, complemented or even displaced by a government of government. The argument here is that the concern to govern through processes external to the formal apparatuses of political authority is to some extent reinscribed within a programme to reform and secure governmental mechanisms themselves, often by folding back the ends of government upon its instruments. This narrative begins to make intelligible the reconfiguration of the social as a set of quasi-markets in services and expertise at the end of the twentieth century, of the governed as customers or consumers of such services and expertise, and explores the way in which this is inflected with themes of community and identity. This narrative also allows me to suggest why current transformations of government are better conceived as post-welfarist regimes of social government rather than as forms of 'post-social' government.

In elaborating this diagram, and the concept of reflexive government, I now realize that in trying to fulfil my initial aim to write a clear introduction to the field, I have over-reached the limits that are required by such an exercise. What I have discovered, in a sense, is the impossibility of writing an introductory textbook to this field. If writing such a text means to write in a manner that does not represent a particular perspective, I have failed utterly. For in attempting to write an authoritative and clear account of the field, I have had to come to terms with both the limitations and the fecundity of my own viewpoint. This viewpoint constitutes no privileged and authoritative voice on the topic, but simply a provisional and modifiable statement of how these studies might be used to understand aspects of the present, including their own existence. I hope, then, that this book will function not only as an impossible introductory text, but also as a form of research that introduces the reader to one type of argument and perspective that can be constructed with the help of the materials here under discussion. If knowledge is always partial and provisional, then surely we need to find ways of writing and reading texts that deny the authoritative voice they have conventionally sought. If this book is lucky enough to gather some readers I trust they will forgive its hybrid status as a kind of 'perspectival' text. They will undoubtedly use it as they might without any directions for use.

Foucault said somewhere that he left the initial titles of his books as they were in order to mark how far the writing of the text had led him away from its conception. I have been more than once tempted to change the title of the present volume and give up its pretensions to the status of a text. Should the title have been *After Governmentality*, or *Governmentality and Beyond*, or *Forget Governmentality*? Should 'governmentality' be abandoned altogether for 'reflexive government'? What I have learnt by holding to the initial title is that even texts are experiments that lead you to 'think otherwise', to use another of Foucault's felicitous phrases. I have learnt that there can be no authorized textbook on governmentality. 'Governmentality' itself is a mixed substance and one that only works when alloyed with others. This book then is text as experiment, or rather a series of little experiments, sometimes using the same compounds and elements, which stand as exemplifications of how far, starting from this literature on governmentality, it was possible, given a certain set of necessarily limited intellectual resources and capacities, for me to think otherwise.

It may be that intellectuals can no longer stand at the barricades leading the masses. It may be that they can no longer in good faith tell others how to act and live, or what to change or leave alone. But they can induce a little movement in the world of thought. If this book has any value, it is in offering its own efforts toward a collective project in making one small and still barely perceptible shift in our thinking.

Notes

1 The acknowledgements of *The Foucault Effect* (Burchell et al., 1991: vii) state that the 'first publication was in Italian translation by Pasquale Pasquino, in the journal *Aut...aut* no. 167–8 (September–December 1978)'. It is unclear whether the first English translation by Rosi Braidotti in *Ideology and Consciousness* no. 6 was from that Italian version. It is also unclear as to whether the source of the Italian version was a tape, a written text by Foucault, a series of notes by a member of the audience, or whatever.
2 In this context, I should mention the exemplary genealogy of the language of modern constitutionalism provided by James Tully (1995) from the perspective afforded by the politics of cultural diversity and the resources of the alternative traditions of common constitutionalism. Tully draws on the work of the later Wittgenstein to challenge the assumptions of modern constitutionalism.
3 I am only mentioning book-length studies here. I must also note the appearance of three important books that have appeared, or will appear, while the present volume was in press: Cruikshank (1999), Rose (1999) and Valverde (1998a). I am also aware of my neglect in failing to discuss Hacking's work on statistics and 'bio-power' (1982; 1986; 1991) and Thomas Osborne's work on medicine as liberal profession (e.g. 1993).

1 BASIC CONCEPTS AND THEMES

We are accustomed to a certain set of received ways of thinking about questions of government. These ways of thinking have been largely derived from ideas clustered around the ubiquitous but difficult and somewhat obscure concept of 'the state'. In most cases the question of government is identified with the state, i.e. with a sovereign body that claims a monopoly of independent territorial power and means of violence, that inheres in but lies behind the apparatuses or institutions of organized and formal political authority and that is separate from the rulers and the ruled. Central concerns of such ways of thinking involve the search for an origin or a source of the power held to reside in the state, the attempt to identify which agents hold or possess that power, and whether that power is legitimate or not. To the extent that we seek to analyse the language associated with government, it is construed as ideology, as a language that arises from and reflects a dominant set of power relations. The study of governmentality is continuous with such a theoretical framework in that it regards the exercise of power and authority as anything but self-evident and in need of considerable analytical resources. It does, however, break with many of the characteristic assumptions of theories of the state, such as problems of legitimacy, the notion of ideology, and the questions of the possession and source of power.

This chapter provides a basic introduction to the general approach associated with the concept of governmentality. The first section starts by defining key terms and spelling out the implications of those terms. The second outlines the nature of this perspective, which it terms an 'analytics of government'. The third suggests some fundamental precepts for those who are sufficiently persuaded to wish to employ at least some elements of this analytics. The second and third sections include some reflections on what distinguishes this analytics of government from more conventional approaches to questions of power and authority that can be typecast as the 'theory of the state'.

The style employed in this chapter is deliberately didactic, in order to fulfil the aim of presenting an exposition of concepts, methodological precepts and axioms. This should not, however, obscure the status of the following as but one account of a particular perspective on problems of power, authority and government. Various thinkers have put together arguments and forms of knowledge derived from studies of governmentality with a variety of intellectual and political positions, theoretical arguments and value orientations.

These thinkers stand in different relations to Foucault's own work and by no means represent a 'Foucauldian' stance. The position presented in this book is shaped not only by Foucault's work but also by a range of twentieth-century social thinkers and by a number of researchers in the contemporary humanities and historical studies.[1] I want to emphasize the analytic power of the governmentality framework and to avoid eliding that power with particular positions or orientations that are for or against government. In stating this, however, I do not wish to abandon the reader to the fashionable yet sterile relativism of the view that one account is as good as another. The present account should be judged in terms of its coherence, clarity, completeness and, above all, capacity to convince. To admit the perspectival character of knowledge should be to sharpen rather than blunt our critical stance.

Government and governmentality

Government as the 'conduct of conduct'

Let us start, then, with a short definition of the term 'government' by the phrase the 'conduct of conduct' (Gordon, 1991: 2; Foucault, 1982: 220–1). What should we take this to mean?

This definition plays on several senses of the word 'conduct'. 'To conduct' means to lead, to direct or to guide, and perhaps implies some sort of calculation as to how this is to be done. The ethical or moral sense of the word starts to appear when we consider the reflexive verb 'to conduct oneself'. Here one is concerned with attention to the form of self-direction appropriate to certain situations, e.g. at work and at home, in business dealings, in relation to clients or friends. Another sense of the term is as a noun. 'Conduct' here refers to our behaviours, our actions and even our comportment, i.e. the articulated set of our behaviours. Again the sense of self-guidance or self-regulation may often be involved as, say, in the case of discussions of our 'professional conduct' or the conduct of schoolchildren. Such discussions are almost invariably evaluative and normative, i.e. they presume a set of standards or norms of conduct by which actual behaviour can be judged, and which act as a kind of ideal towards which individuals and groups should strive. Such discussions also presume that it is possible to regulate and control that behaviour rationally, or at least deliberately, and that there are agents whose responsibility it is here to ensure that regulation occurs, e.g. teachers or professional associations and their 'codes of conduct'.

Putting these senses of 'conduct' together, government entails any attempt to shape with some degree of deliberation aspects of our behaviour according to particular sets of norms and for a variety of ends. Government in this sense is an undertaking conducted in the plural. There is a plurality of governing agencies and authorities, of aspects of behaviour to be governed, of norms invoked, of purposes sought, and of effects, outcomes and consequences.

This short general definition of government as the 'conduct of conduct' can be expanded:

Government is any more or less calculated and rational activity, undertaken by a multiplicity of authorities and agencies, employing a variety of techniques and forms of knowledge, that seeks to shape conduct by working through our desires, aspirations, interests and beliefs, for definite but shifting ends and with a diverse set of relatively unpredictable consequences, effects and outcomes.

An analysis of government, then, is concerned with the means of calculation, both qualitative and quantitative, the type of governing authority or agency, the forms of knowledge, techniques and other means employed, the entity to be governed and how it is conceived, the ends sought and the outcomes and consequences.

This would appear to be an extremely wide, if precise, definition. There are several immediate implications that orient research into such an area. First, government is interesting, from this perspective, not simply because to govern means to order people about or to move things around. Rather, government here involves some sort of attempt to deliberate on and to direct *human* conduct. From the perspective of those who seek to govern, human conduct is conceived as something that can be regulated, controlled, shaped and turned to specific ends. Thus, students of governmentality might be interested in the regulation of a heterogeneous range of things – economies, populations, industries, souls, domestic architecture, bathrooms, exhaust emissions, etc. – but only in so far as the government of these things involves the attempt to shape rationally human conduct.

This brings us to a second implication. The term 'rational', it should be noted, refers to the attempt to bring *any* form of rationality to the calculation about how to govern. For present purposes, rationality is simply any form of thinking which strives to be relatively clear, systematic and explicit about aspects of 'external' or 'internal' existence, about how things are or how they ought to be. Since Max Weber, we have known that there is no single Reason or universal standard by which to judge all forms of thought and that what we call Reason is only the 'specific and peculiar rationalism of the West' (1985: 26; Dean, 1994a: 78–91). After Foucault, we know that, even within the latter, there is a multiplicity of rationalities, of different ways of thinking in a fairly systematic manner, of making calculations, of defining purposes and employing knowledge.

The rational attempt to shape conduct implies another feature of this study of government: its links with moral questions. If morality is understood as the attempt to make oneself accountable for one's own actions, or as a practice in which human beings take their own conduct to be subject to self-regulation, then government is an intensely moral activity. One can approach the morality of government in a number of ways. It is moral because policies and practices of government, whether of national governments or of other governing bodies, presume to know, with varying degrees of explicitness and using specific forms of knowledge, what constitutes good, virtuous, appropriate, responsible conduct of individuals and collectives. Thus a film and literature censorship board directly regulates access to materials and is easily recognized as concerned with moral matters. The requirement that persons receiving various social benefits perform certain tasks, e.g. attendance at meetings, counselling, even training and retraining programmes, is linked to assumptions about how such persons ought to conduct themselves. One can also discuss the morality of the 'governors' manifested in concerns for probity, honesty, impartiality and so on and regulated by parliamentary registers of private interests, codes of conduct for politicians, professionals and public servants. At a further level, government is intensely moral in that it seeks to engage with how both the 'governed' and 'governors' regulate themselves, e.g. a taxpayer can be constituted as an individual capable of self-assessment or a judge as someone with a duty to exercise fair, impartial and reasonable judgement.

Notions of morality and ethics generally rest on an idea of self-government. They presume some conception of an autonomous person capable of monitoring and regulating various aspects of their own conduct. Further, to define government as the 'conduct of conduct' is to open up the examination of self-government or cases in which governor and governed are two aspects of the one actor, whether that actor be a human individual or a collective or corporation. Thus the notion of government extends to cover the way in which an individual questions his or her own conduct (or *problematizes* it) so that he or she may be better able to govern it. In other words government encompasses not only how we exercise authority over others, or how we govern abstract entities such as states and populations, but how we govern ourselves.

The government of the prison, of the economy and of the unemployed, as much as the government of our own bodies, personalities and inclinations, entails an attempt to affect and shape in some way who and what we are and should be. The criminal might be regarded as a victim of circumstance and environment who requires reformation; the unemployed person as someone at risk of welfare dependency who requires group counselling to provide self-help and increase self-esteem; and the national population as lacking the capacities of enterprise and entrepreneurship required to be internationally competitive. All these examples illustrate how government is crucially concerned to modify a certain space marked out by entities such as the individual, its selfhood or personage, or the personality, character, capacities, levels of self-esteem and motivation the individual possesses. Government concerns not only practices of government but also practices of the self. To analyse government is to analyse those practices that try to shape, sculpt, mobilize and work through the choices, desires, aspirations, needs, wants and lifestyles of individuals and groups. This is a perspective, then, that seeks to connect questions of government, politics and administration to the space of bodies, lives, selves and persons.

One of the points that is most interesting about this type of approach is the way it provides a language and a framework for thinking about the linkages between questions of government, authority and politics, and questions of identity, self and person. It offers us some novel ways of thinking about the relation of politics to ethics. Indeed, if we take our cue from another aspect of Foucault's (1985) later thought, ethics can be reconceived in these terms as the arena of the government of the self, as a form of action of the 'self on self'.

It is not difficult to come by examples of this kind of practical ethics in this sense of an action of 'self on self'. Think of the way in which many people problematize their eating habits and bodily shapes in practices of self-government called dieting. This is ethical in as much as such practices imply that it is good to be slim and virile, to have control over one's body, to regulate the intake of fatty foods, to reduce the risk of certain diseases, to be healthy and to increase the probability of longevity. Another example might be the way adulterous spouses may problematize their sexual conduct by seeking therapy to help with the propensity to infidelity. In both cases we find an attempt (often failed, at least in terms of its immediate aim) to act upon oneself. The practices by which we endeavour to govern our own selves, characters and persons, then, are a subset of this broader domain of the 'conduct of conduct'.

In most of the present text I shall discuss practices concerned to conduct the conduct of others rather than those concerned to conduct one's own conduct. I shall thus deal with 'practices of government' in a narrower sense than that encompassed by the phrase 'conduct of conduct'. To the extent I discuss 'practices of the self', I shall tend to discuss the way in which they are utilized in programmes and rationalities of government, particularly that of the government of the state. This entails largely ignoring the sense in which practices of the self are relatively independent of practices of the government of others or of the state. One of the implications of acknowledging this autonomy of the ethical from the political, of practices of the self from practices of government, is that practices of the self can be not only instruments in the pursuit of political, social and economic goals but also means of resistance to other forms of government (cf. Krinks, 1998).

If government is linked to ethics in this way, it also raises the question of freedom. Government as the 'conduct of conduct' entails the idea that the one governed is, at least in some rudimentary sense, an actor and therefore a locus of freedom. Government is an activity that shapes the field of action and thus, in this sense, attempts to shape freedom. However, while government gives shape to freedom, it is not constitutive of freedom. The governed are free in that they are actors, i.e. it is possible for them to act and to think in a variety of ways, and sometimes in ways not foreseen by authorities. Government presupposes the existence of subjects who are free in the primary sense of living and thinking beings endowed with bodily and mental capacities (cf. Patton, 1998).

Government as the 'conduct of conduct' entails living human beings who can act. This is clearly the case when the governed are to be empowered by expertise, or required to act as consumers in a market, as in many forms of contemporary liberal government. Consider, however, the apparent counter-examples of a condemned man sentenced to death or – to use Rejali's (1994) example – of a woman subject to political torture. Surely, one might think, their fate has very little to do with the shaping of freedom. The condemned man is to be treated in a certain way, such as being offered a last meal and religious counsel and rites. He is to be executed in some manner, whether by firing squad, electrocution or lethal injection. In some jurisdictions, e.g. in the USA, he may even have the choice of the type of execution. Once executed, his body and personal effects are to be disposed of in some fashion. Before and up to his death, he is a subject to be governed as well as a prisoner to be killed. His death does not merely involve the perpetration of the ultimate form of violence on his being; it also involves forms of thought, deliberation, and calculation about his actions and reactions, including forms of knowledge of his living body made possible by medicine, psychiatry and so on. After his death, there is merely a corpse to be disposed of according to particular rituals, routines and beliefs. Yet even the burial or cremation of the corpse also entails a more or less calculated set of activities. However, after his death authorities no longer attempt to govern the conduct of the prisoner, but they continue to govern that of his family and friends, groups against capital punishment, even the general public, media, prison wardens and officers, undertakers, etc. They govern his body prior to the execution because, even in chains, it is the locus of a rudimentary freedom given shape through such legal and political discourses on rights, religious beliefs and certain forms of knowledge and expertise. In death he may commit his last act. Through the choice of a firing squad rather than lethal injection he may seek to publicize the brutality of capital punishment. After death, however, he cannot act in that he can no longer do something that will affect others' actions. To govern, in this sense, is to structure the field of possible action, to act on our own or others' capacities for action. Capital punishment entails simple brutal violence (a human being to be killed) and rudimentary forms of physical domination (chains, leg-irons, cells); but to the degree that it requires the deployment of forms of knowledge and expertise, and the calculated action and coordination of the behaviour of actors who are free in that they can act otherwise, it is a form of government.

In the case of the woman under torture, the point can be seen even more clearly. The modern victim of torture is subject to a range of techniques derived from medical and psychiatric disciplines and a calibrated knowledge of the human body. The relation of torturer and tortured often takes on a therapeutic character in which the prisoner is invited to cooperate in a certain course of action. 'The prisoner was conducted (in the double sense of being led or learning to lead oneself) according to a requested norm. She was invited to recant, to condemn, to inform, to admit guilt, or to cooperate . . . A certain freedom was essential to the torture interrogation and "follow-up" procedures' (Rejali, 1994: 75–6). The torturer, in this example, takes the position of a therapist. The prisoner is urged to take responsibility for her own state, and the pain she is causing herself, and to take such action as will remove that pain. She is thus urged to exercise her freedom in a specific fashion. She is hardly in a position to decline the offer because of the calibrated violence being inflicted on her body, the threat of rape, and so on. The margin of the exercise of freedom is of course extremely narrow. She can, however, refuse to cooperate by refusing to admit guilt, sign a confession or denounce others.

There is an even more fundamental and primary sense in which both the condemned man and the woman subject to torture are beings who remain loci of freedom. They can both exercise a capacity to think, i.e. to describe and re-describe their situation in ways that differ from that of their jailers. She can attempt to remind herself that it is the torturers, and not she, who are responsible for her current state of pain. He can understand his execution as one of rank injustice and racial discrimination. Both can redescribe their situation as a spiritual test or a travail on the way to salvation. This primary sense in which thinking is an action of freedom available to human agents is encapsulated in Hitler's dictum that even 'thinking exists only by virtue of giving or executing orders' (Arendt, 1958: 325). Such a pronouncement indicates, by the fanatical and 'totalitarian' desire to eradicate it, the close proximity of thinking and the exercise of freedom and the fact that the capacity to think is always a danger to the practice of 'giving and executing orders'.

Government concerns the shaping of human conduct and acts on the governed as a locus of action and freedom. It therefore entails the possibility that the governed are to some extent capable of acting and thinking otherwise. As we shall argue, certain ways of governing, which we will broadly define as *liberal* modes of government, are distinguished by trying to work through the freedom or capacities of the governed. Liberal ways of governing thus often conceive the freedom of the governed as a technical means of securing the ends of government. To say this is to say that liberal mentalities of rule generally attempt to define the nature, source, effects and possible utility of these capacities of acting and thinking. They also vary according to their conception of this freedom. For example, freedom may be conceived as a natural attribute of *Homo œconomicus*, as in the case of Adam Smith's 'system of natural liberty'; as a product of the discipline of civilization, as for Friedrich Hayek; as the exercise of rational choice in a market, as in many contemporary programmes of reform of the welfare state; or as a 'game of competitive freedom' whose rules are secured by a juridical and bureaucratic officialdom, as in the German 'ordoliberals'. Any specific conception of freedom, however, can never capture or define the possibilities of the exercise of freedom.

The notion of government as the 'conduct of conduct' presupposes the primary freedom of those who are governed entailed in the capacities of acting and thinking. It also, furthermore, presupposes this freedom and these capacities on the part of those who govern. One of the consequences of this latter proposition is that when we govern our selves and others we exercise our capacities for thinking. This brings us to our next point – what is meant by this strange term, *governmentality*.

Governmentality

It is possible to distinguish two broad meanings of this term in the literature. The second is a historically specific version of the first. In this chapter we shall deal principally with its most general meaning.

In this first sense, the term 'governmentality' suggests what we have just noted. It deals with how we think about governing, with the different mentalities of government. What does it mean to talk about how we think about governing? Thinking here is a collective activity. It is a matter not of the representations of individual mind or consciousness, but of the bodies of knowledge, belief and opinion in which we are immersed. The notions of collective mentalities and the idea of a history of mentalities have long been used by sociologists (such as Emile Durkheim and Marcel Mauss) and the *Annales* School of historians in France (Burke, 1990). For such thinkers, a mentality is a collective, relatively bounded unity, and is not readily examined by those who inhabit it. A mentality might be described as a condition of forms of thought and is thus not readily amenable to be comprehended from within its own perspective. The idea of mentalities of government, then, emphasizes the way in which the thought involved in practices of government is collective and relatively taken for granted, i.e. not usually open to questioning by its practitioners. To say that these mentalities are collective is not necessarily to identify them with specific social groups or classes, although it might also be possible to examine the relation between the different mentalities of specific ruling or subordinate groups. It is to say that the way we think about exercising authority draws upon the theories, ideas, philosophies and forms of knowledge that are a part of our social and cultural products. In contemporary liberal polities, for example, these mentalities are often derived from the human sciences (such as psychology, economics or medicine).

This point can be elaborated in relation to some examples. The way we think about the government of nations crucially involves knowledge of the national economy and its trends. This knowledge is provided by a certain class of specialists, economists, drawing on theoretical and technical knowledge, such as models of the economy, economic statistics, forecasts and so on. This knowledge and its implications are provided by economists within the national treasury or the national bank, or even by international agencies such as the World Bank or the International Monetary Fund. Politicians choose between different 'macro-economic' policies. Electorates may choose officials who take 'soft' or 'hard' options with regard to the economy, as the case may be. Authorities may argue that it is becoming more difficult or even impossible to manage national economies owing to economic globalization. However, that it is necessary to attempt to properly manage the economy is one feature of the mentality of national governments that is completely taken for granted.

Similarly, if I undertake that ubiquitous exercise in self-government, the diet, I do so by drawing upon certain forms of knowledge and expertise provided by dieticians, health professionals, the purveyors of the latest health fad, or my religious or spiritual beliefs. Depending on why I undertake a diet, I may calculate my cholesterol intake, my calories or kilojoules, or whether certain foods are proscribed by my religious beliefs. In all cases, I diet for specific sets of reasons (to attain a virile body, to prevent heart disease, to conform with divine law, to respect taboos), employ certain forms of knowledge and seek to act upon a certain aspect of my being (whether of my energy intake and expenditure or my spiritual state). All these various ways of dieting, then, employ different mentalities of the government of the conduct entailed in eating and drinking. Indeed, the same activity can be regarded as a different form of practice depending on the mentalities that invest it. To restrict or prohibit the intake of certain forms of meat could be regarded as a component of a low-fat diet or as part of a fast, i.e. a practice of self-denial necessary to purify one's soul. The part of ourselves we seek to work upon, the means by which we do so, the reasons we do it, and who we hope to become, all vary according to the nature of the ascetic practice in which we are engaged.

This can be put in a more formal language, as I have done elsewhere (Dean, 1995). The analysis of the ethical government of the self, or of an attempt to govern the self, involves four aspects (Foucault, 1985; 1986a; 1986b; 352–7). First, it involves ontology, concerned with *what* we seek to act upon, the *governed or ethical substance*. This may be the flesh in Christianity, the pleasures in ancient Greece, or the 'soul' of the criminal in modern penology (on the latter example, see Foucault, 1977: 16–31). Second, it involves ascetics, concerned with *how* we govern this substance, the *governing or ethical work*. This may include the spiritual exercises studied by Pierre Hadot (1995), or the procedures of surveillance, management and normalization applied to deviant individuals. Third, it involves deontology, concerned with *who* we are when we are governed in such a manner, our 'mode of subjectification', or the *governable or ethical subject* (as one prey to the weakness of the flesh in Christianity, or as an active jobseeker in social programmes). Fourth, it entails a teleology, concerned with *why* we govern or are governed, the ends or goal sought, what we hope to become or the world we hope to create, that which might be called the *telos of governmental or ethical practices*. All practices of government of self or others presuppose some goal or end to be achieved – whether other-worldly salvation, the sculpting of a beautiful and noble life and memory, an enterprise culture or an active citizenry and society.

The ways in which we think about government are multiple and heterogeneous, involving different types of agency and authority and employing different types of thought. Thought, however, is a collective product. Social and cultural historians and sociologists have sought to analyse the collective nature of thought by examining its social, political and economic conditions. Studies of governmentality, however, are more concerned with how thought operates within our organized ways of doing things, our *regimes of practices*, and with its ambitions and effects (Foucault, 1991b). Moreover, where historians of ideas and social thinkers have concentrated on the theoretical and abstract dimensions of thought, the analytics of government is more concerned with thought as it is embedded within programmes for the direction and reform of conduct. The analysis of government is concerned with thought as it becomes linked to and is embedded in technical means for the shaping and reshaping of conduct and in practices and institutions. Thus to analyse mentalities of government is to analyse thought made practical and technical.

An analytics of government thus views practices of government in their complex and variable relations to the different ways in which 'truth' is produced in social, cultural and political practices. On the one hand, we govern others and ourselves according to what we take to be true about who we are, what aspects of our existence should be worked upon, how, with what means and to what ends. We thus govern others and ourselves according to various truths about our existence and nature as human beings. On the other hand, the ways in which we govern and conduct ourselves give rise to different ways of producing truth. National government in contemporary states is unthinkable without some conception of the economy – whether that is conceived as a national or global economy – and the attempt to govern economies leads to the production of knowledge about employment, inflation, trade and so on.

We have already seen (in the general definition of government as the 'conduct of conduct') that government entails not only relations of power and authority but also issues of self and identity. It might now be said, very schematically, that power, truth and identity mark out three general dimensions of government corresponding to what I shall call (later in this chapter) its *techne*, its *episteme* and its *ethos*.

If government involves various forms of thought about the nature of rule and knowledge of who and what are to be governed, and it employs particular techniques and tactics in achieving its goals, if government establishes definite identities for the governed and the governors, and if, above all, it involves a more or less subtle direction of the conduct of the governed, it can be called an *art*. The object of our studies, then, is not the simple empirical activity of governing, but the *art of government*. To refer to the art of government is to suggest that governing is an activity which requires craft, imagination, shrewd fashioning, the use of tacit skills and practical know-how, the employment of intuition and so on. The undertaking does not comprise an empirical description of how various people or agents in positions of authority rule. An analytics of government is not a 'sociology of rule' if the object of this is solely actual relations of authority and domination. Rather, it is a study of the organized practices through which we are governed and through which we govern ourselves, what we shall call here *regimes of practices* or *regimes of government*. These regimes, however, involve practices for the production of truth and knowledge, comprise multiple forms of practical, technical and calculative rationality, and are subject to programmes for their reform. It is important to realize that regimes of practices exist within a milieu composed of mentalities of rule, without being reducible to that milieu.

As well as indicating the relation between government and thought, the notion of governmentality has a second meaning in Foucault's work. Here, 'governmentality' marks the emergence of a distinctly new form of thinking about and exercising of power in certain societies (Foucault, 1991a: 102–4). This form of power is bound up with the discovery of a new reality, the economy, and concerned with a new object, the population. Governmentality emerges in Western European societies in the 'early modern period' when the art of government of the state becomes a distinct activity, and when the forms of knowledge and techniques of the human and social sciences become integral to it. We shall address the details of the emergence of this historical form of governmentality and its relation to sovereignty and bio-politics in Chapter 5. Here, we shall note some aspects of this historically delimited meaning of the term following Foucault's lecture, 'Governmentality' (1991a: 102–3).

First, the emergence of this modern governmentality can be identified by a particular regime of government that takes as its object 'the population' and is coincident with the emergence of political economy (and its successor, economics). Government, henceforth, will be required to be a government of 'each and all', evincing a concern for every individual and the population as a whole. Thus government involves the health, welfare, prosperity and happiness of the population. The notion of population is crucial to the definition of the ends of the government of the state. Yet, at the same time, government must become an *economic* government. To govern properly, to ensure the happiness and prosperity of the population, it is necessary to govern through a particular register, that of the *economy*. Moreover, government itself must be economical, both fiscally and in the use of power.

Second, the notion of governmentality implies a certain relationship of government to other forms of power, in particular sovereignty and discipline. Sovereignty emerges as a theory and practice of monarchical rule that is later democratized through liberal and democratic states with their representative institutions. Its characteristic mechanisms are constitutions, laws and parliaments. Sovereign power is exercised through the juridical and executive arms of the state. It is exercised over subjects. Discipline, on the other hand, has a long history, with diverse origins in monastic, military and educational practices (Foucault, 1977). It concerns the exercise of power over and through the individual, the body and its forces and capacities, and the composition of aggregates of human individuals (classes, armies, etc.). The expansion and intensification of regimes of discipline in the seventeenth and eighteenth centuries – in schools, hospitals, workhouses, manufactories, armies and so on – is roughly correlative with the development of the bureaucratic and the administrative apparatus of the state.

While governmentality retains and utilizes the techniques, rationalities and institutions characteristic of both sovereignty and discipline, it departs from them and seeks to reinscribe and recode them. The object of sovereign power is the exercise of authority over the subjects of the state within a definite territory, e.g. the 'deductive' practices of levying of taxes, of meting out punishments. The object of disciplinary power is the regulation and ordering of the numbers of people within that territory, e.g. in practices of schooling, military training or the organization of work. The new object of government, by contrast, regards these subjects, and the forces and capacities of living individuals, as members of a population, as resources to be fostered, to be used and to be optimized.

Third, governmentality seeks to enframe the population within what might be called *apparatuses of security*. These apparatuses of security include the use of standing armies, police forces, diplomatic corps, intelligence services and spies. It also includes health, education and social welfare systems and the mechanisms of the management of the national economy. It thus encompasses those institutions and practices concerned to defend, maintain and secure a national population and those that secure the economic, demographic and social processes that are found to exist within that population. As Foucault (1991a: 102) warns us, it is best now to see these three forms of power as a 'sovereignty–discipline–government' series which is fundamental to modern forms of authority. Rather than replacing discipline or sovereignty, the modern art of government recasts them within this concern for the population and its optimization (in terms of wealth, health, happiness, prosperity, efficiency), and the forms of knowledge and technical means appropriate to it.

The final characteristic of 'governmentality' stressed by Foucault is the long process by which the juridical and administrative apparatuses of the state come to incorporate the disparate arenas of rule concerned with this government of the population. This is the process he calls the 'governmentalization of the state'. Much of the present text is dedicated to tracing the multiple lines that constitute the history of governmentality. That history will include a specification of the most characteristic rationality of government, that of liberalism, and the relation of this rationality of government to not only sovereignty but also the administrative imperative to optimize the health, welfare and life of populations, or what shall be referred to as *bio-politics*. These historical concerns constitute the themes of many of the later chapters of this book. For present purposes it is perhaps more important that we understand the first, more general meaning of the term.

An analytics of government

The perspective introduced here can be called an *analytics of government*. An *analytics* is a type of study concerned with an analysis of the specific conditions under which particular entities emerge, exist and change. It is thus distinguished from most theoretical approaches in that it seeks to attend to, rather than efface, the singularity of ways of governing and conducting ourselves. Thus it does not treat particular practices of government as instances of ideal types and concepts. Neither does it regard them as effects of a law-like necessity or treat them as manifestations of a fundamental contradiction. An analytics of government examines the conditions under which regimes of practices come into being, are maintained and are transformed. In an elementary sense, regimes of practices are simply fairly coherent sets of ways of going about doing things. They are the more or less organized ways, at any given time and place, we think about, reform and practice such things as caring, administering, counselling, curing, punishing, educating and so on (Foucault, 1991b). Regimes of practices are institutional practices, if the latter term means the routinized and ritualized way we do these things in certain places and at certain times. These regimes also include, moreover, the different ways in which these institutional practices can be thought, made into objects of knowledge, and made subject to problematizations.

An analytics of government attempts to show that our taken-for-granted ways of doing things and how we think about and question them are not entirely self-evident or necessary. An analytics of a particular regime of practices, at a minimum, seeks to identify the emergence of that regime, examine the multiple sources of the elements that constitute it, and follow the diverse processes and relations by which these elements are assembled into relatively stable forms of organization and institutional practice. It examines how such a regime gives rise to and depends upon particular forms of knowledge and how, as a consequence of this, it becomes the target of various programmes of reform and change. It considers how this regime has a technical or technological dimension and analyses the characteristic techniques, instrumentalities and mechanisms through which such practices operate, by which they attempt to realize their goals, and through which they have a range of effects.

Within any given society, there is a large, but finite, number of intermeshing regimes of practices. In contemporary liberal-democratic societies, there are regimes of practices of punishing, of curing, of relieving poverty, of treating mental illness and maintaining mental health and so on. These regimes involve and link up particular institutions so that we can talk of a 'criminal justice system', a 'health system', a 'social welfare system' and so on. However, such regimes are never identical with a particular institution or even system. Thus the regime of practices of punishing may find a central institutional support in the prison. However, how we punish also affects what happens in schools, families, barracks and so on. The existence of such regimes of practices makes possible borrowings across institutions and innovation within them. In addition, there are borrowings across these regimes themselves, and forms of cooperation, overlap, intersection, fragmentation and contestation between them. One regime may attempt to colonize and subjugate another, e.g. the way in which regimes of calculation drawn from accounting and auditing appear increasingly to be used to subsume alternative practices of accountability such as those drawn from professional and collegial norms (Power, 1994).

These regimes of practices give rise to and are informed and reshaped by various forms of knowledge and expertise such as medicine, criminology, social work, therapy, pedagogy and so on. Such forms of knowledge define the objects of such practices (the criminal, the unemployed, the mentally ill, etc.), codify appropriate ways of dealing with them, set the aims and objectives of practice, and define the professional and institutional locus of authoritative agents of expertise.

This dependence of regimes of practices on forms of knowledge accounts for a related feature. Regimes of practices are associated with and become the objects of definite, explicit *programmes*, i.e. deliberate and relatively systematic forms of thought that endeavour to transform those practices (Gordon, 1980; Foucault, 1991b). In fact, the practices of curing, punishing, etc. are invested with multiple programmes that employ certain types of knowledge to reform or radically challenge their operation, to reorient them to new goals and objectives, and to act upon the desires, aspirations, needs and attributes of the agents within them. Regimes of practices, while having a material and institutional locale, exist in the milieu of thought, one feature of which is these programmes of the reform of conduct. A part of the practices of punishment centred on the prison is the various programmes for reducing recidivism, reforming the prison system, sentencing and so on.

An analytics of government often commences analysis by examining the way aspects of regimes of practices are called into question (or *problematized*) by such programmes. However, as we shall see, these programmes do not exhaust the intelligibility of these regimes of practices. An analytics of government will seek to constitute the intrinsic logic or *strategy* of a regime of practices that cannot be simply read off particular programmes, theories and policies of reform. The strategic logic of a regime of practices can only be constructed through understanding its operation as an intentional but non-subjective assemblage of all its elements (Gordon, 1980). That is to say that regimes of practices possess a logic that is irreducible to the explicit intentions of any one actor but yet evinces an orientation toward a particular matrix of ends and purposes. It is necessary to be extremely careful to distinguish between the strategy of regimes of practices and the programmes that attempt to invest them with particular purposes. These programmes are internal to the workings of a regime of practices and not their *raison d'être*. The critical purchase of an analytics of government often stems from the disjunction between the explicit, calculated and programmatic rationality and the non-subjective intentionality that can be constructed through analysis – as we shall illustrate by an analysis of the logic of empowerment in Chapter 3. The key point to underline here is that, unlike many analyses in the social sciences, an analytics of government grants to these regimes of practices a reality, a density and a logic of their own and hopes to avoid any premature reduction of them to an order or level of existence that is more fundamental or real, whether that be the level of institutions, of structures, of ideologies and so on, or even any one of the particular programmes that seeks to invest them with certain purposes and orient them toward specific goals.

To put all this in a very simplified framework, an analytics of government takes as its central concern *how* we govern and are governed within different regimes, and the conditions under which such regimes emerge, continue to operate, and are transformed. An analytics of government thus emphasizes 'how' questions. It is possible to distinguish at least four dimensions of this:

1   characteristic forms of visibility, ways of seeing and perceiving
2   distinctive ways of thinking and questioning, relying on definite vocabularies and procedures for the production of truth (e.g. those derived from the social, human and behavioural sciences)
3   specific ways of acting, intervening and directing, made up of particular types of practical rationality ('expertise' and 'know-how'), and relying upon definite mechanisms, techniques and technologies
4   characteristic ways of forming subjects, selves, persons, actors or agents.

These four dimensions are developed in the final section of this chapter. It is sufficient to note that the axes of visibilities, knowledge, techniques and practices, and identities are co-present within each regime of practices, that each constitutes a line of continual transformation and variation, and that each presupposes the others without being reducible to them. An analytics of government tries to recover the intelligibility of regimes of practices through each of these dimensions, to give due weight to their independence, without falling into any kind of reductionism or determinism.

An analytics of government admits to being a perspective on questions of power and authority. This does not mean that it is a subjectivist, 'anything goes' enterprise. Rather it seeks to formulate and consistently employ a specific set of questions that follow from this concern with how regimes of practices of government operate. To admit its perspectival nature is to say that there is no absolute standard of truth by which this analytics can be judged. To evaluate it, we might simply compare the intelligibility and understanding it yields with alternative accounts.

In regard to such comparative evaluation, it is perhaps useful to draw a notional distinction between an analytics of government and theories of the state, if one is allowed to typecast the latter somewhat. The state, in the political and social sciences, is usually presumed to be a relatively unified set of institutions that are the source of political power and through which political authority is exercised within a particular territory. As Max Weber (1972: 78) put it, the state claims a monopoly over the use of violence within this territory. In the modern liberal-democratic nation-state, the executive, either popularly elected or appointed by a representative parliament, makes decisions that are carried into practice by a professional and nominally politically neutral administration. This executive is bound, however, by a tacit or codified constitution and the rule of law, and is accountable to the law-making agency of the parliament. The laws, enacted by the parliament, are in turn interpreted and enforced through the judiciary and through institutions of security such as the police. Moreover, the state pursues and protects what it understands as its external interests by means of its diplomatic corps and standing army.

As historical sociologists have shown, the processes by which nation-states were constructed and took on the various functions we assume of them today were complex.[2] The internal pacification of a territory, the establishment of monopoly over the use of legitimate violence and taxation, the imposition of a common currency, a common set of laws and legal authorities, certain standards of literacy and language, and even stable and continuous time–space systems, are all integral to the process of state formation. The nation-state was historically constructed through the subordination of various arenas of rule to a more or less central authority and the investment of the duty of the exercise of that authority to long-standing, if not permanent, institutions and personnel. A central part of this process of state formation is the recognition by the state that the health, happiness, wealth and welfare of its population were among the key objectives of its rule.

Despite the complexity of the relations between the institutions that constitute the state, and our growing understanding of how agencies and domains of rule are integrated within the nation-state, our images of the state generally assume that the state can be addressed as a relatively unified actor, both in the diplomatic and military pursuit of 'geopolitical' interests and in its internal systems of authority. Indeed, social scientific theories of the state assume this unity when they typically seek to discover the source of the state's power, who holds it, and the basis of its legitimacy. Democratic, liberal, pluralist, elitist, Marxist and feminist theories of the state pose these same questions, however differently they might answer them. Thus, the source of power can be variously identified as the people, individuals, elites, the relations of production, patriarchy. Those who hold power may be the people, elites, ruling classes, men and so on, and the legitimacy of their rule may rest upon the rule of law, class hegemony, dominant ideologies, the consent of the governed, patriarchal culture, etc.

Theories of the state could be said in a general sense to memorize the trajectory of Western European states from feudal and absolutist monarchical rule to parliamentary democracy to the extent that they focus on the problem of *sovereignty* (Foucault, 1980: 103). This is the problem of the relation between the sovereign and its subjects. On the one hand, such theories examine the legitimacy of the sovereign, the basis of its authority and its right as the law-making and law-enforcing agency within a territory. On the other, they examine the issue of the consent and obedience of the governed, of those who are subjects to this authority. The foundations of sovereignty may be discovered in divine will, the rule of law or the rule of the people. The consent of the governed may be found in tradition, in religious belief, in a primal compact between the governed, in different forms of authority or in ideology. In any case, the problems of who or what is sovereign (and hence who holds power), of the legitimacy of this sovereignty, and of the relation of sovereign and subjects, deeply permeate our images and theories of the state and our political philosophies.

One of the sources of the development of an 'analytics of government' was a fundamental interrogation of these images and the suspicion of their inadequacy to an understanding of the key political problems with which we are faced in the present. We know Foucault's famous aphorism that 'in political theory we are yet to cut off the king's head' (1980: 121), by which he ventured that the problem of the foundations of sovereignty and our obedience to it needs to be supplanted by an analysis of the multiple operations and mechanisms of power and domination. To do this, he at first turned to the language of war and domination. This is present in his suggestion that we invert Clausewitz's aphorism that war is politics continued by other means (1980: 90–1). If politics is war continued by other means then we should attend to the mobile relations of strategy and tactics, to struggles and battles, and to the disposition of forces, that are employed in the exercise of political rule and in the resistance it provokes.

These statements by Foucault should be taken as revisable provocations to our thinking about social regulation and political order rather than as a fully fledged alternative theoretical position. One can track a number of points along the line of development of his thought on power and domination during the 1970s, although one must be cautious about assuming anything like a fundamental discontinuity. He first sought to question the grounding of a theory of power in the images of law and sovereignty. To do so, he experiments with the language of war and domination as a way of reconceptualizing power. His 1976 lectures, 'Il faut défendre la société' ('Society Must Be Defended') (1997b), bear witness to this experiment. One of the consequences of this is an apparent dichotomy between the 'sovereign', juridical form of premodern power of the European absolutist monarchies and modern, normalizing 'disciplinary' power or 'bio-power'. Second, he later abandoned this language of war as leading to an 'extremist denunciation of power' as *repressive* (Pasquino, 1993: 73). He thus turned in the late 1970s to problems of government, as we have described it here, and related themes of security, liberalism and population. This latter move should therefore be placed in the context of an attempt to rethink problems of power and regulation outside *both* the images of law and sovereignty *and* the discourse on war. However, there are certainly fundamental continuities between Foucault's characterization of 'bio-politics', or a form of power operating at the level of *living* individuals and populations, and his thought on government. Indeed, a full view of the analytics of government will need to visit the relation between liberal government, bio-politics and sovereignty, as we shall in Chapters 5 and 6.

This second shift opened up new ways of thinking about law, discipline and government. Law now needs no longer to be regarded as the archaic survival of sovereignty and its juridical and political institutions, and discipline no longer as the pre-eminent modern form of power. Rather the problem becomes the need to rethink the place of both law and disciplinary domination within contemporary governmental forms.

Indeed, having rejected the opposition between sovereign and disciplinary power, Foucault sought to consider the manner in which the art of government has transformed and reconstituted the juridical and administrative apparatuses of seventeenth-century Western European states. This is how we should take a further deliberation offered by Foucault (1991a: 103) on the excessive value accorded the image of the state in our political culture. This overvaluation consists in all the hopes and fears, love and horror, we invest in the state as a 'cold monster' confronting us, either as the means to our secular salvation (found in the glory of the nation, the superiority of the race, the attainment of social justice and equality, etc.) or as a fact of brute domination repressing our genuine humanity (located in civil society, the private sphere, even the market, etc.). Another overvaluation paradoxically reduces the state to a number of functions, such as the development of the productive forces and the reproduction of the capitalist relations of production, and thus makes the state the focus of political struggles. Perhaps, remarks Foucault in the same passage, the state possesses neither this unity nor this functionality, and we should recognize that the state is but a 'composite reality' and a 'mythicized abstraction'. Perhaps, he suggests, what is important for us 'is not so much the *étatisation* [state domination] of society, but the "governmentalisation" of the state'.[3]

Neither the image of sovereignty nor the language of domination and repression can account for the emergence of governmental authority and the place of law and legal institutions within it. Both approaches remain transfixed by a kind of political *a priori*: of the division between subjugation and liberation in one case; and of the sovereign and its subjects in the other. Both are concerned with the identification of who holds and wields power. Questions of how we govern and are governed are reduced to the problem of how the dominant group or sovereign state secured its position through legitimate or illegitimate means. Indeed, the problem of legitimacy – deeply tied to a conception of the state as a 'law-making' body – lies at the base of our thinking about power and the state. An analytics of government, by contrast, assumes that discourses on government are an integral part of the workings of government rather than simply a means of its legitimation, that government is accomplished through multiple actors and agencies rather than a centralized set of state apparatuses, and that we must reject any *a priori* distribution and divisions of power and authority (cf. Latour, 1986a).

In challenging these centralizing images of power and the state, this analytics affirms that these divisions and distributions are something to be analysed as constructed, assembled, contested and transformed from multiple and heterogeneous elements. The mobile, changing and contingent assemblages of regimes of government and rule have analytic precedence over the resultant distributions of power and divisions between state and civil society and between public and private spheres. This is why it is necessary to attend to what is put together in these assemblages: the routines of bureaucracy; the technologies of notation, recording, compiling, presenting and transporting of information; the theories, programmes, knowledge and expertise that compose a field to be governed and invest it with purposes and objectives; the ways of seeing and representing embedded in practices of government; and the different agencies with various capacities that the practices of government require, elicit, form and reform. To examine regimes of government is to conduct analysis in the plural: there is already a plurality of regimes of practices in a given territory, each composed from a multiplicity of in principle unlimited and heterogeneous elements bound together by a variety of relations and capable of polymorphous connections with one another.

Regimes of practices can be identified whenever there exists a relatively stable field of correlation of visibilities, mentalities, technologies and agencies, such that they constitute a kind of taken-for-granted point of reference for any form of problematization. In so far as these regimes concern the direction of conduct, they form the object of an analytics of government.

Analysing regimes of government

The existing research into governmentality provides us with a number of indications as to how to undertake an analytics of government. Here, I shall endeavour to identify, clarify and state the characteristic moves of the analytics of government.

The identification of problematizations

The key starting point of an analytics of government is the identification and examination of specific situations in which the activity of governing comes to be called into question, the moments and the situations in which government becomes a problem. This action of calling into question some aspect of the 'conduct of conduct' is generally referred to as a 'problematization'. Problematizations are something relatively rare. They have particular dates and places, and occur at particular locales or within specific institutions or organizations. Thus, rather than starting from a global theory of the state or of power relations, an analytics of government directs us to examine the different and particular contexts in which governing is called into question, in which actors and agents of all sorts must pose the question of how to govern.

A problematization of government is a calling into question of how we shape or direct our own and others' conduct. Problematizations might thus equally concern how we conduct government and how we govern conduct. To start with these problematizations is to start with the questions various actors and authorities ask concerning how 'governors' (politicians, parents, the professions, corporate entities, etc.) conduct themselves and how 'the governed' (citizens, children, clients, consumers, workers, etc.) conduct themselves. Indeed, from the perspective of these problematizations it is often difficult to make this division between governed and governor, e.g. in the attempts to make professions accountable to clients, boards of management of corporations accountable to shareholders, or academics in public universities to taxpayers. In each of these examples those who might be thought to exercise authority (over clients, investment decisions, workers, students) are subject to the exercise of other forms of authority.

Problematizations are made on the basis of particular regimes of practices of government, with particular techniques, language, grids of analysis and evaluation, forms of knowledge and expertise. It is possible that the same vocabulary and array of techniques can be used to govern those we might usually regard as belonging to either side of the division. Thus the now ubiquitous language of 'enterprise' and 'entrepreneurship' can equally be applied to public organizations and services (under the rubric of 'entrepreneurial government': e.g. Osborne and Gaebler, 1993) or to sub-populations such as the unemployed. Again, in Chapter 3 we shall consider how techniques of empowerment can be applied to populations whose conduct is problematized as 'disempowered' or 'dependent', with low morale and self-esteem. The techniques and language of empowerment can be used to problematize what is understood as the overly paternalistic, rigid and disempowering bureaucratic administration of welfare states. To study empowerment, or to study any other ways of reforming the exercise of authority (e.g. forms of managerialism, mechanisms of accountability, codes of conduct, etc.), is to interrogate the way we ask questions about how we govern and the conduct of both the governed and the governors. An analytics of government, then, starts from the questions we ask concerning our conduct and that of others rather than from a general theory or set of theoretical principles. If this is the starting point, then how does an analytics of government proceed?

The priority given to 'how' questions

The literature on governmentality gives a certain priority to 'how' questions. It asks 'how do we govern?' and 'how are we governed?' What does it mean to say this? It surely doesn't mean that we simply describe how authority operates in a particular situation, say a workplace or a school. Rather, it directs us to attend to the practices of government that form the basis on which problematizations are made and what happens when we govern and are governed. This means, first of all, to examine all that which is necessary to a particular regime of practices of government, the conditions of governing in the broadest sense of that word. In principle, this includes an unlimited and heterogeneous range of things. If one wanted to examine the government of recipients of income support for the unemployed this would encompass such things as: the administrative structure, integration and coordination of various departments of state and other agencies, organizations and businesses; the forms of training of public servants and other professionals (counsellors, case managers) and the expertise expected of them; the means for the collection, collation, storage and retrieval of information about specific populations of clients; the design, layout and location of various offices; the procedures of reception of clients, and methods of queuing, interviewing and assessing them; the design and use of assets tests, eligibility criteria, waiting periods, forms of certification; the use of forms, publicity, advertisements, etc. To list such conditions of governing, however, is not to say that analysis is merely the description of the empirical routines of government. It is an attempt to understand, in addition, how all the above has to be *thought*. All of these things are formed in relation to specific forms of knowledge and expertise of a variety of authorities from architects to social workers, occupational psychologists to management consultants. Moreover, certain forms of thought (party political platforms and policies, programmes of reform of welfare systems, social planning and policy-making) seek to unify and rationalize these techniques and practices in relation to particular sets of objectives, diagnoses of existing ills, schemata of evaluation and so on.

This approach thus stands in contrast to theories of government that ask 'who rules?', 'what is the source of that rule?' and 'what is the basis of its legitimacy?' An analytics of government brackets out such questions not merely because they are stale, tiresome, unproductive and repetitive. It does so because it wants to understand how different locales are constituted as authoritative and powerful, how different agents are assembled with specific powers, and how different domains are constituted as governable and administrable. The focus on 'how' questions, then, arises from a rejection of the political *a priori* of the distribution of power and the location of rule. Power, from this point of view, is not a zero-sum game played within an *a priori* structural distribution. It is rather the (mobile and open) resultant of the loose and changing assemblage of governmental techniques, practices and rationalities.

Finally, these resultant power relations and situations are among the consequences of how we govern and are governed. To ask 'how' questions of government, then, is also to ask what happens when we govern or are governed. Crucial to the resultant power relations are the capacities and liberties of the various actors and agencies formed in practices of government. To ask how governing works, then, is to ask how we are formed as various types of agents with particular capacities and possibilities of action.

'How' questions lead us to problems of the techniques and practices, rationalities and forms of knowledge, and identities and agencies by which governing operates. Another way of putting this is to say that to ask 'how' questions of government is to analyse government in terms of its 'regimes of practices'.

Practices of government as assemblages or regimes

Practices of government cannot be understood as expressions of a particular principle, as reducible to a particular set of relations, or as referring to a single set of problems and functions. They do not form those types of totalities in which the parts are expressions or instances of the whole. Rather, they should be approached as composed of heterogeneous elements having diverse historical trajectories, as polymorphous in their internal and external relations, and as bearing upon a multiple and wide range of problems and issues. Thus the 'modern' regime of punishment brings together multiple elements (from the history of the use of firearms and pedagogical practices to British empiricism and utilitarianism), evinces polymorphous relations (of the application of theory, the borrowing of architectural models, the employment of tactics formed in relation to local issues), and can be brought to bear upon all sorts of problems (discipline in the military, the education of children, the securing of a capitalist economy) (Foucault, 1991b). The term 'regime of practices' refers to these historically constituted assemblages through which we do such things as cure, care, relieve, punish, educate, train and counsel.

An analytics of government is a materialist analysis in that it places these regimes of practices at the centre of analysis and seeks to discover the logic of such practices. However, since regimes of practices partly comprise the forms of knowledge and truth which define their field of operation and codify what can be known, and since these regimes of practices are penetrated by all types of programmes that seek their reform, one would need to add that this materialism must be concerned with thought. Practices are of interest, then, in that they exist in the medium of thought, given that thought is a non-subjective, technical and practical domain.

Following the work of Deleuze (1991) we are able to analyse these regimes of practices along four different, reciprocally conditioning, yet relatively autonomous dimensions. These are addressed by the next four points.

The examination of fields of visibility of government

The first of these dimensions concerns the forms of visibility necessary to the operation of particular regimes. We might ask what the field of visibility is that characterizes a regime of government, by what kind of light it illuminates and defines certain objects and with what shadows and darkness it obscures and hides others. An architectural drawing, a management flow chart, a map, a pie chart, a set of graphs and tables, and so on, are all ways of visualizing fields to be governed. These all make it possible to 'picture' who and what is to be governed, how relations of authority and obedience are constituted in space, how different locales and agents are to be connected with one another, what problems are to be solved and what objectives are to be sought. So much do studies of governmentality emphasize this visual and spatial dimension of government that they seek to draw attention to these *diagrams* of power and authority (Bentham's Panopticon being only the most famous). Such diagrams allow us to 'think with eyes and hands', to use Bruno Latour's (1986b) nice phrase, to capture the sense in which seeing and doing are bound into one complex or in which drawing or mapping a field and visualizing it are interconnected. More generally, we can identify different regimes of practices with certain forms of visibility. Thus clinical medical practice presupposes a field of visibility of the body and its depths while public health regimes locate the individual body within a visible field of social and political spaces. Practices of imprisonment and confinement may presuppose different forms and levels of visibility. Thus we could cite the anonymous and omnipresent surveillance of the prison and contrast it with the banishment from the field of visibility and light characteristic of the castle dungeon. To use another example, risk-management strategies today present social and urban space as a variegated field of risk of crime in which high-risk spaces suffer from a lack of visibility and inspectability.

The concern for the technical aspect of government

A second dimension concerns the technical aspect of government, what I have called elsewhere the *techne* of government (Dean, 1995). Here the literature on governmentality asks: by what means, mechanisms, procedures, instruments, tactics, techniques, technologies and vocabularies is authority constituted and rule accomplished? In a more specific sense, one might discuss 'technologies of government', although it is perhaps worthwhile limiting that term to a certain class of phenomena within the *techne* of government (Dean, 1996b).

One of the key implications of this emphasis on government as technique is to contest those models of government that wish to view it solely – or even mainly – as a manifestation of values, ideologies, worldviews, etc. If government is to achieve ends, or seeks to realize values, it must use technical means. Those technical means are a condition of governing and often impose limits over what it is possible to do, e.g. in order to attempt to manage national economies it is necessary to use certain economic models and instruments. A concern for such things as 'balance of payments', inflation rates, public sector debt levels and so on is not simply an expression of a set of 'economically rational' or even capitalist values. This does not mean that government is purely technical, or that it is reducible to the technical aspects of government, or that it precludes discourses and rhetorics of value (see next point). It is to say, however, that the *techne* of government – like all other aspects of governing – is necessary, somewhat autonomous and irreducible.

The approach to government as rational and thoughtful activity

The third dimension of practices of government concerns the forms of knowledge that arise from and inform the activity of governing. I have elsewhere called this the *episteme* of government (Dean, 1995). Here the literature on governmentality asks: what forms of thought, knowledge, expertise, strategies, means of calculation, or rationality are employed in practices of governing? How does thought seek to transform these practices? How do these practices of governing give rise to specific forms of truth? How does thought seek to render particular issues, domains and problems governable? It is important to underline that 'thought' is something relatively rare. It has a particular time and place and takes a definite material form (a graph, a set of regulations, a text, etc.). It is this connection of government and thought that is emphasized in the hybrid term 'governmentality'.

To analyse regimes of practices of government, then, the literature on governmentality eschews a sociological realism that simply describes or analyses what exists, or how practices work in that sense. One of the features of government, even at its most brutal, is that authorities and agencies must ask questions of themselves, must employ plans, forms of knowledge and know-how, and must adopt visions and objectives of what they seek to achieve. The 'welfare state', for example, can be understood less as a concrete set of institutions and more as a way of viewing institutions, practices and personnel, of organizing them in relation to a specific ideal of government. Similarly, the 'neo-liberal' critique of the welfare state is not first an attack on specific institutions but is a problematization of certain ideals of government, diagrams of citizenship, and the formulas of rule they generate.

Government, moreover, has an intrinsically programmatic character. Here the governmentality literature attends to all the more or less explicit, purposive attempts to organize and reorganize institutional spaces, their routines, rituals and procedures, and the conduct of actors in specific ways. Programmes or 'programmes of conduct' are all the attempts to regulate, reform, organize and improve what occurs within regimes of practices in the name of a specific set of ends articulated with different degrees of explicitness and cogency.

The attention to the formation of identities

The final dimension of regimes of practices is concerned with the forms of individual and collective identity through which governing operates and which specific practices and programmes of government try to form. We might ask in relation to this final axis: what forms of person, self and identity are presupposed by different practices of government and what sorts of transformation do these practices seek? What statuses, capacities, attributes and orientations are assumed of those who exercise authority (from politicians and bureaucrats to professionals and therapists) and those who are to be governed (workers, consumers, pupils and social welfare recipients)? What forms of conduct are expected of them? What duties and rights do they have? How are these capacities and attributes to be fostered? How are these duties enforced and rights ensured? How are certain aspects of conduct problematized? How are they then to be reformed? How are certain individuals and populations made to identify with certain groups, to become virtuous and active citizens, and so on?

The forms of identity promoted and presupposed by various practices and programmes of government should not be confused with a *real* subject, subjectivity or subject position, i.e. with a subject that is the endpoint or terminal of these practices and constituted through them. Regimes of government do not *determine* forms of subjectivity. They elicit, promote, facilitate, foster and attribute various capacities, qualities and statuses to particular agents. They are successful to the extent that these agents come to experience themselves through such capacities (e.g. of rational decision-making), qualities (e.g. as having a sexuality) and statuses (e.g. as being an active citizen). Much of the problem of government here is less one of identity than one of 'identification', if we follow the language of Maffesoli (1991).

How is someone who buys goods at a supermarket to be made to identify as a consumer? How is someone who depends on social security relief from a public authority made to identify as an active job seeker? How are certain men made into or make themselves into a 'gay community'? How are we all to become good citizens? All these imply a work of government, a way of acting on conduct to elicit various identifications for various reasons.

These four dimensions of government presuppose one another. However, they are not reducible to one another. They are each relatively autonomous and it would be erroneous to reduce a regime of practices to any one of its dimensions. Transformation of regimes of practices may take place along each or any of these axes, and transformation along one axis may entail transformations in others.

The extraction of the utopian element of government

Mentalities of government contain a strangely utopian element. To govern, according to this logic, is to do something rather more than simply exercise authority. It is to believe that government is not only necessary but possible. It is to suppose that such government can be effective, that it can achieve its desired ends, or, to use the parlance of contemporary public policy analysis, that there can be a match between outcomes and intentions of policies. This implies that it is possible to re-form human beings, to form or shape them or their attributes in some way, and that our exertions can be effective in this regard. It is to assume that we can draw upon and apply forms of knowledge to that task, that we can gain a secure knowledge of the world and of human beings in that world, that we can 'make things better', improve how we do things, and so on. In this the art of government, as distinct from merely governing, is irreducibly utopian. It is necessary for an analytics of government to extract this utopian aspect.

Another way of putting this is to say that one means by which we might make intelligible regimes of government is to isolate their ultimate ends and their utopian goals. This is, if one likes, the *telos* of government. Every theory or programme of government presupposes an end of this kind – a type of person, community, organization, society or even world which is to be achieved. Notions of an enterprise culture, an entrepreneurial government, an active society, an active or enterprising citizen, an informed consumer, are so many examples of this (Heelas and Morris, 1992; Rose, 1992; Dean, 1995). Even at its apparently most bureaucratic and managerial, or its most market-inspired, government is a fundamentally utopian activity. It presupposes a better world, society, way of doing things or way of living. The *teloi* of advanced liberal, neo-conservative or welfare-state modes of governing, or specific programmes of national renewal (e.g. Newt Gingrich's Contract with America and President Roosevelt's New Deal), are extraordinarily different. Yet they are all not only ways of thinking about the mundane activity of administering things and people but also ways of leading them to a new and better existence.

The circumspection about the role of values

When actors in positions of authority ask 'how to govern' they are asking how we should govern, what is the best way to govern, from what value position and with what objectives. Thus public policies are often considered on the Left to be associated with the realization of the values of social justice, equity or citizenship rights, and on the Right with the securing of personal freedom, national efficiency and military strength. An analytics of government is careful not to reduce practices of government to such objectives and the values which are claimed or presumed to underlie them. Rather claims to be operating in the service of 'values' must be scrutinized as components of the rhetorical practice of government and as part of different forms of governmental and political reason.

The question of values is a complex one. It is extremely important not to view regimes of governmental practices as expressions of values. Values are enunciated in relation to the programmes and practices of government and form a key part of the rhetoric of government. This rhetoric is internal, and often necessary, to the functioning of regimes of practices and thus cannot make intelligible their conditions of existence. Values form a part of the mentalities of government along with specialist knowledge and more practical (and often tacit) know-how, expertise and skills embodied in, say, the training of public servants, professionals of various kinds and so on. They are attached to and assembled with various technologies and techniques of government. These techniques and technologies, however, cannot be understood as emanating from these values. Thus rather than viewing regimes of practices as expressions of values it is important to question how 'values' function in various governmental rationalities, what consequences they have in forms of political argument, how they get attached to different techniques and so on. Values, knowledge, techniques, are all part of the mix of regimes of practices but none alone acts as guarantor of ultimate meaning.

The avoidance of 'global or radical' positions

An analytics of government, finally, turns away from 'all projects that claim to be global or radical' (Foucault, 1986b: 46). At its most general such a position would eschew any position that claims that all the activity of governing is bad or good, necessary or unnecessary. More specifically, such a position would entail a rejection of the idea that the point of an analytics of government is to show how humans can be liberated from or, indeed, by government. At first approach, government works through practices of freedom *and* states of domination, forms of subjection *and* forms of subjectification. It sometimes takes the form of coercion and, at other times, seeks consent, without either coercion or consent being its essential form. Government as 'the conduct of conduct' is as necessary to certain practices of liberty as it is anathema to others. It presupposes and even creates forms of unfreedom and inequality as it seeks to create various kinds of equality and to foster the exercise of certain types of liberty.

My own viewpoint is that we need to adopt a stance that is neither enamoured with the 'will to govern' nor utterly opposed to the practice of governing. Government – particularly the government of the state – does not lead to utopia despite the fact that it is a fundamentally utopian enterprise. Whatever it may achieve, those achievements will not amount to a global emancipation; whatever its deficiencies, we shall never be free from it. Even those practices of government that have as their objective the specific emancipation of a certain group in a particular way may result in – or even require – intentional or unintentional domination of other groups. All organised social existence, including all practices of liberty, presupposes forms of the 'conduct of conduct'. Many of these forms of the 'conduct of conduct' will require relatively durable, fixed, irreversible and hierarchical relations of power, which Foucault (1988a) called 'states of domination' in his later work.

A corollary of the rejection of all global or radical positions with respect to government would be the suspicion of any general principle by which we might rationalize or reform government. Thus one of the problems of using the language of domination and emancipation – as I just have – is that such terms often imply a normative framework, largely inherited from certain forms of critical theory, in which the task of analysis is to identify forms of domination that act as obstacles to the emancipation or fulfilment of human beings. A key problem here is the assumption that human subjects and the liberty they exercise stand outside relations of power and forms of domination. By contrast, an analytics of government reflects its Foucauldian inheritance by showing how the capacities and attributes of subjects and the kinds of freedom which they make possible are shaped within regimes of government. Such regimes of government will include relations that are hierarchical, irreversible, fixed and durable, that is – in Foucault's sense – states of domination.

The distinction between relations of power that are open, mobile and reversible and those that are not is a useful analytical and descriptive tool. However, to the extent that an analytics of government endeavours to avoid global or radical projects, such a distinction cannot be used to construct a general normative stance. Thus an analytics of government should be wary of the use of such a distinction to offer a general critique of domination. It would reject certain formulations that suggest that the point of doing analysis is to distinguish between good or legitimate forms of government and bad or illegitimate ones, or to distinguish between what is good within regimes of government and what is bad within them. Unfortunately, such a position seems to be taken up in several of the late interviews of Foucault when he appears to endorse the general idea that we should learn to exercise power 'with a minimum of domination' (see especially Foucault, 1988a).[4] Domination is here identified with certain states in which 'relations of power, instead of being variable and allowing different partners a strategy which alters them, find themselves firmly set and congealed . . . in such a state the practice of liberty does not exist or exists only unilaterally or is extremely confined and limited' (1988a: 3). It is indeed hard not to be sceptical of the juxtaposition of domination and liberty in such a formulation, given Foucault's insistence on the myriad ways in which subjects are formed through the exercise of power and forms of domination such as discipline (Hindess, 1996: 154). My point here is that making the opposition between domination and liberty into a feature of relations of power – or of regimes of government – does not absolve that opposition of its general declamatory functions and the possibility of using it for 'an extremist denunciation of power' (Pasquino, 1993: 79).

I thus want to insist that an analytics of government marks out a space to ask questions about government, authority and power, without attempting to formulate a set of general principles by which various forms of the 'conduct of conduct' could be reformed. The point of doing this, however, is not to constitute a 'value-neutral' social science. Rather it is to practise a form of *criticism* (Foucault, 1988d). This is a form of criticism that seeks to make explicit the thought that, while often taking a material form, is largely tacit in the way in which we govern and are governed, and in the language, practices and techniques by which we do so. By making explicit the forms of rationality and thought that inhere in regimes of practices, by demonstrating the fragility of the ways in which we know ourselves and are asked to know ourselves, and the tissue of connections between how we know ourselves and how we govern and are governed, an analytics of government can remove the taken-for-granted character of these practices. The point of doing this is not to make the transformation of these practices appear inevitable or easier, but to open the space in which to think about how it is possible to do things in a different fashion, to highlight the points at which resistance and contestation bring an urgency to their transformation, and even to demonstrate the degree to which that transformation may prove difficult.[5]

An analytics of government is thus a way of thinking about how we conduct ourselves and others, and how we think about ourselves and others when we are doing this. It is thus an attempt to gain clarity about the conditions under which we think and act in the present. While this attempt to become clear about how we think and act upon ourselves and others does not necessarily stem from any particular set of values or principles it does, as Max Weber suggested, stand in the service of 'moral forces' (1972: 152).[6] This is to say that, by making clear what is at stake when we try to govern in a particular way and employ certain ways of thinking and acting, an analytics of government allows us to accept a sense of responsibility for the consequences and effects of thinking and acting in certain ways. One of the things that such an analytics allows us to do is raise what Weber calls 'inconvenient facts' (1972: 147). Such facts force us to consider the ramifications of our actions and commitments and point to the disjuncture between the self-representation of particular programmes and their strategic effects. Thus – to use an example we expand upon in Chapter 3 – by noting that notions of 'empowerment' are capable of being used by very different political stances and are themselves imbricated in definite sets of power relations, we produce a certain discomfort for the advocates of such notions of all political persuasions, particularly those who imagine themselves to be standing outside relations of power. Similarly, a consideration of how the self-governing capacities of the governed are a key feature of contemporary liberal rule problematizes the radical view of emancipation as the liberation of the agency of those who are oppressed.

Serving moral forces in Weber's sense increases our sense of responsibility about techniques, practices and rationalities of government and self-government. It thus enhances our capacities for governing the way in which we attempt to govern ourselves and others. In this sense, the moral forces for which an analytics of government might work are those that favour the possibilities of the enhancement of self-government or – to put it negatively – those that seek to diminish *specific* 'states of domination'. Here the problem is not of taking a principled stance against all forms of domination, but of examining the points at which regimes of government meet forms of resistance that reveal possibilities for doing things otherwise. There is no single standard for deciding whether a form of power or state of domination is contingent or necessary. Such evaluations are made by various actors in the course of contestation and resistance to regimes of government as acts of the exercise of capacities for self-determination. All an analytics of government can do is to analyse the rationalities of resistance and the programmes to which they give rise and to make clear what is at stake and what are the consequences of thinking and acting in such a way.

This is what I take Foucault to mean when he speaks of the 'stakes' of this type of analysis in 'What is Enlightenment?' (1986b: 47–8). The stakes of an analytics of government concern the question of how governmental practices, including practices of self-government, form and increase the capabilities and autonomy of individuals and collectives and how they also lead to what he calls an 'intensification of power relations'. By becoming clear on how regimes of practices operate, we become clear on how forms of domination, relations of power and kinds of freedom and autonomy are linked, how such regimes are contested and resisted, and thus how it might be possible to do things differently. The enhanced capacity for reflecting on how we govern others and ourselves makes it possible to adopt an experimental attitude where we can test the limits of our governmental rationalities, the forms of power and domination they involve, and thus investigate how we might think in different ways about the action on the actions of self and others. An analytics of government might thus serve moral forces in that it makes it possible for us to consider how we have come to conduct ourselves and others, and hence the possibility of thinking and acting in new ways. Some of these ways might thus concern how particular forms of the relation between liberty and domination are being transformed. An analytics of government is thus in the service not of a pure freedom beyond government, or even of a general stance against domination (despite some of Foucault's comments), but of those 'moral forces' that enhance our capacities for self-government by being able to understand how it is that we govern ourselves and others. It thus enhances human capacity for the reflective practice of liberty, and the acts of self-determination this makes possible, without prescribing how that liberty should be exercised.

An analytics of government removes the 'naturalness' and 'taken-for-granted' character of how things are done. In so doing, it renders practices of government problematic and shows that things might be different from the way they are. Rather than prescribing a general stance against forms of domination (such as would take the form of the injunction to 'resist all domination' or 'minimize all domination') it allows us to reveal domination as a contingent, historical product, and hence to be questioned. It offers no general prescription of what the result of such questioning might be. In this sense there is a normative character of the project of an analytics of government. The normative character is one of 'exemplary criticism', as David Owen (1995) has called it, rather than foundational critique and prescription. This means that an analytics of government reveals a commitment to self-rule by practising a type of criticism that demonstrates the contingency of regimes of practices and government, identifies states of domination within such regimes, and allows us to experience a state of domination as a state of domination. It does not tell us how we should practise our freedom.

The final point to mention here is that there is another side to this ethos of an analytics of government. It is that all political projects, including and perhaps especially those that endeavour to undertake a radical critique of forms of government, contain apparent and not so apparent dangers. Another sense in which an analytics of government could serve 'moral forces' is to make us permanently aware of the dangers that shadow the desire to augment, improve and fulfil our lives and those of others by governmental rationalities, practices and technologies. This is the point at which the next chapter on the 'ethos' of genealogy begins.

Notes

1 Among the former stand Norbert Elias (1978; 1982), Karl Polanyi (1957), Emile Durkheim (1992), Marcel Mauss (1978) and Max Weber (1927; 1968; 1972; 1985); among the latter, Pierre Hadot (1995), Paul Veyne (1987; 1990), Peter Brown (1987; 1992), Gerhard Oestreich (1982) and Quentin Skinner (1989).
2 From an immense literature, see Tilly (1975), Poggi (1978), Skocpol (1979), Giddens (1985), Corrigan and Sayer (1985) and Mann (1988).
3 Foucault's view of the overvaluation of the notion of the state in modern politics finds confirmation in Skinner's (1989) survey of the etymology and use of the term in various types of early modern political theory. Skinner argues that the only kind of political theory to enunciate a conception of the state as an entity separate from both the rulers and the ruled, and standing behind the institutions of civil government, was that which was concerned to defend the emergent absolutist form of monarchy. Among these writers are Suarez, Bodin and, of course, Hobbes.
4 An excellent and cogent criticism of such formulations by Foucault is found in Hindess (1996: 152–6).
5 I have distinguished between conventional accounts of critique and notions of criticism elsewhere (Dean, 1994a: 117–9). I am on this point completely in agreement with the view that 'the need for a practice of critique as a troubling of truth

regimes remains' (O'Malley et al., 1997: 507). On the ethos of criticism see Foucault (1988d).

6 The following discussion owes much to David Owen. My thinking draws here upon several of his important papers (1995; 1996; 1999) and on Foucault's discussion of critique (1996).

2 GENEALOGY AND GOVERNMENTALITY

> My point is not that everything is bad, but that everything is dangerous, which is not exactly the same as bad. If everything is dangerous, then we always have something to do. So my position leads not to apathy but to hyper- and pessimistic activism. (Foucault, 1997a: 256)

In the previous chapter, we have described an 'analytics of government' – a way of analysing those regimes of practices that try to direct, with a certain degree of deliberation, the conduct of others and oneself. Such an analytics does not constitute anything more than a critical method for investigating the forms of intelligibility of such practices. An analytics of government gains a critical purchase on regimes of practices by making clear the forms of thought implicated in them. It may point to 'inconvenient facts' such as the disjunction between the stated aims of particular programmes and other explicit rationalities and the logic or strategy of such practices that can be known through their diverse effects. More broadly, however, an analytics of government can be employed from a variety of ethical and political perspectives.

This chapter provides a discussion of one such perspective, that which animated the meeting of 'genealogy' with issues of government and liberalism in France in the 1970s in the work of Foucault and his colleagues. There is a dual purpose to this task. The first purpose is to show how the analytics of government grew out of and can thus be situated in relation to a critical ethical and political perspective and a particular style of intellectual work. In other words, it is to ask how and what style of genealogy came to investigate questions of liberalism and government. The second purpose might be described as a self-reflexive one: in order to maintain this analytics of government as an instrument of criticism, it is necessary to recover and make explicit the intellectual, ethical and political orientation in which it was located.

This chapter thus discusses different styles of genealogy and their ethico-political outlooks in order to come to an understanding of how an analytics of government and liberalism emerged in France in the 1970s and to make visible its critical impulse.

Genealogy and government

Under what conditions, and in what fashion, did genealogy come to pose the questions of government and to consider issues of liberalism? How did it come to bring the analytical resources of genealogy to our 'political reason' – to use the term favoured by a recent volume (Barry et al., 1996)? What is this style of study called genealogy? And is there more than one version of it? These questions are themselves not merely of academic interest. They indicate a whole ensemble of issues of the political and intellectual orientation of genealogy conceived as a 'history of the present', and of its ethos and manner of conceiving its own purposes and interrogating itself. Where the 'critical theory' of Jürgen Habermas grounds itself in a meta-historical account of the emancipatory dimension of all social conduct (understood as communicative action), genealogy – at least after Foucault – approaches the historicity of social conduct via its own particular set of ethical and political concerns 'grounded' in the present. I shall suggest that Foucault and his colleagues came to the problem of government at the juncture of a particular style of genealogy and a particular set of historical-political conditions which, following Colin Gordon, might be characterized as ones of 'limited political adversity' (1986: 79). We might infer that this genealogy of government has flourished precisely in those situations in which an independent Left intellectual culture has found itself in varying degrees of opposition to a recharged and militant liberalism, such as that found in much of the Anglophone world in the 1980s and 1990s. The conditions of this genealogy help us account for the ethos or ethical orientation of the milieux that gave birth to the analytics of government.

Consider first some different styles of historical writing and historico-political analysis that allow us to situate this most recent interest in genealogical studies. Gordon (1986: 77–80) has pointed out that there are a number of examples of the genealogical genre of historical writing in the twentieth century. Although it has most often been associated with a broadly liberal tradition, it has had a number of minority and heterodox exponents on the Left. He discerns a first type of genealogy as a 'semiology of catastrophe'. This is exemplified in the writings of the German and Austrian émigrés of the 1930s. It cuts across the liberal–Left divide to encompass the Frankfurt School, Karl Polanyi, Ernst Cassirer, Alexander von Rüstow and Friedrich Hayek. This genealogy addresses the present through the past to decipher the signs of impending or accomplished catastrophe. Gordon contrasts this to a genealogy as the 'permanent pragmatics of survival' found in Max Weber or Joseph Schumpeter, in which genealogy reveals the limits of what can be hoped for. The latter form 'addresses the endogenous hazards and necessities of a system, not the unrecognised incursions of an alien, pathological mutation' (1986: 78).

The revival of genealogy in the 1970s might be regarded, to keep following Gordon's (1986: 79) suggestions, as having greater affinities with this second current to the extent that it does not arise from a position of exile, commenting on the present as portending or realizing catastrophe. In the 1970s in France genealogy approached the present as a set of limits and possibilities, as evidenced by Foucault's own work on the question of enlightenment (e.g. 1986b: 32–50). Rather than a wan acceptance of such limits, however, the specificity of this most recent form of genealogy would lie in the way in which it brings the historical and analytical resources of genealogy to bear on problems raised in the course of particular forms of political action – in particular the localized struggles of the 1970s such as the work of the Groupe D'Information de Prisons (GIP) in France (Macey, 1993: 257–89). On the other hand, one might detect temperamental affinities with previous forms of critical theory such as that of Adorno and Horkheimer, as Foucault himself admits on several occasions (e.g. 1994) and Thomas McCarthy (1994) has sought to analyse. The key points of this latter intersection are: the radicalization of Kantian critique toward a critical history of rationality; the rejection of the autonomous rational subject; the suspicion of the claims of the human and social sciences; and the priority accorded practice over theory. One might note that both styles of genealogy have similar intellectual forebears in Nietzsche and Weber.

Most importantly, there is a strong case to be made for a certain commonality between the Frankfurt thinkers and Foucault in the use of genealogy as a means to gain a degree of critical distance from the Enlightenment philosophy of history and its 'prospectuses of progress' (Gordon, 1986: 77). Nevertheless, we might broadly contrast the dialectical genealogy of the Frankfurt School with Foucault's more analytic approach. While the former would regard the Enlightenment claims as turning into their very opposite so that genealogy investigates reason becoming domination, the latter eschews such frontal attack for more circumspect analysis. To put it in Foucault's (1986b: 42–3) striking formula, genealogy refuses the blackmail of the Enlightenment, to be for or against it. Some critics, such as Bernstein, suggest that this formula leads to a 'specious "either/or"' because it 'seduces us into thinking that we are confronted with only two possibilities: either there are universal ahistorical normative foundations for critique or critique is groundless' (1994: 234). One might argue that Foucault's critical ethos is precisely that we should *not* be 'seduced' by such a false alternative. The critical ethos of genealogy can be positively described as an incitement to study the form and consequences of universals in particular historical situations and practices grounded in problems raised in the course of particular social and political struggles.

We can begin to supplement Gordon's account by considering contemporary 'modernist' social theory and 'postmodernist' cultural critique. Both of these can be read as taking up a position in response to this 'simplistic and authoritarian alternative' of being for or against the Enlightenment (Foucault, 1986b: 43). Despite the overplayed antagonisms between these 'theoretical' genres, both share a common antipathy to genealogy. Within 'modernist' social theory we find what might be called 'the meta-histories of promise', found again both on the Left and within the liberal tradition, which assure us that, despite present detours, the movement of history confirms the ideals of the Enlightenment. Jürgen Habermas is perhaps today the most prominent of those thinkers who disqualify genealogy in an attempt to purify political action of all its historical accretions so that the Enlightenment can be fulfilled as it gives itself guarantees against the repeat of the catastrophe. His themes support a meta-history of the potential for emancipatory fulfilment: the incompletion of modernity as a project, the discernment of fundamental rationality in human communication, and the dynamics of a rationalization that is both oppressive and liberating. From this perspective, genealogy is little more than a tracking of the impure and confused contents of a history without drawing the fundamental lines which can both justify political action and act as a normative prophylactic against the potential of such action for catastrophe.

The real partner of this meta-history of promise is not genealogical circumspection but the anti-Enlightenment mode of cultural critique which regards the present as a moment of barely endurable despair, emptiness, shallowness, fragmentation and nihilism. According to this stream of thought the effects of late capitalism have displaced both identity and community with the consumer gratification of, as Foucault puts it, 'signs, speed, and spectacles' (Gordon, 1986: 81). This form of thought encompasses both the later Marcuse with his thesis of one-dimensionality and a whole current of French thought stemming from the situationism of the 1960s. A certain 'postmodern' diagnosis of the present as a moment of rupture, fragmentation and cultural upheaval is but one version of this. Another, perhaps less fashionable one, is the kind of conservative cultural critique best represented by Daniel Bell (1979), who invokes Sombart's thesis of the acquisitiveness of capitalism with its tendency to 'mass society', consumerism, hedonism, and the implosion of the rational individual imbued with a work ethic of deferred gratification. The period from the late 1960s has never been short of prophets of a new doom as well as those of a new dawn. In a period of undoubted intellectual hubris and excess, it is somewhat difficult to maintain a sense of modesty about one's claims, of limits about one's project, and of perspective about the nature of the present. To its credit, this is one of the enduring features of the ethos of genealogy. For genealogy, by contrast, it is necessary to approach the present 'with the proviso that we do not allow ourselves the facile, rather theatrical declaration that this moment in which we exist is one of total perdition, in the abyss of darkness, or a triumphant daybreak, etc. It is a time like any other, or rather, a time which is never quite like any other' (Foucault, 1994: 126).

The take-up of genealogy in the 1970s thus evinces a very particular and deliberate set of orientations to the task of intellectuals. It can be characterized from the outside by a series of negatives. It is neither for nor against the Enlightenment, neither a theoretical harbinger of a fully realized Reason nor a lament at its corruption. It refuses the meta-narratives of progress as much as the embrace of contemporary nihilism. It is elaborated neither as a semiology of catastrophe nor as a dialectics of salvation. Moreover, it refuses the prophetic and apocalyptic tone of contemporary social and political theory as much as it refuses its triumphalist twin. It refuses to take its own analysis as a species of that realism which stands convinced of its own certainties about the present.

The ethico-political impulse of this kind of critical intellectual work can also be described in positive terms. This practice of genealogy might be said to have two impulses meshing behind the critical orientation to historical material. The first of these might be called *diagnostic* in the sense detected by Deleuze (1991). This is an orientation to the present as an open set of possibilities rather than as portending catastrophe, witnessing decay or promising fulfilment. Yet it is a present subject to knowable limits and constraints, not least of which would be the vocabularies and forms of reason by which we make politics thinkable, the mechanisms by which this politics is accomplished and the manner in which we understand ourselves as those who govern and are governed. The ethos of this type of genealogy is of militancy grounded in scholarly moderation. It is militant in that the problems it addresses are called into focus by social and political movements and localized struggles. Yet it does not urge such movements to overturn everything or to 'subvert all codes'. Genealogy is led to undertake a task of some complexity requiring considerable erudition: to sort out what we take to be necessary and contingent in the ways in which we think and act in regard to the 'conducting' of our lives and those of others, and to discover what problematizations of this are possible. Further, it is the attempt to discern which of these problematizations indicate lines of fracture and transformation and which indicate a consolidation of regimes of government. In this diagnostic mode, genealogy is less a refuge from disaster and more a cautious initiation into the conditions of a renewed task of political invention. Its cautious militancy and intellectual moderation places the ethos of genealogy against all the dire prognostications on the fragmentation of identity and the ills of 'mass society'. Genealogy is thus an attempt to renew acquaintance with the strangeness of the present against all the attempts to erase it under the necessary dialectic of reason in history or to mark it as a moment of millenarian rupture, final dénouement or irreversible loss.

If genealogy is diagnostic in its relation to the present, it is *anti-anachronistic* in relation to the past. By making explicit the immersion of its historical analyses in an experience of the present, genealogy – in a move redolent of the ethos, if not the letter, of Max Weber's (1948) discussion of the value relevance of the social sciences – seeks also to limit the tendency to read the past through that experience. Past formations are not read as antecedents or necessary stages towards the present. There is thus the attempt to guard against anachronistic readings of historical materials. This is not done by an impossible reading of such materials *in* their own terms, i.e. by a magical reconstruction of lost worlds. Rather, genealogy seeks to grasp regimes of practices *by means of* their own terms (Dean, 1992: 219). This opens two possibilities. The first is to grasp the foreignness of that land which is the past. By doing so, we are depriving ourselves of certain forms of self-assurance:

that things have always been pretty much the same, that there are universals which animate the conduct and experience of human beings in every age, and that there is a fine thread linking our experience with these other humans which makes both our and their experience intelligible and necessary. Genealogies and other historical studies have shown, for example, that it is only about two centuries since 'the economy' can be said to have emerged as a 'theoretical-programmatic' reality (e.g. Foucault, 1970; Tribe, 1978; Meuret, 1988; Dean, 1991; Burchell, 1998). It is only at the end of the eighteenth century that the governable world came to be characterized by an economy, conceived as a quasi-naturalistic, semi-autonomous reality, composed of laws, tendencies or processes that we must at least respect when we attempt to guide our societies. A genealogy of terms such as 'labour', 'capital', 'production', 'circulation' and even 'economy' reveals that, not long ago, they belonged to a quite different form of knowledge and vocabulary of government. The past as a strange land sharpens the contingency and singularity of the present, and our experience within it, and our 'historical sense' – to use Nietzsche's phrase – of what can and cannot be subject to our action.

The second possibility is to use the analysis of the past to make the unfamiliar familiar, to show that the past is not so different from today in certain respects. Here genealogy sets itself against the immodesty of all those attempts to turn the present into a momentous, apocalyptic time of massive ruptures and dire public and personal troubles. A key example of this is the tendency to regard a concern with self-identity, its fulfilment or transcendence, as a feature of the present moment defined as 'late' or 'post' modern times (e.g. Giddens, 1991). Drawing on the work of historians of culture and ideas, it is possible to show that many of the features held to be specific to the quest for self-identity in late modernity are part of the longer and more complex trajectory of techniques of conscience formation and 'spiritual exercises'. Thus we find the use of 'autobiographical' techniques among Roman philosophical schools, including the keeping of notebooks, writing letters to friends, and mnemonic devices such as the nightly self-examination recommended by Seneca (Foucault, 1988e; 1993; Hadot, 1995). Continuous or regular acts of self-interrogation, the scrutiny of innermost thoughts in the search for truth and authenticity, and the verbalization of that which provokes resistance, are all present in John Cassian's fourth-century exposition of the practice of confession (Foucault, 1993). The point is not that we should erase all historical narratives of identity, fulfilment and transcendence, or that there are no differences between recent movements of personal liberation and ancient philosophical and religious schools, but that attention to particular regimes of ethical practices or forms of asceticism reveal awkward continuities for those who claim, or even simply assume, the ruptural nature of the present.

The style of genealogy that formed the milieu of our analytics of government was not that of a 'semiology of catastrophe' recounting signs of an impending or realized doom from a position of exile. It is endogenous to a political system, and practised in a time of limited political adversity. It shares with various other critical genealogies a scepticism toward the eman-cipatory claims of a universal reason and a historicization of rationality, and a pragmatics of survival in a situation of limited adversity. It succumbs nei-ther to the anti-historical promises of modernist theory, nor to the postmodernist macabre dance of death on the grave of universal values. Rather it views the hard and patient labour of detailed historical and empir-ical work as necessary to question and reformulate presumed continuities and discontinuities so that it is possible to offer diagnoses of the limits and possibilities of the present.

How then did this style of genealogy come to elaborate an analytics of government and begin to investigate liberalism in France in the late 1970s? The answer seems to lie in the intersection of this intellectual trajectory with a certain historical and political situation. Let us deal with the former before placing it against the latter. On the one hand, genealogy had come to a kind of theoretical impasse in its analysis of power. It had recognized that it was necessary to reject the language of law and sovereignty to investigate power relations – what it termed a 'juridico-discursive' conception of power. It sought an alternative in the discourse of war (Foucault, 1997b). However, in using the language of war, battle and struggle, genealogy found itself uncomfortably close to a position which tended to identify all forms of power with domination, and thus much like that of Adorno and Horkheimer. As Pasquale Pasquino (1992: 79) recalls, by the second half of the 1970s it was necessary to shift from this theoretically unsatisfying and politically naïve conception of power as domination to investigate 'global problems of the regulation and ordering of society as well as modalities of conceptualising this problem'. This included the study of the development of a science of the state in the modern West. Such a study would include, as Foucault's (1989b: 99–104) course summaries make clear, a detailed inquiry into the notion, means and mechanisms that ensure the *gouvernement des hommes* in any given society and the formation of what he calls a political *gouvernementalité*, the latter defined as the way in which the conduct of the totality of individuals becomes implicated in the exercise of sovereign power. It would also include the elaboration of a concern for liberalism as a critique of excessive government and as a form of political reasoning that needs to be located against another governmental imperative which is derived from bio-politics: to optimize the life of each and all within the gov-erned population.

The result of this was a new conceptual architecture of power. In Foucault's late work, the notion of government is elaborated within a kind of typology of forms of power that seeks to displace the immediate identifica-tion of power with domination. Government comes to be viewed as a kind of intermediate region which is not purely one of either freedom or domination, either consent or coercion. It is located by Foucault (1988a) *between* a pri-mary type of power as an open, strategic and reversible set of relations between liberties, *and* domination as the fixing and blocking of these relations into permanent, hierarchical distributions. Government is between these two in that it involves a form of power over others that is made operable through the liberties of those over whom it is exercised.

The elaboration of a notion of government marks the definitive rejection of a certain type of radical declamatory rhetoric of power and the beginning of a project to think about the problem of regulation outside earlier models of power. The focus on government seeks to displace *both* the notion of power as repression or interdiction that Foucault had traced to the 'juridical-political theory of sovereignty' *and* his own earlier attempts to rethink power in terms of 'the discourse of war and domination'. 'Power is less a confrontation between two adversaries or the linking of one to the other than a question of government . . . [which] did not refer only to political structures or to the management of states; rather it designated the way in which the conduct of individuals or groups might be directed' (Foucault, 1982: 221). Importantly, then, the notion of government stands as an attempt to pose the question of the epistemological and technical conditions of existence of the political, to analyse the historical *a priori* by which we construct politics as a domain of thought and action, and to analyse the instrumentation, vocabulary and forms of reason by which this is done. If, for Kant, 'critique' is the study of the conditions of true knowledge, the study of governmentality is a kind of critique of political reason, in as much as it seeks to investigate some of the hitherto silent conditions under which we can think and act politically. Perhaps, as we have suggested before, given the association of critique with the universal foundations of truth and right, it is better to refer to Foucault's task as a *criticism* of political reason, as he does in the English title of his lectures at Stanford (Foucault, 1981).

We should also note that the term 'government' does not exhaust the terrain of politics, but makes intelligible certain of its practical, technical and epistemic conditions of existence. The emphasis on the agonistic nature of power as a 'strategic game between liberties' suggests that the analysis of the arts of government is not the only component of the study of politics. 'In my analysis of power, there are three levels: the strategic relationships, the techniques of government, and the levels of domination' (Foucault, 1988a: 19). One of the limitations of Foucault's analyses of government and liberalism is that they tend to focus on the second and perhaps third of these three 'levels' at the expense of the first. As Hindess (1997) has argued, it is also necessary to examine the implications of those forms of political rationality and action which concern the struggle over government rather than the rationalities and actions of governmental organizations themselves.

Consider now the historico-political horizon for these deliberations. This might be first characterized – for better or worse – by the decreasing salience of Marxism as a political theory on the independent Left, paralleling its decline as a form of party political practice in Western Europe and as an established social formation in the East. As I have argued elsewhere (Dean, 1994a: 142–4), the changing thematic of power in genealogy in the 1970s can be viewed as an attempt to evacuate the intellectual terrain dominated by a Marxist theory of the state. Such a theory is inadequate to the analysis of power relations because it is characterized by a functionalism and economism in which the state is reducible to a set of necessary functional requisites of capitalism, and liberalism to capitalism's most characteristic ideology.

Second, one finds several references to the 'welfare-state problem' in Foucault's work of the late 1970s (e.g. 1981; 1988b). This attempt to rethink the conditions of the political, and the rejection of the identification of power with domination, coincides quite precisely with the problematization of the post-war welfare-state compact in Europe by a renewed and recharged liberalism. But if a Marxist schema is not adequate to the analysis of power relations, the view of liberalism as a 'bourgeois ideology' preparing the way for and disguising the fundamental realities of capitalist exploitation and property relations would appear similarly problematic. If genealogy is to track a kind of history of the conditions of our political reason in which the ideal of the welfare state becomes a problem, it must find an approach to liberalism which neither accepts its normative and substantive claims nor condemns it as a misrepresentation of a more fundamental reality. Rather than view a materialist and historical account of liberalism as referring to a more fundamental historical process of which liberalism is a function and a reflex, genealogy strives to make intelligible forms of liberalism in relation to the practices of government to which they are linked. To analyse liberalism in relation to these practices of government, rather than as a period, philosophy or form of state, is to seek to understand its plurality, capacity for reinvention and sheer longevity.

In brief: genealogy is the patient labour of historico-political analysis and contestation of existing narratives. It is animated by a particular ethos of permanent and pragmatic activism without apocalyptic or messianic ends. It evinces a tension between 'pessimism of the intellect' and 'optimism of the will' (O'Malley et al., 1997: 508). In the 1970s in France, it is taken up by an independent Left, grounded in the localized struggles against specific power relations, deprived of Marxism as a form of political theory and practice, and facing a recharged and newly militant liberalism. Perhaps all this is summed up by Foucault's statement cited at the beginning of this chapter.

Liberalism, critique and 'the social'

First a word of caution. It is tempting to use these studies of governmentality as simply another more or less successful account of the development of the institutional form of government of the state and the forms of thought that either influence or reflect it. In such an account, one would find a succession of forms of state that compose the 'normal' stages of development of liberal polities: a pre-history of the formation of the territorial state under absolutism and its attempt to institute a police state, the emergence of the liberal constitutional state, the development of the welfare state, and the emergence of a neo-liberal form of state. At each stage, different philosophies of government would predominate: reason of state (*raison d'Etat*), classical liberalism, welfarism, neo-liberalism and so on. An elementary criticism of this schema is that it ignores the complex continuities and discontinuities revealed by the genealogy of government in these societies. Much more fundamentally, however, it fails to comprehend *what* is understood by these terms, or what is distinctive and characteristic of this approach to liberalism.

Liberalism is approached genealogically neither as a coherent set of ideas nor as a definite institutional structure. Rather than view liberalism as a philosophy based on the 'rule of law' and the protection of individual rights and freedom against the unnecessary encroachments of the state, we can approach it as a characteristic way of posing problems. Graham Burchell (1996: 21) emphasizes its critical and problematizing character. For Foucault (1989b: 113), it is a polymorphous and permanent instrument of critique which can be turned against the previous forms of government it tries to distinguish itself from, the actual forms it seeks to reform, rationalize and exhaustively review, and the potential forms it opposes and whose abuses it wishes to limit. This means that the key targets of liberalism can change according to the circumstances in which it is located: at the end of the eighteenth century, it was notions of 'reason of state' and police; at the end of the nineteenth century, it was earlier forms of liberalism; after the Second World War in Europe, it was forms of national and state socialist totalitarianism; at the end of the twentieth century, it includes not only the ideal of a welfare state but also the very concept of the nation-state. These are the actual and previous forms of government in regard to which various kinds of liberalism have been posed as a critique. As we shall see in Chapter 6, liberalism sets itself against not only existing forms of governmental rationality but also potential ones, particularly the potential form contained within a bio-politics of the population. Utilizing resources drawn from the theory and practice of sovereignty on the one hand, and from the discovery of the economy on the other, liberalism will seek to balance the bio-political imperative of the optimization of the life of the population against the rights of the juridical-political subject and the norms of an economic government.

'Police' and 'reason of state' comprise elements of governmental rationality in early modern Europe, which we shall develop in Chapter 4. Whatever their own internal logic, they stand accused by early liberalism of the desire for the obsessional regulation of all aspects of life and of the attempt to establish a police state. For liberalism, reason of state assumes that it is possible to have an adequate and detailed knowledge of the reality to be governed, the state itself, and to use this knowledge to shape that reality for certain ends, usually to increase the power and wealth of the state (Burchell, 1996: 21–2). Police is the name given to the knowledge and means by which this is achieved. Against this, liberalism – especially in the work of the writers of the Scottish Enlightenment such as Adam Smith and Adam Ferguson – argues that it is not possible for the state or its agents to possess a detailed knowledge of the governed reality or to use its powers to shape that reality at will. The governed reality is neither as transparent nor as amenable to manipulation as German *Polizeiwissenschaft* (science of police) and 'reason of state' assume.

Liberalism can thus be characterized as a critique of state reason, as Gordon (1991: 15) puts it, a doctrine of the wise limitation and restraint on the exercise of authority by sovereign bodies and a form of pedagogy of sovereigns and statesmen. As such, as Rose (1996b: 43–4) has pointed out, it proposes two kinds of limits to the action of the state. The first concerns what it is possible to know and shape at will. For liberalism, the reality to be governed is constituted by several processes that are both necessary to the ends of good government and not directly visible to the agents of sovereignty. The exemplar of these autonomous processes is 'the economy' construed as a sphere of quasi-natural processes having a law-like quality, although similar critiques of state reason can be made in the name of the realities of 'the population' or 'civil society'. These are spheres construed as outside the domain of political authority and having forces and relations intrinsic to them that must be respected by the exercise of that authority. A key component of liberalism as an art of government is to find a set of political norms that can balance the competing imperatives that can be derived from a knowledge of the processes that constitute these spheres. Thus a knowledge of the processes that constitute the health, happiness and well-being of the population might lead to a coordinated and centralized apparatus for the administration of life. This 'bio-political' norm for liberalism needs to be set against norms of economic government. The latter are derived from a knowledge of economic processes, whereby excessive interference can endanger the security of the economic processes on which the material well-being of the population depends.

The second limit to state action concerns the nature of political subjects who, liberalism asserts, are individuals with rights, desires, needs and interests that cannot be dictated by governments. Liberalism takes up the language of right that it has inherited from another form of rule, sovereignty, and applies it in a host of different domains – first to the rights of economic subjects but later to the rights of consumers and users of publicly provided, as well as private, services. The real innovation of the study of liberalism as a rationality of government, however, is not the emphasis on the respect for the rights and freedoms of subjects. Rather, it is that such rights and liberties are necessary to the operation of the autonomous processes (of the economy, population and society) which are both external to political authority and necessary to its ends. For an analytics of government, liberalism can be approached then as a loosely related set of problematizations, interrogations and critiques of past, present and potential forms of government rather than as a juridical political philosophy, worldview or ideology.

Nor does this analytics of government approach liberalism as a form or period of state or a set of policies. Rather, more than either earlier versions of reason of state or socialism's entrenched state rationality, liberalism can be approached as an *art* of government, i.e. as a more or less subtle activity that interlaces interventions and withdrawals, connects different agencies, and utilizes the interests, needs and choices of individuals construed as more or less autonomous agents. It is an art in the sense that it recognizes the existence of several 'non-political' spheres and the necessity of such spheres to the ends of government. Liberalism as an art must decide under what circumstances and in what combination to allow the play of the forces of the market, the affections of families, the sympathies of community, and the laws of population, and when to intervene to protect and invoke the rights and liberties of individuals that are vital to securing such processes. Liberalism is an art of government not only because it recognizes that there are limits to the role of the state but because what it determines as falling outside the political sphere is itself necessary to the ends of government. In the analysis of a characteristic formula of rule of early liberalism, *laissez-faire*, Foucault shows that what is at issue is not the rejection of regulation but how 'to make regulations that ensure the play of necessary and natural modes of regulation' (Gordon, 1991: 17). As Hindess (1996: 127–8) has shown, considered as a political philosophy, liberalism is usually held to be committed to limited government owing to its prior commitment to individual liberty; considered as an art and rationality of government, it views the operation of individual liberty as necessary to the ends of government.

One might further describe liberalism as a critical ethos in relation to government rather than either a form of the state or a juridical and political philosophy. It is an ethos first of review under which it is always necessary to suspect that one is governing 'too much' ('on gouverne toujours trop') (Foucault, 1989b: 111). It insists on the need for continual review of the means of government, and asking whether such means are not inimical to the ends of governing. Governing too much in this sense might be worse than not governing at all because it would interfere with the processes that are necessary to government and hence endanger their security. For example, according to the Malthusians, to provide too much public poor relief tampers with the natural economic responsibility of men for their wives and children and leads them to marry and procreate without foresight and prudence. This therefore produces an unnatural increase in the size of the population beyond its means of subsistence resulting in wars, famine and other forms of vice and misery. In this sense, liberalism takes its place in the long lineage of forms of thought that have proffered advice to princes and politicians but have counselled them about the need to govern in moderation, with prudence, probity, deliberation, caution and economy (Barry et al., 1996: 8).

This ethos of review is also central to another feature of liberalism considered as an art of government: its capacity for self-renewal. Considered as a political philosophy there is not one but several, if not many, liberalisms: classical liberalism, economic liberalism, social liberalism, welfare liberalism, neo-liberalism (itself taking several versions). As a practice animated by an ethos of critique, liberalism displays a remarkable degree of political invention and self-renewal. Thus the liberal regime of government not only prepares the way for positive forms of knowledge of economy and society but establishes them as absolutely necessary. In order to enframe the processes of the economy, population and civil society in 'mechanisms of security' (Gordon, 1991: 20) – such as health and social security systems, internal police forces and standing armies, practices of national economic management – liberalism must be open to the diverse specialist knowledge of these processes and their effects, particularly those that comprise the self-acting capacities of the governed. This does not mean that these forms of knowledge are reducible to liberalism or that liberalism is ready to accept everything they produce. Rather, it means that liberal government contains within it a space of contestation and dissent in which various forms of knowledge are constituted as 'dialogical partners' of liberalism (Weir, 1996: 385). Over the last two centuries, liberalism has entered into dialogue with various social, economic and political forms of knowledge, from social economy to policy science, vital statistics to welfare economics, feminism to theories of management. In its concern to establish a set of linkages between a government of subjects active in their own rule and a knowledge of processes necessary to the security of the state, liberalism hollows out a space in which it is open to a dialogical self-critique in relation to forms of positive and interpretative disciplines and critical discourses.

It would thus be mistaken to imagine a phase of pure liberalism followed by a phase in which liberalism is diluted by the collectivist principles of welfarism, after the manner of A.V. Dicey's (1914) famous thesis. The forms of knowledge with which liberal government engages in this complex and sometimes difficult dialogue reveal the dangers to the security of these autonomous processes and the capacities of the individuals they depend on. Thus, in the nineteenth and early twentieth centuries, a number of disciplines from social economy to welfare economics can show that the economy is only self-regulating within certain parameters, that it results in urban misery, is subject to 'business cycles' creating unemployment and so on. Similarly, medical and public health authorities chart the threat to the population in the forms of epidemics, premature death and pauperism resulting from the unsanitary conditions of the working populations in the cities and towns. Philanthropists, educationalists and physicians can show the effect on the moral and physical development of children of factory labour and families deficient in relation to norms of hygiene and domestic economy. Criminologists and researchers can show the threats to civil society of the 'dangerous classes' and of *Homo criminalis*. Social reformers can substantiate the insecurity of segments of the population in sickness, old age and unemployment.

We could speak of roughly a century (between the mid nineteenth and mid twentieth centuries) in which the liberal governmental regime was subjected to a series of problematizations and critiques. In the interstices of this liberal space of government are to be found those new agencies and figures that claim expertise or whose domain is defined or redefined in relation to the problems diagnosed by such expertise: social workers, philanthropists, police officers, clinical psychologists, general practitioners, schoolteachers, public servants and so on. Such critical discourses find new institutional supports in public (i.e. state) schools, juvenile courts, government departments, police stations, unemployment exchanges, baby health and family planning clinics. If we link these problems, agents, institutional sites, forms of knowledge and types of action, we might discern the outline of a government of the *social*, one that emerges, if not directly out of liberalism, from the structured space of legitimate dissent from liberal government.

It is worthwhile reflecting at this point on this term 'the social', a theme first elaborated in the literature by Donzelot (1979; 1984). The social may be viewed as the privileged space in which the self-review and self-renewal of liberal government takes place for most of the twentieth century. It is important to underline its status: it is neither internal to liberal government, in that it cannot be derived from liberal political philosophy, nor external to it, in so far as it does not form a fundamental position of opposition to liberalism. Rather it is a set of problematizations of the liberal governmental economy (e.g. the 'social question', social problems, social issues), a set of institutions and practices (e.g. social welfare, social insurance, social work), a set of laws and legal jurisdictions (e.g. the juvenile court, family law) and a variety of actors, agencies and authorities (e.g. social workers, schoolteachers, police officers, general practitioners). All these represent solutions to problems of liberal government – of proper childrearing, of the effects of the industrial economy, of divorce, of urban crime – that maintain and interconnect formally constituted 'private' and 'public' divisions (between business and the state, between the family and the state). Yet, at the same time, the social threatens and ultimately does take liberal government beyond its founding images of society: those of the contract and atomistically conceived rational and autonomous individuals. For Deleuze the social is thus 'a particular sector in which quite diverse problems and special cases can be grouped together, a sector comprising specific institutions and an entire body of qualified personnel' (1979: ix).

Several points can be made here about the social. The first is that many of the interventions and practices conducted in its name rely upon the aspirations of those toward whom these interventions are directed. Thus Donzelot (1979) discusses the desire for 'social promotion' on behalf of families that is mobilized by medical, philanthropic and educational practices and their agents such as doctors, teachers and social workers. Many interventions relied on members of the family, even of poor families, to act as accomplices. Such interventions sought to elicit and then work through the active commitment and cooperation of families and family members to pursue their own well-being, and to collaborate with medical, educative and hygienic norms. Thus the social is a form of liberal government in that it seeks to work through a mass voluntary commitment to bettering the quality of family life.

The second point concerns the general problem of a form of social citizenship that is compatible with the existence of a liberal economy on the one hand, and a depoliticized sphere of family life on the other. Despite the empirical character and apparent diversity of the concerns through which 'the social' came to take on a kind of solidity and self-evidence, it must also be viewed as a response to a more general question of liberal ways of governing. This question, as Giovanna Procacci (1993) has succintly put it in relation to the French situation between the Revolution and 1848, is how a society which is founded on the juridical and political contract between citizens deals with the issues and effects of inequality and poverty. That problem, as she puts it (1993: 24), is how to diffuse the potential for conflict due to inequality and poverty in a society founded on civil and political inequality. Given that this problem is not visible from the perspective of the contract and of civil and political rights, i.e. from a juridical and political perspective, this had to be resolved in a new way. 'As a result of such tensions, a new field of policies, institutions and scientific disciplines – the social – was promoted' (Procacci, 1998: 11).

A final point concerns the relation between the notion of society and the social. For Donzelot, '"the social" is not society understood as the set of material and moral conditions that characterize a form of consolidation. It would appear to be rather the set of means which allow social life to escape material pressures and politico-moral uncertainties' (1979: xxvii). The social does not arise from the implementation of a theoretical model of society; rather, it is the condition of such a model. There is a sense in which the discovery of civil society is a component of the liberal critique of police at the end of the eighteenth century. However, the notion of society is never static or conclusively fixed. It might be better to think of society (conceived as a reality independent of state and politics and the real milieu in which the economy exists and has effects) as something that is always already waiting to be discovered in the development of various local critiques of the liberal governmental regime. In this sense, society was less a discovery of social theorists and more an artefact of the formation of the social. It was discovered and rediscovered: by philanthropists and social workers in the causes and effects of poverty; by doctors in the correlation between living conditions and mortality and morbidity rates; by educationalists in the attributes appropriate to the properly socialized citizen; by social economists in the ill-effects of political economy (Procacci, 1978); by sociologists in the forms of solidarity of different societies, and in the correlation of suicide with various social facts (Donzelot, 1988; 1991); by criminologists as something to be defended (Pasquino, 1980). For over a century, and across various liberal polities, the critique of government would lead to the formation of the social and to forms of social provision, agents, specialists and institutions that, in a piecemeal, incomplete and unplanned way, would be embraced within the newly drawn lines of the institutions of the national state. Such a critique, however, would pave the way for a vision of society no longer tied to the juridical categories of the individual, his or her rights and responsibilities and the contract. As we shall see in Chapter 9, the discovery of the reality of society as a reality *sui generis* has, among its conditions, the elaboration of the technology of social insurance and the related political doctrines of *solidarisme*.

This social government was the condition for the emergence of a specific rationality of government that might be called *welfarism* (Rose, 1993).

Welfarism gave rise to a host of intellectual edifices: triumphalist historical analyses, sociological narratives of citizenship, visions of the future, and political-economic programmes. Moreover, new academic disciplines and research were partly justified in relation to welfarism: public health, sociology, welfare economics, social administration and social policy. Such analyses and disciplines made it possible to understand localized, piecemeal criticisms and innovations of the classical liberal economy as part of a unified process that would culminate in a specific diagram of the operation of national governments – the 'welfare state'. The 'welfare state' was more an ethos of government or its ethical ideal and much less (and to varying degrees in different national contexts) a set of accomplished reforms and completed institutions. Above all, the welfare state was to be the *telos* (i.e. the final end or goal) of particular problematizations, interventions, institutions and practices concerning unemployment, old age, disability, sickness, public education and housing, health administration, and the norms of family life and child-drearing. It is important, as we shall see, to keep the notions of the social and of welfarism quite distinct so that the liberal critique of the latter might mean a reconfiguration rather than the end of social government.

Liberal government, then, is a manner of doing things that can be analysed as a principle and a method for the rationalization and review of the exercise of government (Foucault, 1989b: 110). While liberalism seeks a perpetual vigilance concerning an excess of government, it contains but does not determine the possibility of a social government within its internal regime. This is because, unlike early notions of police and certain variants of socialism, liberal government presumes a non-political dimension of existence governed by processes that are autonomous from the operation of sovereign authority. The security of these processes (of the economy, of the population, of civil society, of the family) is furthermore necessary to the ends of government. If liberalism assumes that 'the state' is a limited and somewhat artificial sphere, liberal government constructs the division between the state and its outside as necessary to its ends. In this sense, the social is a way of seeing, thinking and acting that is neither internal nor external to liberalism; rather, it arises on the basis of myriad critiques of the liberal governmental economy. Liberalism itself, however, today finds renewed force in its critique of the 'welfarist' edifice built from this social domain. Thus the relation between liberalism and the social is illustrative of the way in which the forms and targets of liberalism change, as does its conception of the governed subject and of the boundaries of the political. Given that, we shall now turn to Foucault's analysis of forms of 'neo-liberalism' and its views of the dangers of 'too much' government.

Neo-liberalism and Foucault

Foucault's own work on post-war liberalism stresses the specific contexts of the elaboration of its critiques of the irrationality of the excess of government and the return to a technology of what Benjamin Franklin called 'frugal government' (Foucault, 1989b: 117; Gordon, 1986; 1991). He also emphasizes the plurality of liberalisms, and the particular character of the intellectual formation of each instance. To this end he examines German liberalism from 1948 to 1962, particularly that published in the journal *Ordo*, and the American neo-liberalism that goes under the name of the Chicago School of Economics.[1]

The so-called *Ordoliberalen* are exceptionally interesting. They were intellectuals associated with the Freiburg School of the late 1920s whose work was defined at the intersection of neo-Kantian philosophy, Husserl's phenomenology and Weber's sociology, and was concerned with the connections manifested in history between economic processes and juridical structures (Foucault, 1989b: 117). Mostly exiled during the Third Reich, they returned to a position of pre-eminence after the war in the Federal Republic of Adenauer and Ludwig Erhard. Their response to the totalitarianism of the 1930s stands in marked contrast to that of the members of the Frankfurt School (Gordon, 1986: 80–1). Like the latter, they are lineal descendants of Weber and the Weberian theme which Foucault characterizes as the 'irrational rationality of capitalist society' (1991b: 78). However, where the Frankfurt neo-Marxists find themselves in a search for a broader, more social reason to overcome the irrationalities of capitalist instrumentalism, the Freiburg neo-liberals sought a new capitalist reason capable of overcoming the social irrationalities of previous forms of government and earlier epochs.

The 'ordoliberals', then, held that the German catastrophe was the consequence not of the failure of the capitalist economy but of the failure to implement a capitalist market regime. 'The market system had not been tried and found wanting, it had been denied a trial' (Gordon, 1986: 80). They accuse earlier types of social government, particularly Soviet socialism, National Socialism and Keynesian techniques of intervention, as remaining systematically ignorant of the market mechanisms that ensure stable price formation (Foucault, 1989b: 118). The ordoliberals recommend the implementation of the competitive market as 'an artificial game of competitive freedom', but under particular institutional conditions. Their conception of the market is profoundly anti-naturalistic and 'constructivist': it is no longer a domain of quasi-autonomous processes but a reality to be secured by an appropriate juridical, institutional and cultural framework. They therefore proposed that the market be organized, but not planned or directed, by an institutional and juridical officialdom, of which one part would offer the guarantees of the rule of law, and the other part would ensure that the freedom of economic processes would not be subject to social distortion (1989b: 118). Moreover, the market would be protected by vigilant social interventions that would include policies of unemployment assistance, health coverage and housing (1989b: 119). Finally, it would be necessary to ensure – by means of what Alexander von Rüstow called a *Vitalpolitik* or 'vital policy' – that the market as a game of competitive freedom was matched by a culture in which all aspects of life, not purely economic ones, would be restructured as the pursuit of a range of different enterprises (Gordon, 1991: 42).

There is here a basic identification of individual freedom and a free society with freedom of the market. It is this identification which allows these thinkers to offer both a means of political legitimation and a principle that would ensure both civil cohesion and future prosperity. However, the admission of a totalistic policy over the 'conduct of life' – over what Weber would have called the *Lebensführung* – appears to admit that the socially divisive effects of the market need to be kept in check not only by a professional bureaucratic and legal hierarchy but also by the judicious regulations of executive government, thus renewing contact – as Gordon (1991: 42) notes – with a statist strain in German political thought.

Foucault's (1989b: 118–19) approach to the Chicago School similarly brings into focus what is opposed, criticized and problematized. Here the examples of 'too much' government are the New Deal, war planning, and the post-war macro-economic and social programmes associated with Democratic administrations. He suggests that the danger of these forms of government is here represented as having an ineluctable logic: economic interventionism leads to excessive public sector growth, over-administration, bureaucracy and rigidity, which in turn create new economic distortions leading to a new cycle of interventions. The logic of the American neo-liberals moves in an opposite direction to that of the ordoliberals. For the latter, the mechanism of price formation is so fragile that it needs to be supplemented by an ever-vigilant internal politics and a complex set of policies and social provision. For the former, there is such a confidence in market rationality that it can be extended to all sorts of areas that are neither exclusively, nor even primarily, concerned with economics, such as the family, the birth rate, delinquency and crime. Economic rationality then can be used to analyse all aspects of human behaviour and provide guidelines for policy.

Gordon (1991: 43–4) draws on Foucault's lectures to show how this is possible. First, American neo-liberalism employs a notion of *choice* as a fundamental human faculty that overrides all social determinations. Second, this neo-liberalism radically inverts the notion of *Homo œconomicus* of earlier liberalism and proposes a form of 'manipulable man'. Rather than the subject who rationally calculates its interests as an economic actor, the choices of the subject are capable of being modified by its environment. *Homo œconomicus* here meets behaviourism to the extent that modifications in behaviour follow from remodelling the environment according to this market rationality. Third, this neo-liberalism presents, particularly in the theory of 'human capital' of Gary S. Becker, a map of this subject as an entrepreneur of herself or himself. Here the individual, composed of both innate and acquired skills and talents, invests in human capital to obtain both monetary earnings and psychic and cultural satisfactions. As Becker puts it, investments in human capital are 'activities that influence future monetary and psychic income by increasing the resources of people' (1964: 1).

What do these examples of neo-liberalism show? In a very basic sense, they alert us to the fact that there is more than one type of neo-liberalism. This is to say not that there is a good and a bad neo-liberalism but that it is necessary to analyse particular forms of political rationality and the ways in which they connect themselves to regimes of government. Nothing, in this sense, could be more remote from the ethos of genealogy than to imagine that we can somehow do away with an analysis of the specificity of political and governmental reason and discourse by identifying an 'ideal type' abstracted from the variety of current philosophies of government in advanced liberal democracies. They show us, second, that none of the forms of neo-liberalism are opposed to government understood as the 'conduct of conduct' and that they rely on specific mechanisms of regulation. In one version, the German social market economy (much like many contemporary forms of labour politics in Anglophone countries: Dean, 1998a), the apparatuses of national government have an activist and interventionist role in the organization of the conditions of a market economy and the production of types of subjects appropriate to its requirements. In another, closer to the Chicago School and contemporary conservative politics, the ends of the government of the state are folded back upon its means. Here we find the extension of market rationality into ever-new domains and the establishment of 'quasi' or artificial markets in areas of previously public provision of services.

Finally, these examples recapitulate and underline the critical and problematizing character of liberalism and the way in which the targets of this critique change according to historico-political circumstances. This leads us to remind ourselves of the singularity of the genealogical approach to liberalism. As Foucault (1989b: 110) puts it, liberalism is not to be approached as a theory, an ideology, a juridical philosophy of individual freedom or a set of policies, or even as a way in which a society 'represents itself', but as a 'manner of doing things' (*manière de faire*), oriented toward certain objectives and self-regulated by continuous reflection. It should be analysed, he suggests, 'as a principle and method for the rationalization of the exercise of government – a rationalization which obeys, and this is its specificity, the internal rule of maximal economy'. The variant forms of liberalism – and indeed of neo-liberalism – stem less from fundamental philosophical differences and more from the historical circumstances and styles of government which are met by a certain form of critique, an ethos of review and a method of rationalization.

We have, then, sketched the relationship between genealogy, government and liberalism in the work of Foucault and related literature in the late 1970s. This provides us with a springboard to begin to consider the kinds of issue confronting those of us who inhabit a world shaped by an international system of states, and in particular those who live in liberal-democratic states, at the beginning of the twenty-first century. In the next chapter we shall illustrate both the conceptual and methodological orientation, and the distinctive ethos of an analytics of government, outlined in these first two chapters, by means of two studies of key concepts of the critique of the welfarist mentality of government.

Note

1 Keith Tribe has suggested that the *Ordoliberalen* were not 'neo-liberals' in the sense that 'they envisage a wide-ranging programme of social reform, whereas the attention of neo-liberals is focused on competition policy' (1995: 207n). While this may be so from the viewpoint of economic *theory*, the ordoliberals can be regarded as neo-liberals, on Tribe's and Foucault's accounts, from the perspective of economic *governance*. They are neo-liberals in the latter sense in that they sought to reconstruct the operation of a market economy and the regime of the price mechanism, even if this did entail extensive social provision.

3 DEPENDENCY AND EMPOWERMENT: TWO CASE STUDIES

Many of the issues raised at a general conceptual and methodological level in the preceding chapters can be illustrated and clarified by a relatively brief discussion of two studies of key concepts in the contemporary government of welfare and poverty. These studies are close to the central analytical and substantive concerns of the present book. The first is an investigation into the history of the notion of welfare *dependency* by Nancy Fraser and Linda Gordon (1994). The second is a study of strategies of *empowerment* found in the US Community Action Programs in the 1960s by Barbara Cruikshank (1994). They both bear, to varying extents, the influence of post-Foucauldian concerns with power and government and with how we might understand the concepts and strategies through which governing is accomplished in contemporary liberal democracies. Both take up themes in public policy in the recent history of the United States and both display contemporary feminist concerns. Most significantly, they orient us toward how we might deal with the question of the agency of the governed raised in Chapter 1. Nevertheless, they illustrate rather different approaches to the relation between governing and agency. At the most general level, Cruikshank's study sits squarely within the analytical methodology and ethos of a Foucauldian genealogy. Fraser and Gordon's study, despite drawing on the language of genealogy, remains locked into the framework of critical theory with its meta-historical perspective and romance of emancipation.

Dependency

Since at least the 1970s, not only in the United States but also in other liberal-democratic countries, there has been much public policy discussion around notions such as a 'culture of poverty', 'permanent poverty', and the formation of a new 'underclass' composed of welfare dependants. Indeed welfare dependency is understood, on both right and left, as a key problem that follows from what is seen as the welfare-state mentality of the provision of benefits and services to passive recipients (e.g. OECD, 1988). The situation of being economically dependent on welfare benefits for one's subsistence is said to foster a culture in which individuals expect to receive such assistance, and in which that expectation becomes a component in the lifestyle of families, communities and neighbourhoods. Welfare dependency is most closely associated in the USA with the 'welfare mother', the invariably single, inner-city dwelling, African-American woman supporting children, often with the assistance of Aid to Families with Dependent Children (ADFC). However, welfare dependency can also be used to describe the situation of those who are identified as the 'long-term unemployed'. A central aspect of this notion of welfare dependency is that the *economic* state of being dependent upon benefits for one's subsistence is linked to a *moral-psychological state* of dependency that is reproduced within the lives and lifestyles of individuals, families and communities.

Nancy Fraser and Linda Gordon (1994) have sought to debunk this notion of 'dependency' by pointing to what they call its 'genealogy'. They borrow the notion of genealogy from Foucault to suggest a kind of historical analysis that questions our common-sense understanding of terms by examining how the meanings of such terms are constructed within diverse practices. As a first approach, we can note that this analysis shares with an analytics of government the focus on a specific problematization of the welfarist mentality of government. Further, these thinkers borrow the term 'genealogy' to denote a methodological strategy of 'defamiliarization'. However, to the extent that their analysis inscribes that methodology within a meta-historical narrative of modernity that endeavours to reveal the emancipatory agency of the governed, the ethos of their analysis is closer to that of critical theory than of genealogy.

Fraser and Gordon (1994: 312) identify four general registers of meaning of the term 'dependency':

1   an *economic* register in which one depends on another for subsistence, e.g. the case of a housewife or a servant
2   a *socio-legal* register in which one's legal status is subsumed under the legal personality of another, e.g. the case of married women under the common-law principle of coverture until well into the twentieth century
3   a *political* register of dependency, entailing subjection to an external power (in the case, for example, of a colonial dependency) or exclusion of certain individuals and groups from citizenship rights
4   a *moral-psychological* register in which the character traits of individuals or groups are known through moral or religious beliefs or forms of expertise, e.g. a drug addict.

Having identified these different registers of meaning of dependency, Fraser and Gordon then argue that they are differently assembled and understood within different types of societies. In *pre-industrial* society dependency is applied to the vast majority of people as serfs, apprentices, servants, retainers and wives (1994: 312–14). Those belonging to this differentiated group are found in a position of economic subordination and socio-legal subsumption under another (e.g. the master, lord or household head). They have no political rights because landed property ownership is a condition of access to such rights. Dependency here is a normal, not a deviant, condition, and implies inferiority without moral disapprobation. In *industrial* society, under the combined influences of certain forms of radical Protestantism, democratic struggles and the emergent labour market, dependency comes to be understood as inimical to human dignity and self-determination. White working men throw off political and legal subordination and understand the system of wage-labour as a form of independence. There are several figures left outside this notion of the 'independent labourer': the pauper, the native, the slave and the housewife. While the first three are largely understood through the moral-psychological register, the housewife complements the male worker's independence by combining the pre-industrial socio-legal and political dependency of wives within patriarchal households with a more recently intensified economic dependency. Dependency, in its economic sense, is hence feminized. Within feminist struggles against the law of coverture, this dependency becomes increasingly stigmatized. Nonetheless, it was possible to distinguish between the 'bad' dependency of, for example, the pauper, and the 'good' dependency of the housewife.

In *post-industrial* society, however, Fraser and Gordon (1994: 323–5) argue that there have been two changes which have seriously undermined the classical industrial system of dependency: the formal abolition of many of the socio-legal and political statuses of dependants; and the 'decentring' of the family wage. First, then, housewives, paupers and natives are no longer excluded from civil and political rights. Second, under forces of economic restructuring and the proliferation of new family forms, the family wage ideal is no longer hegemonic. This has led to claims that the bases of dependency have been removed and that only the moral-psychological meanings remain. These claims, however, have mostly emanated from forms of expertise such as the 'psy' disciplines, ensuring that dependency has become 'pathologized' and associated with therapy. 'Dependent personality disorder' becomes codified in the *Diagnostic and Statistical Manual of Mental Disorders* (APA, 1994). We now can talk about 'drug dependency'; about 'co-dependency', that is relations where one person, usually female, supports another's dependency; and, of course, about 'welfare dependency'. As a consequence, the pejorative overtones increase and the term becomes increasingly individualized. Even the feminist critique of housewives' psychological dependency, as evidence of their social subordination, provided by Betty Friedan in the 1960s becomes translated into a gender-based depth psychology of women's hidden fear of independence. According to this account, in post-industrial society there is no longer any good dependency.

When applied to welfare, the central contention is that poor people have something more wrong with them than their poverty. Welfare dependency is hence a syndrome lurking behind the welfare state that can be related to biology, psychology, upbringing, culture or behaviour, or several or even all of these factors. The particular coalescence of the notion of welfare dependency on the African-American, unmarried, teenaged, welfare-claiming mother in the USA is extremely interesting. The way in which this figure of the welfare mother works within political discourse is exemplified in the then Vice-President Quayle's comment after the 1992 riots in Los Angeles: 'Our inner cities are filled with children having children . . . with people who are dependent on drugs and on the narcotic of welfare' (Fraser and Gordon, 1994: 327). The particular attention given to the welfare mother can be understood, Fraser and Gordon suggest, as resulting from the place that ADFC has within the administrative structure of US social benefits and the problematization of the African-American family that can be traced back to the Moynihan Report of the 1960s and further.

There is much to Fraser and Gordon's account of dependency that is strong and compelling and repays close study. It critically engages with a key component of the problematization of welfarism. In this sense it can be read as a contribution to the examination of the mentality or rationality of government characteristic of recent neo-liberal and neo-conservative critiques. It demonstrates the fruitfulness of attention to the language of social problems, to the way the terms of that vocabulary are contested, and to the ways in which they change over time. In their most perceptive passages, Fraser and Gordon demonstrate how notions of dependency and independence are written into the logic of the US system of public provision, and how they intersect in a particular fashion within the 'second-track', gendered, form of assistance of ADFC.

Nevertheless, there are important limitations to the analysis. The employment of the great sociological schema of 'industrial society' risks a certain homogenization of insights revealed by the empirical material. This might be thought of as contrary to the ethos of genealogy – that ethos which leads the genealogist to a careful, detailed analysis without acceding to the hubris of claiming a pivotal status for the present. More central, however, is the way in which this schema is allied with a form of analysis known as 'ideology critique', derived at least in part from the inheritance of the Frankfurt School of critical theory. The objective of ideology critique is to unmask the ideological content of language to reveal real relations of subordination. Consequently, the notion of dependency is understood as an ideological 'keyword' that changes its meaning in relation to broad institutional and social-structural shifts (Fraser and Gordon, 1994: 310–11). Another approach, occasionally hinted at by the authors, is to regard the notion of welfare dependency as a component within a particular mentality of government and its vocabulary of rule, a vocabulary that conditions and is conditioned by the ways in which we govern others and ourselves. More simply, where ideology critique views language as condensing meanings generated by social structures, an analytics of government attempts to grasp what language makes possible and what it does, i.e. how it functions within what Miller and Rose (1990) call an 'intellectual technology'. For ideology critique, the task of the analysis of language is to unmask the ideological content to reveal the possibility of alternative, emancipatory truths. For an analytics of government, concepts such as 'dependency' figure within regimes of practices concerning the relief and welfare of the poor in countries such as the USA in several different ways. They figure within the problematization and critique of existing or past operations of such regimes. They enable an alternative visualization and representation of the problems to be addressed and they invest the reform of these regimes with particular objectives. As a central element in a mentality of rule, the language of dependency and associated concepts can be approached as problematization, representation and programme of reform.

What are the consequences of these different ways of approaching terms such as 'dependency'? Fraser and Gordon's analysis approaches dependency as comprising a set of meanings that arises from the broad configurations or structures of various types of society. Such terms are ideological in that they embody and condense perceptions and values that are derived from the structures of domination within those societies. This is a fairly straightforward version of the kind of ideology critique much beloved of critical theorists and sociologists of knowledge. The key problem with this approach is that it still regards language as a second-order phenomenon shaped by more fundamental forces and conditions. It cannot then view language as an integral component within ways of doing things; nor can it examine how language shapes what are taken to be problem areas of social and political life and how they might be addressed. This is not to say that the language and vocabulary of rule should be accorded a causal priority in analysis. It is simply to hold that we should not underestimate the role of language in constructing worlds, problems and persons as governable entities.

Key terms in vocabularies of rule – such as dependency – are not simply ideological condensations of the meanings of broad social structures. They are integral components of government, of our organized systems of acting upon and directing human conduct. From the perspective of an analytics of government, notions of 'dependency' are primarily intelligible as components of various systems of governing or regimes of practices. One such regime of practices concerns problems of poverty and the administration and treatment of the poor. Thus in England at the beginning of the nineteenth century, the notion of 'independent labourer' is first of all a key aspect of the Malthusian programmes that sought the reform of the Poor Laws and the guidance of philanthropy so that propertyless able-bodied men, and those construed as their 'dependants' (wives, children), were no longer legitimate objects of assistance. Such classes were to be granted public relief only under the 'less eligible' and deterrent conditions of the workhouse. Here, categories of independence and dependence played a key role in providing a code which functioned as the means of discrimination between legitimate and illegitimate objects of relief in the reformed Poor Law administration after 1834 (Dean, 1991). While this is but an episode in the history of the notion of dependency, it clearly demonstrates the inscription of such concepts in particular regimes of practices of relieving the poor. In the case of recent notions of 'dependency' focusing on such groups as single parents or long-term unemployed people, we can detect a critique of welfare provision that presages particular types of reform which will contrast, to use the language of 'New Labour' in Britain, a 'hand-out' with a 'hand-up'. In order to make intelligible terms such as 'dependency', we need to shift our analysis from the study of the relation between ideology and social structure to the operation of regimes of practices of welfare and assistance. By doing this, we can show not simply how notions of dependency are symbolic of social relations, but how they actually allow practices and programmes of reform to operate. Such practices include those which constructed the very shape of the nineteenth-century industrial labour-market, or those which today form what we shall call in Chapter 8 of this book a 'post-welfarist' regime of social government. This kind of analysis also makes it possible to grasp the reason for the longevity and difficulty of abandoning such notions within public policy. How we think about governing and the reform of government, the way in which we construct domains of government, the instruments and means by which we govern – and hence the entire field of what might be called public policy – are not secondary reflections of more fundamental relations of, say, the market and the family. Rather, rationalities of government are among the permanent conditions that help give shape to those domains we know as the labour market and the space of familial life. When we contest or attempt to reshape ways we think about governing in any sphere, we call into question the very fabric of our forms of life.

Several points follow from this displacement of ideology critique. First, analysis must move from the ways in which categories such as the 'sole parent' and 'the long-term unemployed' are contingent upon changing social structures, to focus on how such categories arise from, and are necessary to, particular regimes of practices concerning the provision of welfare. They are not simply components of ideology. These are first of all governmental categories that are produced within specific practices and within attendant forms of knowledge and expertise. Such categories – and related forms of knowledge – are necessary to the processes of the distribution of welfare benefits and other social services in liberal democracies. It is thus somewhat absurd to imagine that we can do without such categories. An analysis of such categories that disregards the practices of which they are a part, and which they allow to function in specific ways, is thereby limited.

Second, we must abandon the idea that by demystifying notions of dependency we shall uncover *real* relations of subordination. Given the politically controversial nature of welfare-state measures, and the proliferation of the human sciences and derived forms of expertise, such categories as 'sole parent' will be invested with meanings and subject to programmes of action that derive from such knowledge. This will include the employment of moral and psychological judgements. We cannot simply wish away such forms of knowledge or the programmes of reform they make possible. In order to contest such notions, we must rely on similar types of knowledge, or at least some other form of expertise. To assert that the condition of the sole parent is a result of 'social relations of subordination' and not the moral or psychological condition of the individual, we employ social scientific knowledge and show its priority over arguments derived from psychology or moral philosophy. Contestation often takes the form of competing – and sometimes the same – kinds of expertise (e.g. that of social policy versus economic models) derived from the human sciences.

Third, we should reject the romanticization of the 'victim' often coupled with the critique of ideology. Here ideology critique meshes with the 'meta-histories of promise' characterized in the preceding chapter. Ideology critique characteristically invokes, in one way or another, the experience or understandings of those who are the objects of governmental practices and perceptions, e.g. the victim, the oppressed, the powerless, the marginalized, the poor. Sometimes this is linked to the widespread sociological theme of resistance and, beyond that, to broader notions of agency. In this particular case, Fraser and Gordon (1994) appeal to a higher kind of expertise – the expertise offered as the experience and agency of the welfare recipients themselves. They cite the members of the National Welfare Rights Organization as having an active, rights-claiming relation to welfare rather than a passive, charity-receiving one, and those claiming AFDC who complained of bureaucratic enforcement of dependency (1994: 329–30). Fraser and Gordon thus call upon the expert agency of welfare claimants in articulating needs, demanding rights and making claims. The agency, expertise and experience of the victims or the oppressed link this style of critique to the ethos of the 'meta-histories of promise' by its almost ritualized cashing out of the emancipatory credentials of the analysis.

Fraser and Gordon are right to point to the existence of a field of contestation involving multiple agencies around the governmental expertise of welfare. In so doing they remind us that governmental programmes are produced by diverse agencies in complex relations of antagonism and collusion with one another and that politics should be regarded as a matter of struggle between such agencies whose outcome depends upon these agencies' capacity to mobilize intellectual and material resources, and on their tactics and strategies.[1] However, the point of investigating these alternative discourses of welfare, for Fraser and Gordon, is to question received valuations of dependency in order to 'allow new emancipatory social visions to emerge' (1994: 332). This move rests on the implicit assumption that the oppressed are able to achieve an actual or potential greater access to the truth. Thus the agency of the oppressed indicates the truth of humanity and the path to emancipation because, as such, it stands outside the power relations which maintain ideological representations of that humanity. The problem here, however, is that the invocation of the expertise of the claimants themselves, and more generally of their agency and their capacity for active engagement with authorities of various kinds, no more steps outside relations of power, domination and subordination than does the notion of welfare dependency. For one of the characteristics of contemporary practices of government (that will be stressed and investigated in this book) is the way in which practices of government have come to rely upon the agency of the governed themselves. In this sense, the place where 'emancipatory' social visions emerge, for Fraser and Gordon, is the aim of the very practices of government they hope to criticize. In order to make and illustrate this fundamental point, we shall turn to another recent American study, this time of what its author calls 'the will to empower' (Cruikshank, 1994).

Empowerment

The idea of empowering the disenfranchised, the marginal and the poor has had extremely positive connotations in recent political thought and action. The notion that victims of social inequalities and discrimination, economic deprivation and political subordination be 'empowered' to cast off their status as victims and actively participate in the transformation of their condition has been, since the 1960s, remarkably compelling for thinkers, activists and reformers in liberal-democratic countries. It draws upon the participatory aspects of democratic traditions and preserves, while it radicalizes, the stress on autonomy and self-determination found in many variants of liberalism. It suggests that the value of political arrangements can be measured by the degree to which they enable all citizens to participate in decision-making processes. Empowerment is, in this sense, the normative correlate of the explanatory focus on agency. If human beings are, at least potentially, agents, then they need to be empowered to become so. Programmes of empowerment are particularly clear examples of those contemporary liberal rationalities of government that endeavour to operationalize the self-governing capacities of the governed in the pursuit of governmental objectives.

An American political scientist, Barbara Cruikshank (1994), has recently begun to explore this notion of empowerment as it developed in the USA in the 1960s in the Community Action Programs (CAPs) initiated under President Johnson's War on Poverty and the wider anti-poverty movement of the period. Empowerment, here and in its related feminist variant, emerges as what Cruikshank calls a *technology of citizenship*, a strategy or technique for the transformation of subjectivity from powerlessness to active citizenship. We note here the stress on both the technical aspect – or *techne* – of governing and the manner in which governing is concerned with the fabrication of certain kinds of subjectivity and identity. This technology of citizenship requires consciousness of one's powerlessness, knowledge of its causes, and action to change these conditions (1994: 30–1). The notion that one needs to empower 'victims' so that they may actively engage in the provision of services, and overcome a passive, indeed dependent relation to government, was not only a part of the official jargon of the CAPs but also taken up by the 1960s New Left political activists, the civil rights movement, and the nascent 'second-wave' feminist movement. The notion of empowerment survives and prospers today as a part of official political vocabulary on the Right and in the mainstream of American politics. It is in evidence in the idea of Empowerment Zones, a concept that basically encompasses the use of market solutions such as privatization to problems of urban poverty and housing

(1994: 33). It is also evidenced by its key place in the influential programme for 'reinventing government' put forward by Osborne and Gaebler (1993), in which a core component of the entrepreneurial restructuring of public agencies is that they empower rather than serve. Given that the notion is integral to the contemporary reform of public services, Cruikshank's contribution to the genealogy of the concept is highly pertinent.

As technologies of citizenship, political relations that entail empowerment have four features according to Cruikshank, each of which can be illustrated by the CAPs. First, they are established by a definite, if contested, form of expertise. The notion of empowerment is thus a component in a particular type of rationality of government. In the case of the CAPs, this expertise involved a knowledge of the powerlessness of the poor, and of the means for getting the powerless to participate in anti-poverty programmes. The key object of this expertise was the subjective sense of powerlessness and apathy that prevents the poor from identifying themselves as a constituency for anti-poverty policy and from voluntarily participating in it. In this sense expertise about the poor and their condition was to be secondary to the expertise of the poor themselves (1994: 35–8).

Second, empowerment entails what Cruikshank calls 'a democratically unaccountable use of power' in that one party initiates it. Thus in the CAPs, the US federal government sought to elicit and stimulate the participation of the poor through the legislative creation of local power relations – embodied in the key notion of 'community' – between the poor, the delinquent, social scientists, service providers, street-level bureaucrats and, most importantly, the professional reformer cum radical activist. The central objective of official discourses concerning the CAPs was 'maximum feasible participation' (1994: 38). The poor would not create anti-poverty programmes but would participate as a unified actor replete within the community as constituted within these programmes.

Third, such relations depend upon a knowledge of those to be empowered. We can note here how definite forms of knowledge are a condition of the workings of the practices of empowerment and how, in turn, those practices give rise to various types of knowledge and truth. In the War on Poverty, there were several interesting interconnections between the technologies of citizenship and social scientific knowledge. Above all, the 'poor' had to be known to be governed. Yet before they were known, the 'poor' had to be constituted as a unified grouping. Here 'the poor' was reinvented as a term that crossed racial, geographic, labour market, gender and age barriers to combine disparate groups into what Michael Harrington called *The Other America* (1968). At about the same time, anthropologists spoke of a 'culture of poverty'. There was a massive labour of forming the poor into a knowable object so that they might be governed. At the same time political scientists engaging in the community power debate such as Bachrach and Baratz (1962; 1970) were able to discover what they considered the 'second face of power' which included 'non-participation', 'non-events' and 'non-decision-making'.

Fourth, these relations of empowerment involve what Cruikshank calls a 'voluntary and coercive exercise of power upon the subjectivity of those to be empowered' (1994: 35). Here, relations of empowerment defeat the dichotomies by which we usually pose the problem of power – between power and powerlessness, consent and constraint, subjectivity and subjection. Governmental interventions, such as the CAPs, sought to create a set of conditions which *required* that the poor should act so that government might become effective. The poor were subjected to these programmes and to the authority of their agents in order that they might attain a certain type of subjectivity. Governmental regulation occurred so that the governed might exercise their freedom. Thus Cruikshank's study illustrates how government can depend upon the formation of certain types of subject with the capacity to exercise various forms of freedom and how contemporary government cannot be understood in terms of the dichotomies of conventional understandings of power.

In the CAPs, then, a War on Poverty was to be conducted not only by reformers and bureaucrats but by the poor themselves. The poor were to be armed in this war so that they might struggle for the introduction, improvement and enlargement of measures to defeat poverty. By 1969, the US government withdrew support for the programme of 'maximum feasible participation' – no doubt partially owing to the failure of the programme to constitute a coherent community, but also owing to the effects of the agency granted to activists and the poor themselves. The study thus demonstrates two features of the 'congenitally failing' character of programmes of government: the possibility of unintended outcomes of such programmes, some of which might result from the formation of various agencies, e.g. of the 'poor' themselves, of activists; and the way in which 'failure' is viewed according to criteria of evaluation and judgement which are sometimes internal to the programme itself and sometimes internal to other programmes, e.g. the cost of the War on Poverty and Great Society programmes. Despite such 'failure' and unanticipated outcomes, the programme has wider implications in the larger history of the government of minorities and the marginalized, and in the women's movement, and it established a link between the self-government of individuals and groups and their effective government.

By way of concluding this case study, I want to indicate how we might regard Cruikshank's analysis as critical. Here, critical discourse works not through the unmasking of ideological representations to uncover real relations, as does Fraser and Gordon's ideology critique. Rather it makes clear the immanent disjunction and dissonance between how practices of empowerment are viewed by their advocates and the intelligibility or logic of such practices. In this way we might say, using the language enunciated in the first chapter, that Cruikshank's study gains a critical purchase by making intelligible the *strategy* of which the *programme* of empowerment is only one incomplete part. First, the *logic of empowerment*, as we have seen, tends to dichotomize power and powerlessness, but Cruikshank shows how self-governing can be a component in power relations. While power relations are unequal and hierarchical, they are not 'zero-sum games' in which only certain actors have power at the expense of others. Second, *relations of empowerment* are viewed as outside power relations in that they are understood as merely facilitating the active participation of the poor as agents in the political process. However, Cruikshank's study demonstrates how the relations between the poor and the activist, the poor and the bureaucrat, and indeed the poor and themselves are acted upon by governmental agencies. These relations are constituted within a distinctive rationality, technology and strategy of power. The agency of the poor does not anticipate 'emancipatory visions of society' outside power relations but is an element in a particular set of power relations. Finally, while empowerment is presented as a *quantitative* increase in capacity, it acts as a *qualitative transformation of forms of subjectivity*. It tries to act upon disparate groups so that they come to recognize their common being within a unified administrative category, thereby assuming the identity of active citizens and participants in social reform.

Cruikshank's analysis cannot be called a 'critique', if that implies a position privileged by access to universal morality from which to criticize specific practices. If we mean by criticism a questioning and a shaking of the self-evidence of practices, this analysis is surely critical. One important way in which it criticizes is by demonstrating the disjunction between the intelligibility of such practices and their explicit programmatic rationality.

A second way in which Cruikshank's study allows us to engage critically with practices and programmes of empowerment is that it acts as a kind of 'exemplary criticism' of the kind we discussed in Chapter 1. Her research into our 'will to empower' exemplifies an orientation toward the question of self-rule simply by focusing on it as a research topic. In so far as it provides greater intelligibility to claims that certain practices serve to foster forms of self-rule, and thus reveals the dangers, delusions and states of domination to which such practices give rise, it enables us to think more carefully and critically about our own will to empower.

Conclusion

Why tell this story of the CAPs when it is merely an episode in the short history of techniques of empowerment? It can be read as a sobering restraint on our will to empower and, perhaps more generally, on our embracing of governmental programmes that seek to optimize the agency of the governed. This is not to say that we should abandon or not join in with such programmes. One of the themes of this book will be the way in which the active agency of the governed is a necessary component of many of the ways in which we both govern and are governed. This suggests, however, that the agency of the marginalized, the poor, minorities, welfare claimants, victims and so on does not point to an emancipatory vision of free, consensual social relations, i.e. relations that are outside coercive, regulatory exercises of power. To specify, attempt to use, work with or through this agency is not to escape power relations. It is to seek to establish particular kinds of power relations, and to effect a specific use of expertise. Terms such as empowerment, agency, activity and resistance, as much as dependency, passivity and subordination, are key aspects of our contemporary vocabulary of rule and are constituted in relation to definite regimes of government and power relations. Cruikshank's analysis highlights what is only implicit in Fraser and Gordon's study of welfare dependency: how effective government in contemporary liberal democracies comes to depend on the actions of self-determining individuals and groups. In order to work, governing often concerns the formation of the subjectivities through which it can work.

Cruikshank's analysis thus does a service in favour of 'moral forces' in Weber's terms. It makes us more responsible when we endeavour to participate in programmes of empowerment – or any other programme that tries to elicit the agency of those who are governed. It does this by clarifying how such programmes work and by presenting 'inconvenient facts' about the disjunction between how such programmes represent themselves and their objectives and strategic effects. It serves moral forces to the extent that it increases our circumspection about the value of programmes of empowerment. Moreover, by demonstrating the global and totalizing ambitions of the slogan of 'maximum feasible participation', it prevents us from too readily acceding to the view that maximizing participation is the answer to all social and political ills.

Both of these studies suggest that we can analyse terms such as 'dependency' and 'empowerment' as components of systematic ways of thinking about the population to be governed, the means by which that population is constituted, and the objectives to be sought. Both studies alert us to the various ways in which forms of expertise and knowledge shape the field of visibility of who and what is to be governed and why. They also emphasize the complex and constitutive relations of the language of government to the knowledge provided by the human, social and behavioural sciences. Cruikshank's study, in particular, presents various ways in which forms of knowledge are implicated in the exercise of authority. It demonstrates the massive intellectual labour entailed in forming 'the poor' as a unified object of intervention throughout the 1960s. Moreover, the practices that constituted the CAPs became an arena for political scientists who codified issues of non-participation into the theory of the second face of power. Here is a clear example of the way in which problems raised by practices of government give rise to theoretical knowledge that in turn can be used to refine such practices. These regimes of government thus exist in complex interdependence with the knowledge produced by the human sciences. Such knowledge is their conditions of possibility (there could be no War on Poverty without the unified thought-object of 'the poor') and is among their ramifications (social and political scientists develop their interest in community and community studies).

Cruickshank's study is also exemplary in two further ways. It shows how regimes of government extend far beyond what have been conventionally considered the formal apparatuses and institutions of the state. It demonstrates that governing often seeks to define, connect and coordinate relations between state agencies, legislatures, communities, neighbourhoods, professionals, individuals and so on. This study challenges us to provide a language of analysis which is no longer dependent on the image of the state and on a fixed separation of public and private spheres, and which can accommodate itself to the inherent multiplicity (of programmes, agents, authorities, objectives, etc.) of governing.

Cruikshank also points to what is a tricky theoretical problem, but one from which many studies of governmentality can gain a certain critical purchase. This is the problem of the disjunction between the explicit rationalities of government (the stated intentions of the CAPs, the explicit programmes of empowerment) and the more or less implicit logic of these practices (how these practices operate as revealed by the analysis). The term 'strategy' will henceforth be reserved to describe the non-subjective yet intentional logic that can be discerned when one analyses a regime of governmental practices (cf. Gordon, 1980: 250–1). As we have already noted, it is here that the critical potential of these studies can be located.

Cruikshank's study offers a particularly clear analysis of one key episode in the critical history and diagnosis of our contemporary ways of governing. The following chapters hopefully will contribute to broadening our focus. They examine key elements of a genealogy of the forms of governmentality current within these states and then proceed to a diagnostic of features of our present political circumstances.

Note

1 On both of these points, I am in agreement with O'Malley et al. (1997). Studies of governmentality need to emphasize the plurality of diversity of agencies which shape how a field is to be governed, and to be sure that they do not reduce politics to government. An analytics of government studies the conditions under which politics is possible; it needs to be articulated with an analysis of the 'strategic game of liberties' (Foucault, 1988a) or with politics in Weber's sense of action directed toward affecting government (Hindess, 1997). It does not follow from this, however, that we need to draw a fundamental line between those agencies on the side of power (government, or whatever) and those in a position of resistance to it.

4 PASTORAL POWER, POLICE AND REASON OF STATE

> Government is the right disposition of things, arranged so as to lead to a convenient end. (Guillaume de La Perrière, 1567)[1]

> But with us in England, for want of a due regulation of things, the more populous we are, the Poorer we are; so that, that wherein the Strength and Wealth of a Kingdom consists, renders us the weaker. (Sir Matthew Hale, 1683)

In this and the following three chapters we encounter examples of governing that range from pastoral government of the members of a religious community in ancient societies to the ways in which populations have been managed by national states in the name of various political and social objectives, both liberal and non-liberal, in the twentieth century. Far from representing a simple inventory of different styles and ways of thinking of governing, however, these chapters offer a way of thinking about the historical trajectories of government in Western European countries and their colonial and post-colonial derivatives. They chart what might very broadly be thought about as the trajectory of the 'governmentalization of the state'. This is a trajectory on which government first is elaborated as a government of humans and their conduct in relations to 'things' and later becomes a 'government through processes'.

In this chapter we shall see that the emergence of a secular and autonomous art of government from the sixteenth to the eighteenth centuries in Europe first took the form of what Hale calls a 'due regulation of things', or the 'right disposition of things' as La Perrière put it. This conception understood the task of government to be to ensure the wise and proper distribution of humans and things, and their relations and movement, within the territorial confines of the kingdom or state. There are many other aspects to different rationalities of government from the sixteenth to the eighteenth centuries in Europe that will be developed in this chapter. However, this 'dispositional' theme would seem to be common to many, if not all, of these rationalities.

No matter how naïve it might seem, I want to emphasize that the point of this excursion into the past is to shed light on current problems and values and our understandings of these problems and values.[2] One of the fundamental questions that drives the following investigations, commentaries and development of the literature on governmentality is that of the welfare state and the possible transformation, and even 'death', of social forms of government. Much of this chapter traces the formation of elements of political thought that might be understood as comprising the deep but obscure foundations of the values and ideals encapsulated in our twentieth-century conceptions of a welfare state. It is for this reason that we shall first consider the emergence and consequences of pastoral forms of government in ancient societies. The analyses presented in this chapter are not simply illustrations of a theoretical schema. They are intended to assist in the reflection on those problems usually cast in terms of oppositions between state intervention and the market, public and private provision, values and administration, equality and freedom and so on. They are also offered to help us think about the way in which the provision for human needs has come to be posed as a question of the division of responsibilities between markets, states, communities, families and individuals.

Pastoral power

Where do our notions of 'care' come from? More specifically, what are the sources of the idea that the state should care for the welfare of its citizens? What kind of trajectory is it possible to map of this concern to govern for the welfare of citizens? What kind of problems might be built into this notion? To suggest how we might begin to answer these questions I shall introduce Foucault's notion of 'pastoral power' and develop it in relation to themes concerning the care of the poor in late antiquity.

It is hardly contentious to argue that one key source of a concern for the welfare of individuals and of populations, of each and all, is to be found in the development of pastoral techniques of government in Christianity. Foucault indeed assumes this argument when he proposes to investigate the Christian notion of pastoral care taken over and adapted from ancient Judaism (1988b; 1988c). The pastoral relationship is between God, the pastor (his representative) and the pastorate (the Christian community). The relation between God and his people is conceived within this tradition as the relation between the shepherd and the flock ('the Lord is my shepherd'). Indeed any examination of the *longue durée* – the level of the slow-placed, barely perceptible, historical temporality much beloved by the Annales School of historians such as Fernand Braudel (1980: 25–54) – of social government will show the close connection between the Church, charity, and provision for the poor and the sick and the education of the young. It is only in the last few hundred years that these types of activity have been undertaken under the aegis of secular authority in European societies and their New World outgrowths.

That 'welfare' has become a secular concern is certainly connected with the schisms of Western European Christianity at the time of the Reformation and Counter-Reformation and the religious and sectarian wars that accompanied them. The examination of 'pastoral power' and its evolution within these societies is thus absolutely central to understanding how these societies came to give a special place to collective and secular provision of welfare. It also helps us understand a central paradox of contemporary liberal welfare states: how charity, philanthropy and voluntary activity (what is now sometimes referred to as the 'third sector') can be used both to buttress and also to undermine the ideal of a welfare state.

Following Foucault (1988c: 61–3) we might locate a primary source of our notions of care in the ancient Hebraic conceptions of pastoral power modelled on the shepherd–flock relation. These conceptions are characterized by four themes: the fundamental nature of the relation of the God-shepherd to the flock; the constitution of the flock by the shepherd's activity of gathering them together and guiding them; the salvation of each and all by means of the shepherd's individualized kindness; and, finally, the shepherd's duty to be devoted without rest and to know the flock as a whole and in detail.

Foucault notes that the image of the shepherd-ruler is found in other cultures, including ancient Greece, but without such centrality. Plato, for example, addresses the shepherd–flock relation but impugns it as an inappropriate way of thinking about the task of the politician (1988c: 64–7). While the gods in the Golden Age might act like shepherds, and so too the teacher or physician, the politician's task is not to foster the life of a group but to form and ensure the city's unity. It is not antique political thought but early Christianity that takes up the relation of shepherd and flock. Christ becomes the 'Good Shepherd'.

The theme of the shepherd and the flock, however, is modified in several ways in early Christian thought (1988c: 68–70). First, the shepherd becomes accountable for the actions of all. There are complex and profound moral ties binding the shepherd and the members of his flock. Second, obedience comes to be understood as a key virtue. The members of the Church are bound to the shepherd's will in a relation of complete dependence. They obey the shepherd not because it is the law but because it is his will. Third, the shepherd now requires an in-depth individualizing knowledge of each member of the flock. This is a knowledge of the needs and deeds, and the contents of the soul, of each. Here the early Christians took over ancient Greek and Roman practices of the 'care of the self' including self-examination and guidance of conscience, but uncoupled these from the self-government of free citizens and tied them to notions of total obedience. Finally the practices of guidance, examination and obedience are linked to the objective of getting individuals to work on their own worldly 'mortification'. This is a renunciation of the things of this world for the purity and grace to enter another.

The early Christian pastorate provides us with an image of the exercise of power that is in many ways continuous with certain of our present forms of expertise. Like Christian pastoral power, many forms of expertise in the twentieth century, such as those that involve the 'psy' disciplines, counselling, social work and other therapeutics, seek a knowledge of the individual and his or her inner existence, and require that the individual practise a form of self-renunciation (e.g. of alcohol and drugs, of bad habits, of co-dependent behaviours, etc). However, there is one point on which contemporary pastoral power differs from its early Christian version: the individual is now 'normalized' in relation to scientific knowledge of populations. The effects of pastoral power are intensified through what Foucault called bio-politics, which we examine in the following chapter.

The investigation of these images of government allowed Foucault to open up a questioning of the deep roots of our mentalities of government (1988c: 67, 71). He used it to stress the tensions inherent in the 'welfare-state problem' between the 'shepherd–flock game', inherited by way of Christianity, and the 'city–citizen game', inherited from the Greek model of the *polis*. The first tension is between two ways of conceiving the exercise of power. One might use the image of the *polis* or *res publica* as emblematic of a conception of political power exercised within and by a self-governing political community that will later be understood as a state. Such a community is subject to laws of its own making. By contrast, the image of the shepherd and his flock, or the pastorate, might stand for a long trajectory of pastoral power that is transformed in the eighteenth century into a concern for each and every member of the population, his or her life, death, individual existence and identity. The second is a tension between two types of governed subject. Here the contrast is between a legal and political subject with rights and obligations, encapsulated in notions of the citizen, and the living individual who is the target of pastoral power, a being who is both obedient and needful. Foucault thus argues that the welfare-state problem is one of the 'tricky' adjustment between political power exercised over legal-political subjects and pastoral power exercised over live individuals.

Cities and citizens

Foucault's comments are interesting if somewhat sketchy. In the remainder of this section, I want to provide a more concrete historical account of these two ways of thinking about government and view them in the context of their historical conflict. In order to do so, I shall make reference to Paul Veyne's work on the duties of benefaction of the ruling class in classical antiquity and Peter Brown's work on the challenge to the ruling order provided by the nascent Christian communities.

The notion of the city–citizen game remains relatively unexplored in Foucault's work. Indeed it is tempting to read into it the idea of the community of free citizens that make up the *polis* or the *res publica* and to regard Athenian democracy as a kind of ideal. The fact of 'euergetism', or the obligation of the ruling notables to stand as benefactors of their cities, provides us with a rather different version of the city–citizen game. The term is derived from *euergesia*, Greek for the desire to do good for the city, and *euergetai*, those who engaged in acts of civic beneficence arising from this noble motive. There is no modern equivalent of this phenomenon as motive, practice or social group, with the partial exception of that kind of philanthropy by which, particularly in the USA, the rich bequest permanent foundations to establish museums and other quasi-public institutions. The difference between euergetism and philanthropy, and the fact that we no longer think it necessary to notice that difference, is at the heart of our concerns here.

Veyne's magisterial *Bread and Circuses* (1990) covers over a thousand years (from before 300 BC to AD 300) of euergetism through four social orders. The first is the moment of the beginnings of public gift-giving in the Greek city-states when emergent inequalities of wealth could be tolerated only if the rich acted as benefactors to the community. This took the form of 'liturgy', or leg-islated gift-giving for unnecessary ends such as festivals and choruses, and, in the case of Athens, for equipping and decorating the galley hulks of the navy. The second, from the fourth century BC, is marked by the 'reign of notables' during which full political rights within the Greek city were granted only to those who could ensure the survival of the community. Then magis-trates would be expected not only to provide traditional gifts, entertainments and banquets, but also to pay for the expenses of their own offices and public works and monuments. Each ruling class man became devoted to acts of *euergesiai*. He was esteemed and later remembered accordingly, and his exer-cise of political authority was justified by these acts. Euergetism was the expression of the notable's social superiority.

The republican Roman world was different again. Here, the cities were flush with the bounty of conquest and did not rely on the wealth of the notables to survive. No longer did the rich pay for their own positions. The oligarchy continued the Greek practice less from necessity and more in an effort to win hearts and minds, to gain prestige among the plebs, to extend their networks of influence and dependence (clientship), and for their own glorification. Finally, all of this was centralized under the Emperor and con-stituted both a bond and a meeting-place (e.g. at the Circus) between the sovereign and his people, as well as forming a component in the complex and shifting relations between Emperor, Senate and the plebs.

In later imperial Roman times, even the least local notable could be cajoled, either by acclamation of the plebs or through the urging of his fellow dignitaries, into taking up an office that included gifts of public buildings, gladiator fights, public banquets and festivals, and that might well prove ruinous to him (Veyne, 1987: 105–15). By so doing, notables demonstrated their devotion to the city, their 'aristocratic civism'. This civic devotion was one of the two wellsprings of euergetism in Rome. The other was the display of ostentation that would be manifested on the occasion of a wedding or at a funeral banquet. Of course, the reluctant notable could retreat to his coun-try estate, with his lands and farmers, far from the reaches of the city, but this would be to abdicate public life itself, and thus to abdicate the very essence of his identity as a member of the nobility. More often than not, notables com-peted with each other in displays of ostentation and civic duty. They did so to confirm their luminary status, to receive acclaim, applause and titles, and to be remembered through inscriptions on headstones and statues, as well as by the permanent foundations they established, as generous and noble men. The passion to give was 'self-interested' in that it was a kind of lust for glory, although, given that the desire sought no other end than the acclaim of the populace, it was an ethic of disinterested ambition. Roman euergetism can only be understood as a part of a particular aristocratic *habitus*, to borrow loosely upon Pierre Bourdieu's (1990) term. In using this term I mean a set of characteristic and largely habitual forms of bodily comportment, modes of address, relations to self and others, and moral and intellectual dispositions.

Aristocratic civism grew out of the received culture of the city and was formed within deliberate educational practices known as *paideia*. Peter Brown (1992: 35–58) tells us that the (male) notables of the fourth century of the Eastern Empire were still initiated as late adolescents into a common culture of *paideia*, a form of grooming by which they asserted their own cultivation, communicated with others of their class, with governors and representatives of the Emperor, and expressed their social distance from other classes. *Paideia*, which required the attainment of difficult skills, implied a conception of superior persons who combined discretion, self-restraint and justice in the activity of governing with a cultivation expressed as a 'devotion to the Muses'. The central techniques of this educational practice were those of rhetoric, a training in highly formalized styles of speech that extended to voice modulation, breath control and deportment. The techniques of *paideia* provided the repertoire for the conduct of the complex and tension-laden practice of politics in the late Empire and gave a certain gloss to the murderous intrigue around the Emperor and his officials. *Paideia* and *euergesia* together mark different but related aspects of the ethical habitus of the municipal notables. While the former defined a form of ethical comportment that comprised the relation of the well-born few to themselves and members of their class, the latter defined their relation to their cities and fellow citizens.

One might wish to summarize euergetism as a practice and way of thinking about rule in the city along a number of dimensions: its object, aim, relation of rulers to themselves, and relation of ruler and ruled. The object of rule was the city, conceived as a community of free citizens, within the larger political unity of the Empire. The aim was the nourishment of the city by doing good for it and in so doing to establish oneself as a noble and memorable being. The beneficiaries of rule were the citizenry, those who belonged to the *demos*, by virtue of coming from a citizen family and being a member of a recognized civic group (Brown, 1992: 85). Those who were not citizens, those who lived beyond the boundaries of the city and were the faceless refuse of the ancient economy, were not the object of benefaction; nor were the growing immigrants from the countryside and smaller towns and the refugees from wars. The relation of the ruler to the ruled was thus one of the hardened solidarity that a free citizen feels with his fellow citizens, rather than a feeling of pity or charity (Veyne, 1990: 29). These acts evince a relation of the ruler to himself that can be described as patrician pride. They are manifestations of an aristocracy based not on blood but on deeds that bespoke the *euergesia* that the nobility believed ran in their blood. They thought themselves possessed of *megalopsychia*, the 'high minded zest for open-handed gestures of largesse', and *eunoi*, 'the unfailing goodwill to one's hometown' (Brown, 1992: 83).

The 'city–citizen game', in sum, implies the careful cultivation of a set of attributes and a form of moral personality on the part of the ruling class. These attributes involve a particular relation to oneself, manifest in a particular comportment, which is both physical and ethical. This comportment also entails specific relations to others: to other members of the ruling class, to the city and its citizens, and to those who were outside its limits. In all of these ways, the nourishing of the city stands in marked contrast to the Christian ethic of the care of the poor that would challenge it, at some times by opposing it and at others by accommodating it, but that would gradually take over from it. The transition in gift-giving was, as Peter Brown (1987: 262) puts it, 'one of the most clear examples of a shift from a classical to a post-classical Christianized world'.

Shepherd and flock

Christianity as a form of mundane government of a community involved very different conceptions of rule, persons and their ethical obligations. Its conception of rule was also associated with an injunction to give, but one that contrasted sharply with the culture of the antique city. Rather than an ideal of the studious control of deportment, these communities worked with a conception of the human being that sought single-mindedness, simplicity, transparency to God and openness to others. Here, the material of this 'profound and sombre scrutiny' was the 'heart' (Brown, 1987: 254). Early Christian groups, like Judaic communities, were concerned to root out the 'zones of negative privacy' that contained dangerous opacities to both God and community. The efforts to combat this 'double-heartedness' in early Christianity and the rise of practices of sexual renunciation, particularly among leaders, have specific purposes. They were concerned to maintain the solidarity of a socially vulnerable group, to mark the status of Church leaders within pagan society, and to create a public space for the Church. Moreover the claim to moral leadership of the Church in the fourth century was bound to the radical asceticism of the anchorite monks, rooted in the authority of the desert and the marginalized populations of the ancient economy, and in the claim, manifested in almsgiving, of the new Christian notable, the bishop, to be no longer a *philopatris* or 'lover of the city' but a *philoptochos* or 'lover of the poor' (1987: 292).

This relation to the poor and the sick was a component of the Christian love commandment: first to love God, and then, as a reflection of that love of God, to love thy neighbour as thyself (Nelson, 1996: 67–9). Christian love, *agape*, found one of its expressions in the injunction to practise 'good works' in atonement for sin. The movement beyond exemplary good works including acts of self-abasement and self-mortification to the establishment of philanthropic institutions occurred in the Eastern Empire only after the latter part of the fourth century.

Christianity, as a philosophy of the socially vulnerable, found a vocation for its leaders in the 'care of the poor'. It proposed solidarity between rich and poor as a potent analogue of the relation between God and the sinful individual. The poor person was like an afflicted sinner, and penitents gave alms for venial sins. Its bishops associated themselves with the categories marginalized in the late Empire. Its monks, defined by their elemental move to the desert, crossed the boundaries of the city to join those at the margins of the ancient economy, and made poverty a direct conduit to the new universal truth. These monks found a simple truth (against the 'double-heartedness' of the pagan world) and authority in poverty that ignored the old division between city and countryside, citizen and non-citizen, and concentrated instead on a new universal relation between rich and poor (Brown, 1987: 288–91).

The clash of two different forms of giving and the 'birth of almsgiving' is not simply an episode or aspect of the rise of Christianity but a defining moment in the transformation of authority relations in late antiquity. Indeed, it has lasting implications for the government of those societies that even today claim a Christian derivation or that trace their lineage to the Mediterranean cities of this time. The universal solidarity of souls displaced the exclusive status of citizenship as the object of rule. Authority was founded not on the deeds of benefaction but on the solidarity of rich and poor.

This new authority, grounded in the concern for the poor, proved decisive for a number of reasons. The first concerns the forms of ethical personality of the agents of this authority. On the one hand, the monks – the illiterate heroes of the desert, who abandoned the city and its double-heartedness for a form of plain speaking, a universal truth revealed directly by God – claimed an esteem that had hitherto been based on the cautious orations and precise diction of the ruling elite and its *paideia*. On the other, the bishop, who spoke, like John Chrysostom, of the 'other city' (Brown, 1992: 94), demonstrated the universality of the Christian community and the breadth of its concern, and thus established a moral right to stand for the community as a whole.

The second concerns the inclusion of hitherto excluded groups in the public life of the Christian community, particularly women. Excluded from public life by ancient civic culture, and from public office within the Church, women, particularly those who were wealthy, were able to take on a degree of public status in the late Empire in the role of patroness of the poor, of almsgiver, and of carer for the sick and strangers (Brown, 1987: 279). No doubt, sexual renunciation on the part of the clergy made possible this limited participation of women in the public life of the early Church. The rising status of the bishop was in part due to his ability to associate himself and his Church with those categories of persons whose existence had been ignored by ancient civic models of the notables. At the same time, the Church was able to mobilize the funds controlled by Virgins, that is, by the class of wealthy women, particularly the unmarried or the widowed.

Finally, the bishops proved themselves to be much more effective agents than the old civic aristocracy in the municipal control of the increasingly unruly and riotous plebs of the fourth and fifth centuries. The municipal councils, without any instrument to keep the peace, were faced with discontented plebs under pressure from immigration from the countryside, increased population, massive underemployment, and the factions that developed around Christian controversies. The bishops, by contrast, commanded virtual urban militia, recruited nominally for philanthropic practices of caring for and burying the urban poor. Moreover, the insensible but gradual widening of the term 'poor', and the blurring of the distinction between the *demos* and the poor, meant that the populace was more likely to join the crowds around the basilica seeking succour than look to the traditional notables to discharge their civic duties. In short, the bishops proved the most effective protectors and pacifiers of the mob at the same time as they were able to pose the question of how wealth was best spent.

Of course, the division between the outlook and practice of the new and old ruling groups was nowhere as clear-cut as I have presented it here. There were often disjunctions between the claims of the bishops with regard to the poor and the practice of the Church and, at times, almsgiving took on the attributes of euergetism. There were also desert ascetics and theologians who denied the injunction to do good works and who argued that such worldly activities portended spiritual contagion (Nelson, 1996: 78). However, the clash between these two forms of giving does more than simply concretize Foucault's opposition between the city–citizen game and the shepherd–flock game. It allows us to show that what is at stake is rather more than two principles of rule, or two different philosophies, sets of beliefs, ideologies and so on. The city–citizen game and the shepherd–flock game are mired in practices for the government of the conduct of self and others. Their opposition is not an opposition of principles but one of different forms of ethical self-government (*paideia* and Christian asceticism), different forms of moral personality (the noble and the bishop and monk), and different sets of ethical obligations (embodied in euergetism and almsgiving). These intertwined forms of the relation to self, relation to one's peers, relation to the ruled and relation to the excluded comprise the repertoire of actions, habits, mentalities and styles that entered into this decisive historical struggle.

Care for the poor and the marginalized in the practices of almsgiving was more than a sideline for the Church. Such practices were about the construction of the authority of the Church and the outflanking of existing secular authority. They were about remapping the contours of inclusion and exclusion, acquiring status for its leaders based on a new ethical comportment and, finally, overcoming the old civic culture. It was the universality, holiness and authority of poverty – taken as a vow and way of life by the desert monks – that would finally combat the 'double-heartedness' of the city and its cultivated rulers.

Foucault notes that pastoral power is tied up with a notion of the living individual and his/her needs, with the relation between the collective and the individual, with notions of obedience and duty, with knowledge and, most importantly, with ideas of salvation. We might now add that the exercise of pastoral rule rests on a specific conception of the potential inclusion of all humankind within the community, the solidarity of rich and poor, and the duty of almsgiving.

By contrast, the ancient city is not simply a community of free and equal citizens but a form of systematic exclusion (of the marginalized, of women, of slaves) from the rights and prerogatives of citizenship. The duties of rulers are to fellow citizens as members of the city rather than to all souls as God's creatures. The appropriate attitude of the rulers is one of patrician pride and the relation to the ruled one of the hardened solidarity of free citizens.

The welfare-state problem

At the end of the twentieth century, this episode might contribute to the genealogy of social welfare government. Adopting Foucault's viewpoint, we can understand aspects of the 'welfare-state problem' as one of the complex and difficult adjustment between two diagrams of the political actor corresponding to two different ways of conceiving the governed political community embodied in the shepherd–flock game and the city–citizen game. These diagrams are of:

1   the individual as *citizen* who exercises *freedoms and rights* within the *legal and political structure* of the political community on the basis of *equality* with other citizens.
2   the individual as a *living being* whose welfare is to be cared for as an individual and as a part of a population, as one who must be integrated within complex forms of *social solidarity*.

Given the kind of transition in gift-giving sketched above, our current dilemmas might be even more intricately woven into antique inheritances than Foucault's schema suggests. In the present century we have turned away from the salvation of souls and back to the notion of citizenship for the basis of our collective beneficence. We might thus think that we have rejected the model of almsgiving for an older model of civic culture. To say this, however, requires immediate qualification. As those living in late Roman cities knew, citizenship was based on exclusion and civic duty rather than on universal respect for humanity and compassion for those in need. The twentieth-century return to citizenship as the basis of social welfare is marked by the attempt to be as inclusive as possible of those who make up the citizen body. It is probably more accurate to say that we seek an extremely difficult combination of the rights of a (necessarily limited and therefore exclusive) body of citizens with the universality implied in Christian almsgiving. The ideal of the welfare state thus seeks to fuse the rather different motivations of a kind of collective civic culture with a Christian love of humanity. This seems to me to be at least one part of the welfare-state problem revealed by a brief excursion into late antiquity. This is a problem that is inherent in the ethical ideal of the welfare state itself.

The other part of the welfare-state problem concerns the cultivation of the motivation to give – that is, the cultivation of the forms of ethical comportment and ethical personality that are appropriate to the collective beneficence called social welfare. We are used to questioning the attributes of welfare recipients and of the poor – for example, in the discussions of 'welfare dependency' and the culture of poverty raised in Chapter 3. However, the ethical orientation of those from whom national governments seek to raise the funds for social benefits and services is rarely called into question. The difficulties of and revolts over the raising of taxation, particularly from the rich, suggest that advanced liberal democracies have neglected to cultivate an ethical culture that can sustain concerns for social justice and the alleviation of disadvantage. There is nothing in these societies that parallels either the obligation of a nourisher of the city in ancient Rome or the obligation of the almsgiver in Christianity. At best we seek to draw upon a potpourri of elements taken from such contexts. We might conclude that, at a minimum, if we are to sustain or to revive the ideal of a welfare state into the twenty-first century, we need to think about how to cultivate new forms of ethical comportment appropriate to the transfers of wealth it requires.

Foucault's account of the welfare-state problem indicates the deep disjunction between the conception of the individual and the community found respectively in the 'shepherd–flock' and 'city–citizen' models. However, as I have shown, an analysis of the ancient inheritances of the welfare-state also reveals the novel way in which it tries to fuse Roman civic culture and Christian charity, and the manner in which it neglects a crucial aspect of both these cultures, the cultivation of the motivation to give. Of course, there is no inevitable link between ancient models of government and contemporary welfare-state problems. Our understanding of the former can illuminate the latter, but it cannot show our problems as the necessary outcome of the contradictory aspects of ancient culture.

If most modern conceptions of politics refer back to the ancient model of the *polis,* then most modern conceptions of government and administration refer back to the model of the pastorate. We should note not only the deep disjunction between such models but also the partiality and particularity with which they have been taken up in the contemporary world.

Reason of state and police

The pastorate and the city are two images of the political *community* or, at least, of the community to be governed. They are not yet images of the government of a *state*, i.e. of that body that claims a monopoly of legitimate violence within a particular territory, to use Weber's definition, and that exercises power over the inhabitants of that territory both as citizens and as members of a population, to follow Foucault. It is only by understanding how the pastoral care of this new flock, the *population*, becomes fused with modern citizenship *within* states that we can begin to appreciate Foucault's characterization of modern states as 'demonic' (1988c: 71). The questions we should ask here are: 'how did a secular rationality and art of government come about?' and 'how did we come to pose the problem of the art of government in terms of the government of the state and the welfare of the members of the population?'

To understand this, we again follow Foucault in investigating the development of two aspects of governmental rationality flourishing in the seventeenth and eighteenth centuries, 'reason of state' and 'police'. I have sought to develop his account of reason of state with reference to Gerhard Oestreich's work on neo-Stoic philosophy of government, and to supplement his account of police by drawing on aspects of my own study of the government of poverty (Dean, 1991) and by placing the science of police within the broader *episteme* of government in early modern Europe.

Reason of state

In his exposition of Foucault's lectures on government, Colin Gordon (1991: 8–10) quite correctly points out that the pastoral model is adopted and massively elaborated by a Western Christianity which, however, never unifies the role of sacerdotal pastor and secular ruler. This thus allows for the possibility of both a Christian doctrine and a secular discussion of worldly rule throughout medieval Europe. Neither of these, nevertheless, attempts to invent a secular form of the pastorate which both 'individualizes' and 'totalizes' the members of a polity, that is, a government of each and all like that found since the sixteenth century. In charting how this secular pastorate comes into being, Foucault gives special place to the literature concerned with 'reason of state' found in Italian and German authors (Botero, Palazzo, Chemnitz) from the late sixteenth century and in the French *politique* theorists of the seventeenth century (1988b: 148–53; 1988c: 74–7). His work is complemented and somewhat deepened in this regard by the research of Gerhard Oestreich on the revival of Stoicism, particularly in the writings of the Netherlander, Justus Lipsius, and its implications for the development of the state and by Quentin Skinner's writings on the formation of the modern conception of the state. The key concept for this strand of political thought was *prudentia civilis* (civil prudence), a doctrine and set of techniques for political conduct. This revival of Stoicism provides a link to the reflection on ethical and political conduct undertaken in the late Empire. In a sense, it is possible to discern in these doctrines a new education of rulers that parallels the *paideia* of antiquity. It is in these writings on reason of state and civil prudence that Foucault finds something like the beginnings of an autonomous rationality of government not reducible to a reflection on the personage of the prince or the principles of the divine order. Without overstressing their similarities, many of Foucault's more unsubstantiated hypotheses received qualified support from Skinner's meticulous research.

Foucault first argues that notions of reason of state and civil prudence call into question a Christian literature on prudence and wise government. For the latter, government, if it is to be just, must respect human, natural and above them divine laws (Foucault, 1988b: 149). Government grows out of a divine, cosmo-theological order (Gordon, 1991: 9). This Christian tradition conceives the sovereign's government through the paradigm of God's government of nature. Foucault cites a text of St Thomas in which the king must lead man toward his finality just as God does for natural beings. This finality is neither health nor wealth nor truth. Rather humans need to be led to heavenly bliss through earthly conformity to what is *honestum*. Christianity is not able, then, to separate religious and secular virtue. The virtue of rulers is to be judged by whether or not they lead their subjects to their natural and divine purposes and ends. Ideas such as civil prudence mark what might be called the political secularization of virtue.

Such ideas, suggests Foucault (1991a), also break simultaneously with the tradition of political thought associated with Machiavelli's *The Prince*. He cites a whole late sixteenth-century 'anti-Machiavellian' current that, whether fairly or not, characterizes Machiavelli's problem as one concerning the relation of the prince to his principality (1991a: 89–97).[3] This literature views the prince as external to and in a position of transcendence in relation to his principality. The principality is thus an acquisition by the prince, whether through conquest, treaty or inheritance. The corollary of this is that the bond between prince and principality is tenuous. The conclusion is that the exercise of power is about reinforcing this bond. In practice this means two things: to identify the internal and external dangers to the prince's rule and, second, 'to develop the art of manipulating relations of force that allow the prince to ensure the protection of his principality, understood as the link that binds him to his territory and his subjects' (1991a: 90).

In the course of this anti-Machiavellian literature, especially in a text like La Perrière's *Miroir politique* of 1567, Foucault discerns the elaboration of an approach to government that is obsessed not with the doctrine of the prince and his sovereignty but with practices that are multifarious and are internal to the state or society: governing occurs at many places and through many agents in the body politic (1991a: 90–2). Because of the plurality of the practices and agents of government, one can identify the art of self-government, the art of the government of a family, and the science of a state, and pose questions concerning the relation between morality, domestic economy and politics. The pedagogy of the prince might follow an ascending line through these three disciplines.

At around the same time, Oestreich argues (1982), neo-Stoicism acts as a significant and productive dimension in contemporary political thought and practice precisely because it introduced profound reflection on virtue and self-government, not only in relation to the internal discipline and extension of duties of the rulers but in relation to the moral education of the army, the bureaucracy and indeed the whole people. This neo-Stoic mentality of government might be characterized as following a descending line through these three disciplines: from the government of the state, to the government of the household, to the government of the self.

Foucault shows a particular interest in La Perrière's view that 'government is the right disposition of things, arranged so as to lead to a convenient end' (1991a: 93). Such a definition of government has, he suggests, two aspects. First, to govern is to govern things. 'Things' are in this sense plural and het- erogeneous. The word refers to a complex of humans and things. This complex involves humans' relations with wealth, resources and the means of subsistence; with the territory in its specific qualities, soil, climate, etc.; with each other in their customs and habits; and with eventualities such as acci- dents and misfortunes (1991a: 93). The second aspect of this definition is the notion of leading such things to a convenient end. This means that the ends of government are immanent to the objects of government. The ends of gov- ernment are no longer 'transcendent' in the sense of being specified by divine or natural laws or being ultimately in the service of the sovereign's greatness or majesty. A clear example of this government of things applied to a dethe- ologized political government is reason of state.

The central features of reason of state are summarized by Foucault in the following terms. First, it is government by reference to reason alone. It is a rational 'art' of government – a specific, secular set of techniques conform- ing to rational rules (Foucault, 1988c: 74). Reason of state makes reference neither to the wisdom of God nor to the strategies of the prince (Foucault, 1988b: 150). Government has its own peculiar rationality. Second, it is an art of government that requires that we take account of what is to be governed, namely the state. The state in this context is a kind of natural object despite the juridical concern with how it is constituted (1988b: 151). Third, the aim of reason of state is to reinforce the state itself, its own strength, greatness and well-being, by protecting itself from the competition of other states and its own internal weakness. Reason of state is concerned with the 'holding out' of the state itself rather than with the relation of sovereign to kingdom. Fourth, this art of government presupposes a certain type of knowledge. This is a concrete, precise and measured knowledge of the strength of the state (Foucault, 1988b: 151). In the development of such disciplines as political arithmetic and statistics we witness the first development of the 'expertise' of the politician. This is undoubtedly the type of knowledge Botero sought when he defined reason of state as a 'perfect knowledge of the means through which states form, strengthen themselves, endure, and grow' (1988c: 74). Finally, we can specify the relation of reason of state to a pastoral art of gov- ernment in the following way. Human individuals are of interest only in so far as they contribute to the strength of the state either positively or negatively. Foucault calls this feature the 'political marginalism' of reason of state since what is in question is the marginal political utility of the individual.

There are some points on which Foucault's admittedly sketchy remarks on reason of state are unclear and which can be refined with the help of Quentin Skinner. Skinner (1978, vol. 1: 248–9) places 'reason of state' as clearly within a Machiavellian 'moral universe', particularly Botero's *Reason of State* of

1589. We thus need to be aware of important continuities with Machiavelli in this literature that are not stressed by Foucault. However, Skinner (1978, vol. 2: 353–5), like Foucault, locates the emergence of a modern conception of the state somewhere between the publication of *The Prince* and the response to it by both humanist and reason of state theorists. While Foucault contrasts the 'transcendent' relation of sovereignty to the state as among the 'immanent' objects of government, Skinner argues that the state indeed becomes such an object and is here distinguished from the condition in which the ruler finds himself. A further indication of the close relation between the emergence of a notion of the state as separate from the prince, and the Machiavellian controversy, is found in Budé's *The Education of the Prince* of 1547. Like Lipsius, Budé insists that the principal foundation of good government is found in the value of 'civil prudence' and introduces a discussion of the prince's duty to give 'a proper foundation to the public state' (Skinner 1978, vol. 1: 252; vol. 2: 355).

Reason of state is thus not understood in the somewhat pejorative sense that we give it today when we say things like it is for 'reasons of state' that President Chirac renewed French nuclear testing in the South Pacific in 1995 or that Australia shows continued complicity in Indonesia's 1975 annexation of the former Portuguese colony of East Timor. In using this term we are suggesting that the pursuit of the state's interests contravenes principles of law, human rights and global environmental values. In the sixteenth and seventeenth centuries, reason of state is used to think about how states can be managed in a positive manner according to principles that are intrinsic to them, even if these principles must be balanced against the virtues of justice. Reason of state marks the abandonment of a belief in the unification of all kingdoms in one final empire prior to the Second Coming, or of the project of the reconstitution of the Roman Empire (Foucault, 1988b: 152). From now on, politics must recognize the plurality of competing states with different histories. States are historically limited entities. Hence reason of state is concerned with the 'holding out' of the state. Another way of putting this might be to say that reason of state is founded on the problem of the *security* of the state, a problem that will not disappear even through the liberal interrogation of the limits of government.

Reason of state breaks with Christian and judicial traditions of government. It marks a rupture with both Christian notions of government in terms of God's revelation and commandments, and ideas of government in accordance with divine, natural or even human law. In this sense, it is like the contemporary neo-Stoic idea of civil prudence. As Gerhard Oestreich (1982: 162–5) shows, *prudentia civilis* is the major concept in politics in the seventeenth century, embracing the training of princes, their advisers, the new standing army and emergent bureaucracy. At universities, education was directed not to contemplation and the transmission of knowledge but to *virtus socialis*, active involvement in social life. Indeed civil prudence is understood as insight into the techniques of social and political conduct. The doctrine stressed obedience and discipline as conditions of a well-ordered state and taught the individual to regulate emotions and subordinate himself politically. Its casuistry endorsed the first two of three levels of deception it identified. Thus distrust and secrecy, and bribery and dissimulation, were recognized as necessary, but breach of contract and infringement of law were not.

There is perhaps still something scandalous in these doctrines. Reason of state was widely perceived as such and often identified as an *atheist* art of government and, according to Gordon, was even denounced by the Pope as the 'devil's reason' (Foucault, 1988c: 75; Gordon, 1991: 9). There is certainly much in the neo-Stoic philosophies of government concerning the type of political virtues required of individuals at all levels of the polity that jar our sensibilities today. While we might find some resonance in Lipsius's discussion of *constantia* (steadfastness or endurance) and the related values of *patientia* (patience) and *firmitas* (firmness), it is clear that neo-Stoicism is also concerned to link these to more classical Roman political and moral values of *auctoritas* and *disciplina* (authority and discipline) (Oestreich, 1982: 13-27). The doctrines of Tacitus and Seneca are reframed within the political and military aims of neo-Stoicism, i.e. to increase the power and efficiency of the state through the acceptance of the central role of military force. The idea of civil prudence thus contains a militaristic virility at its core.

On the other hand, one could argue that these doctrines are absolutely vital to the emergence of a 'civil' society, one in which there is a relative and tolerable peace within and between most polities and in which social constraint has become internalized as self-constraint, as Elias (1982) would put it. To understand this, it is necessary to recall the context in which they were elaborated. These doctrines are characteristic of a period of religious wars in which there were wars between great powers as well as confessional civil wars which would last for decades. It is the period of Protestant revolution and Catholic Counter-Reformation, in which a resurgent Catholicism led by the Jesuits faced off the Calvinism of the Protestant minorities. Moreover, it is a period of enormous change in the structure of European states, with the movement toward a form of absolutism and the decline of the feudal estates. The apparatuses of the great territorial states of the eighteenth century are yet to be fully formed and armies are still recruited from mercenaries and run by opportunistic commanders without political allegiance. As Oestreich puts it, referring to the end of the sixteenth century: 'Amid all religious division in the world, no principle governing constitutional, moral, military and social affairs commanded assent . . . Extremes of indiscipline and insecurity were created by the most outrageous conflicts of all, the ideological civil wars which sometimes lasted for decades' (1982: 17). To deal with such conflicts, sovereigns and other bodies issued territorial, local and ecclesiastical ordinances to regulate the lives of their subjects. Such ordinances were often called *police* ordinances. Police, in a sense vastly different from the current English sense of the term, might be described as the internal component of reason of state or as the technique of civil prudence.

These doctrines integrate external and internal components. Today, we largely think of 'reason of state' in the context of the relation between states. This is the sense in which the residual meaning of the term is perhaps more than mildly pejorative. We talk of the interest of state, *realpolitik*, in matters of international relations – especially in military, security or diplomatic matters. Here we recognize that one state, in direct competition with others who are more or less its equal, might discern interests that can be placed above the dictates of its own professed morality or international law. In a classical sense, however, reason of state concerns both relations between states and relations within the state. Externally, it is concerned with maintaining and augmenting the strength of the state in relation to other states, the 'diplomatico-military technique perfected on a European scale with the Treaty of Westphalia' in 1648 after the Thirty Years War (Foucault, 1991a: 23). Internally, it is concerned with the augmenting of the elements and forces that constitute the strength of the state. This internal set of techniques and the rationality they embody is called *police*.

Police

The pre-nineteenth-century meaning of that 'strange little word "police"', as Leon Radzinowicz (1956: 417) put it, is doubly obscure for contemporary readers in the English-speaking world. This is because these meanings have become obsolete and, in any case, because their currency in England, in particular, was never widespread. Nevertheless, police in its archaic sense is absolutely vital to the genealogy of present forms of governmentality.

Let us start with both these obstacles to understanding the notion of police as an element in the formation of the rationality and techniques of government characteristic of what might be designated as the early modern period. At this time, police is *not* a police force, a body of officials or officers, some of whom are uniformed, whose rationale is the prevention and detection of crime, or 'keeping the peace'. An agency that would administer legal regulations was first clearly implied only during the eighteenth century and then only as one of the many branches of the subject (Hume, 1981: 43–4). The 'prevention of robberies' formed one of the eight branches of police in Catherine the Great's *Instructions* of 1768 (1981: 34–5). William Blackstone's concept of the patriarchal state grounded in the rule of law precluded the possibility of police as an institution (Radzinowicz, 1956: 418–29).

Indeed, in Britain, 'police' is a word largely of nineteenth-century currency. Important exceptions are the lectures delivered by Adam Smith (1956) at Glasgow University in 1762–4 and Blackstone's *Commentaries on the Laws of England*. For Smith, police, justice, revenue and arms formed the four 'great objects' of law. For Blackstone, 'public police and œconomy' meant the 'due regulation and domestic order of the kingdom' (1830: 162). Even allowing for these exceptions, Leon Radzinowicz (1956: 1) cites the French visitor to London who exclaimed in about 1720: 'Good Lord! How can one expect Order among these People, who have not such a Word as *Police* in their Language.' Nevertheless, the notion of police appears to have had wide currency in continental Europe from the thirteenth century, particularly in German regions and in France. In Germany, after the seventeenth century, it gave rise to a distinct *science* of police, *Polizeiwissenschaft*. This science of police is closely associated with the 'theory and technique of government' called cameralism to which the American sociologist, Albion Small (1909), devoted a major study.

What, then, did the term mean? According to Knemeyer (1980: 172–81) police was both the condition of order in the community and the ordinances that sought the institution and maintenance of that order in fifteenth- to seventeenth-century German statute law. Later, he continues, it begins to accept a further set of meanings, embracing the concept of commonality itself in humanistic and theological literature. Nevertheless, order remained the paramount focus. When, in the seventeenth and eighteenth centuries, a science of police was formed, it was concerned with the content of that order, and so theorized the specific conditions of its institution and maintenance. This science of police was thus led to an evaluation of the objectives of the *state* and the proper form of *state* activity.

A similar perspective emerges if we take specific examples of writings on police. Gerhard Oestreich (1982: 155–6) cites the political manual of Dr M. von Osse, the chancellor to the Elector of Saxony in the mid sixteenth century. For Osse, police 'was identical both with the government and with the object and nature of the community as a whole'. Osse cites four things necessary to the good police of a town or country: *princeps, consilium, pretorium* and *populus*, understood respectively as a ruler and overlord, good and wise counsel, good and impartial jurisdiction and a well-behaved and obedient people. The object of police is to keep a community thriving, so that its subjects may prosper, and to prevent anything hindering the common good. The subjects have as their obligations respect and obedience.

What range of things is to be regulated by this police and its ordinances? *Polizei* is said to exist when subjects behaved in an 'orderly, modest, courteous and respectful fashion' in every aspect of life (Knemeyer, 1980: 174). Police was thus equated with a society of good manners, or a polite society. At first police ordinances dealt primarily with 'sumptuary' problems of the blurring of distinctions between the estates, such as the wearing of extravagant clothing, the appropriate behaviour of each subject at church or during festivals, the performance of trades and occupations, and the behaviour of servants and journeymen towards their masters (1980: 177). Later were added concerns over monopolies, unseemly vendors, weights and measures, usury, extravagance in all areas, fires, public buildings and streets (1980: 177; Hume, 1981: 33–4).

Something of the breadth of this range is illustrated by the big police ordinance of the free imperial city of Strasbourg in 1628 (Oestreich, 1982: 156–9). Heading this ordinance were regulations of an explicitly Christian content and justification including issues of Sunday observance, divine service, sorcery, blasphemy, cursing and perjury. Other sections involved the upbringing of children, keeping of domestics, expenditure on weddings and christenings, dealings between innkeepers and guests, comprehensive sumptuary regulations, begging and almsgiving, the status of Jews, the prevention of usury and monopolies, the trading of middle-men, faked goods, gaming, breaches of the peace, libel and slander, and, finally, funeral rites. As comprehensive as the Strasbourg ordinance was, however, it did not include measures elsewhere characteristic of police ordinances such as those regulating weights and measures, brewing and baking, and the sale of goods and serving of drinks. These 'economic areas' were the subject of special market ordinances.

The difficulty of defining the primary purposes of police is its 'regulation mania', as Oestreich (1982: 157) put it, its desire to regulate all manner of what appear to us quite heterogeneous things and activities. A first attempt to think about these purposes might be to note its municipal and urban character. In support of this, we could cite the definition of de Lamare as the 'public order of each town' (Hume, 1981: 33). Police was widely regarded as a matter of local authorities, or 'the inferior parts of government' as Adam Smith (1956: 154) put it, concerned with public cleanliness and security, and cheapness and plenty. One commentator (Hume, 1981: 33) characterizes this police, particularly in its 'œconomic' dimension, as the outlook of a relatively isolated community, with a narrow and largely closed market, which dealt with perishable goods of limited supply, and was liable to famines, traders' rings, forestallers and dishonest practices.

However, this approach captures only a partial and static sense of the term. It is partial because it misses the moral dimension, the entwinement of strictly governmental concerns with concerns over the regulation of human conduct and the intercourse between humans. Its attempts at regulation respected few bounds, particularly of a 'private' realm, and extended to manners, morals and the minutiae of everyday life. In this respect, police ordinances could be viewed as an intensive 'coaching' of citizens in how to behave in towns and regions that had become more populous, in which feudal structures of authority were giving way to more centralized forms of internal sovereignty, and in which ecclesiastical authority had ceased to hold sway (Oestreich, 1982: 156–7). Police became a police of 'general morality and respectability' or, to cite Catherine's *Instructions*, a police of 'public decency' (Hume, 1981: 34–5).

To fully grasp the notion of police, we must try to grasp something of its evolution. The development of police, and its movement beyond sumptuary laws to a police of general morality, can be understood, at least in continental Europe, in the context of the specific devolution of authority from the estates to the newly forming local, municipal and central state structures. In fact, German historians argue that police encompassed matters of the regulation of manners as the estates declined and legislative responsibility came to be located in more centralized governmental apparatuses (Knemeyer, 1980: 178–81; Oestreich, 1982: 157). While this is true, it is only one component of a more complex historical trajectory that intersects with Elias's work on the civilizing process and state formation.

As Jeffrey Minson (1985: 104–5) noted, in the late medieval period the multiple sources of police regulation included 'municipalities, guilds, charities, principalities, ecclesiastical and seigneurial authorities as much as . . . royal command'. The emergence of the sovereign state and the formation of internal sovereignty might be first viewed as a take-over and extension of the dispersed police prerogatives exercised by the estates. However, by the eighteenth century, we begin to witness the concentration of some police functions and a sublimation of others onto an emergent private sphere around issues of social morality. The result of this is that police had slowly become identified with the distinctive political sphere, the sovereign state, and the estates were depoliticized. From Norbert Elias's perspective, what we witness is the movement from forms of external constraint and regulation, the comprehensive disciplining of human conduct found in the sixteenth and seventeenth centuries, to forms of self-constraint and self-regulation coeval with the internal pacification of states and the monopolization of the use of violence and taxation. The great flowering of manners at the court of the absolutist state epitomizes this connection between the consolidation of structures of internal sovereignty and the emergence of practices of self-government (Elias, 1983). By the end of the eighteenth century, the greatest heir to the cameralist tradition, von Justi, was able to give a definition of police as 'the enlargement of the internal power and strength of the state' (Knemeyer, 1980: 181).

In stressing reason of state and police, and the emergence of *Polizeiwissenschaft* as the German science of administration, we have followed the emphasis found in the writings and lectures of Foucault himself. However, it is necessary to place these currents of thought and practice against the broader canvas of the development of state sovereignty in Europe and the attendant flowering of many forms of governmental rationality. We might be tempted to speak of this as a period of the formation of a 'state rationality', a term Foucault used at Stanford (1988c: 82). Examples of this would be German cameralism, mercantilism, and the related problem of population.

The history of cameralism has been comprehensively dealt with by Albion Small (1909) at the beginning of the twentieth century. He uses the term to refer to a group of authors of the seventeenth and eighteenth centuries, of whom von Justi is perhaps the most important, but whose antecedents reach back to the end of the fifteenth century and include Melchior von Osse whose work we have already met. Small contests the placement of cameralism within the history of economics and describes it as a theory and practice of governmental management. The chief object of cameralism was to discover how best the welfare of the state might be secured by ensuring the revenue that supplies its needs (1909: viii). The 'cameralists of the books' (who were not theorists, but were drawn from the 'cameralists of the bureaux') worked out and published systems of governmental procedures primarily for pedagogical purposes (1909: 6). The question they had to answer was what programme must a wise government adopt both to supply the fiscal needs of the state and to ensure the fulfilment of the obligations of the state (1909: 6). Foucault (1988c: 82) discerns a central paradox here between the theme of ensuring the strength of the state and the increase of its power and the aim of developing the happiness, prosperity and security of its people.

Cameralism has as its root the Latin word *camera*, literally meaning something with a vaulted roof or arched covering (Small, 1909: 18). *Kammer* refers to the chamber where counsellors charged with the administration of the revenues of a state met. The emergence of cameralistics is integrally connected to the routine of the bureaux first in the fiscal departments and then in the larger sense of routinized governmental rule. In this sense, it might be described as a practical art of governing bureaucratically. For this reason cameralism is far less like an 'economic theory' and more intelligible as a theory and technique of government.

The cameralists were only one, albeit impressive, feature on the topography of an age concerned with government. To construct the governmental *episteme* of the classical age we would need to take into account not only reason of state, *prudentia civilis*, cameralism and *Polizeiwissenschaft*, but also 'Political Arithmetick', 'Political Œconomy', the re-emergence of census taking and statistics, and those writings usually grouped under the vexed term 'mercantilism'. While Small is happy to group cameralism with mercantilistic thinkers outside Germany, he spends considerable time showing that it is mistaken to reconstruct them, or indeed the mercantilists, as economic thinkers. The same can be said of seventeenth- and eighteenth-century writings that used the term 'political œconomy' which, as Tribe (1978) has shown, are unified not by a reference to a theoretical object of the economy but by a concern with the 'wise administration of the state' by the sovereign or statesman. In all these writings, and without erasing their differences, we find elaborated an art of government modelled on the management of the household rather than the laws of the economy.

This *episteme* of government can be characterized in the following ways (Dean, 1991: 27–34). First, the art of government is still enmeshed in a particular image of the household or family as a sphere of patriarchalist relations of service and obligation between sovereign and subjects, heads of households and wives, parents and children, masters and servants, and so on. 'Œconomy' refers, in Foucault's terms, to the 'wise government of the family for the common welfare of all' (1991a: 92) or, as Sir James Steuart said in 1767, the 'art of providing for all the wants of a family, with prudence and frugality' (1966: 15-6). 'Political Œconomy', continued Steuart, is to the state what 'œconomy' is to the family. When Gregory King estimated the size of the English population for 1695 it was based on the number of households within the kingdom (Glass, 1973: 14).

Second, the wealth of the nation is thought of in terms of the *circulation* between households (Tribe, 1978: ch. 5; Dean, 1991: 30–2). The wise administration of the state is concerned with the augmentation of the royal household's wealth through circulation between the nation's households. The art of government concerns the proper distribution of all its objects (households, persons, things) and the fostering of circulation between them. This is what we have referred to as the 'dispositional' problematic of government. In this map of the governed field there is a tension between stasis and movement, between ensuring proper relations and conduct of the various ranks of persons, and facilitating and regulating the flows of money and of communication between them. In this sense, the notion of police is exemplary.

Finally, all these discourses and techniques of government, from police science to census taking, almost simultaneously come to think about their concerns in terms of a new object, the population. This last notion bears some examination.

While we can agree with Foucault (1988c: 82–3) and Pasquale Pasquino (1978) that the notion of population is crucial to the German science of police, some caution needs to be exercised. For Foucault, population is a strongly marked term and it is here that we should be wary about following him. At various places he insists that the concept of population is an index of the modernity of certain political discourses. This is certainly the case in his account of 'bio-politics' (1979: 139–43). Bio-politics – or a politics of life – emerges with the constitution of the population as a field of knowledge (in political economy, statistics, etc.) and a domain of regulation and action in technologies of the management of its health, hygiene and welfare. Foucault refers to this event as one that both marks the 'threshold of modernity' and establishes an 'era of governmentality' and the 'governmentalisation of the State' (1979: 142–3; 1991a: 103). Moreover, Foucault's remarks seem to imply a disjunction between familialistic or householding models of government and population-based rationalities.

Now there is little doubt that the notion of population is central to the early modern *episteme* and *techne* of government. However, such large claims are problematic to the extent that they prevent us from giving a more nuanced account of different conceptions of population. In this area, we should insist on at least a primary disjunction between pre- and post-Malthusian conceptions of population and its ramifications for governmental rationalities. As we shall see in Chapter 6, the later conception is tied to the emergence of an economic rationality and a specific set of 'liberal' techniques of administration of welfare. The earlier conception, however, is mapped onto the householding notion of the art of government. Here the concern with population is not a 'bio-economic' concern for the life of the human species in its struggle to overcome natural scarcity, but a concern for the augmentation of its numbers.

As Small notes of the cameralists, they were not anti-Malthusian because 'the Malthusian problem never distinctly appeared above their horizon' (1909: 15). Their problem was to promote population and ensure that its members were industrious. In this regard, they were like their English 'mercantilist' cousins. In writers such as Josiah Child and Matthew Hale in the mid seventeenth century, in William Petty's contemporary *Political Arithmetick*, and in those writers dealt with by E.S. Furniss (1957) in his classic study of mercantilism, we find a dual concern for government. The first is with the augmentation of the revenues that flow into the national treasury. The second is with the augmentation of the numbers of the population. Until the end of the eighteenth century, the notion that the numbers of people were the riches and strength of the nation went uncontested even if it was on occasion qualified (Furniss, 1957: 16–23). The assertion of this maxim was qualified by a concern with the 'due regulation of things' which principally meant that the numbers of the people, particularly the poor, were to be made industrious, whether this was to be achieved by make-work schemes, the establishment of workhouses, houses of correction and labour colonies, anti-recreational campaigns attacking the sports, leisure activities and holidays of the labouring population, or the lowering of real wages (Dean, 1991: 35–52).

If we use the term 'mercantilism' to describe this English literature, we find mercantilism and cameralism are one on the aims of government considered in terms of the stewardship of the national estate, and on the question of population. Where the 'cameralists of the books' in Germany came from the machinery of the fiscal bureaucracy, in England the 'mercantilists of the books' were more likely to be drawn from the board of the East India Company, or from the ranks of the judiciary from Chief Justice to magistrate, or to be a mayor or local notary. This no doubt accounts for the different tenor of these writings and for the far greater sophistication of the development of the bureaucratic aspects of the state in Germany.

What I want to mark here is that the rise of a liberal political economy and the Malthusian eruption in the discourse on population signal something of an end of the type of constellation of ideas, concepts, habitual ways of thinking and techniques that made up the *episteme* of government during the baroque period. 'Œconomy' as a set of techniques of an art of government conceived as the wise administration of the state as royal household, police as a condition to be achieved equivalent to the good order of the city or territory, and population as the numbers of the people or the 'stock of labour' that makes up the wealth, strength and greatness of the nation, are all the rudiments of a rationality of government that was also a rationality of state in the seventeenth and eighteenth centuries. It is quite literally unthinkable in the eighteenth century that population should be engaged in an epic struggle for survival, family a private sphere outside government, economy an objective, autonomous and quasi-natural reality to be respected by government, and police merely one institution for the security of the state. When police is no longer an ideal to be sought by government but one of its techniques, when economy is no longer an art of household management but a key dimension of reality, when population is inscribed within the laws of scarcity, and when family is no longer contiguous with political authority but external to it, we have crossed the threshold to an entirely new mentality of government.

From the end of the eighteenth century, the art of government of the state will no longer be simply concerned with the proper 'disposition of things'. The term 'disposition of things' comprehends the ordering and regulation of humans in their relations to a whole series of heterogeneous entities (e.g. proper behaviours, dress and diet; wealth, industry and subsistence; the soil, land and climate) and the orderly settlement and movements within and between productive households arranged within the territory. The point at which population ceases to be the sum of the inhabitants within a territory and becomes a reality *sui generis* with its own forces and tendencies is the point at which this dispositional government of the state begins to meet a government through social, economic and biological processes. This government through these processes would come to generalize the pastoral government of religious communities to the entire population within the state. To understand this line of modification in the genealogy of government, we shall need to discuss in more detail what might be meant by the terms 'bio-politics' and the 'governmentalization of the state'. We take up that task in the next chapter.

Conclusion

We can thus distinguish several different types of problem inherited by the 'welfare state' that can be identified by our genealogy of government thus far:

1   the general problem of the relation between the 'city–citizen game' and the 'shepherd–flock game' as identified by Foucault
2   the issues of the relation between the 'care of the self' and the 'care of others' within the Christian pastorate and within late Roman civic culture
3   the problems arising from the fusion between the exclusive status of citizenship and the universal salvation of humanity of the pastorate within the ideal of the welfare state
4   the manner in which this collective welfare is to be secured by sovereign means (through the state and its fiscal instruments) and the relative neglect of questions of the ethical cultivation of the desire to give
5   the way in which the relation between the internal welfare of the population becomes linked, in doctrines such as reason of state, to the security, external strength and power of the state
6   finally, problems of the techniques of discipline, surveillance and bureaucracy needed to foster this welfare of the population – problems condensed in the now derogatory epithet 'police state'.

It is via the last set of problems that we can *begin* to grasp Foucault's provocation in calling the fusion of the city–citizen game and the shepherd–flock game within modern states 'demonic'. What is demonic is the way 'fundamental experiences' of life and death, of health and suffering, of desires and needs, of individual and collective identity, of toil and labour, have become matters for extremely sophisticated regimes of government and complex forms of knowledge and expertise, and that all this is linked to the exercise of the sovereign power of the state. One might be tempted to compare Foucault's point here with Jürgen Habermas's (1987) notion of the 'colonization of the lifeworld' if by 'lifeworld' we mean precisely the world of these fundamental experiences. But this rendering of matters of life and death governable is neither as univocal in its sources, nor as single-minded in its purposes, nor as unidirectional in its effects as the Habermasian image of colonization would have it. The art of governing these matters of life and death will be initiated and undertaken through a multiplicity of agencies within and without the shifting boundaries of the state, for a plurality of ends, and with a variety of effects. We return to the 'really demonic' character of modern politics in Chapter 7.

Above all we must resist the idea of the state as a unitary actor colonizing a realm of authentic experience and communication. Indeed, the identification of governmental rationality with state rationality in reason of state, cameralist police science and national mercantilism, proved to be a brake on the 'take-off' of the arts and techniques of government. It is only with what might be called the liberal critique of state reason that the rapid expansion of the sciences of human conduct and the practices of government will occur. The condition of this liberal critique will be the displacement of the householding and dispositional approach by a bio-political one.

Notes

1 La Perrière cited by Foucault (1991a: 93).
2 This is a point made not only by those who have followed Foucault in adopting the notion of a 'history of the present' but also eminent intellectual historians of political thought such as Quentin Skinner and James Tully. The latter calls Skinner's approach a 'history of the present' to highlight its similarity to Foucault's genealogy (1988: 16–17). He illustrates this by arguing that Skinner used the term 'foundations' in the title of his work, *The Foundations of Modern Political Thought* (1978), to refer to the formation of a vocabulary of political thought that 'becomes foundational for us (moderns)'. Skinner (1998: 116–17) himself has said that the task of intellectual history is to 'prevent us from becoming too readily bewitched. The intellectual historian can help us to appreciate how far the values embodied in our present way of life, and our present ways of thinking about those values, reflect a series of choices made at different times between different possible worlds.'
3 As Foucault himself seems to realize (1991a: 89), to characterize this literature as 'anti-Machiavellian' is perhaps to overstate the unanimity of the range of positions taken up in the sixteenth century in relation to Machiavelli's *The Prince*. Skinner's account is perhaps subtler on this point. His discussion allows the possibility that humanists could both try to sustain their lofty commitment to the ideal of justice as the basis of politics while embracing the Machiavellian theme that 'it may be justifiable to do what is useful rather than what is strictly right' (1978, vol. 1: 251).

5   BIO-POLITICS AND SOVEREIGNTY

> The government of the Prince is not, as is commonly thought, the art of
> leading men; it is the art of providing for their security and for their sub-
> sistence through observance of the natural order and physical laws
> constituting the natural law and economic order, and by means of which
> existence and subsistence might be assured to Nations and to every man
> in particular; this object fulfilled, the conducting of men is fixed, and
> each man leads himself. (V. Mirabeau, 1763)[1]

In this chapter and the next, we shall examine how, from the end of the eighteenth century, the dispositional and householding conception of government
is complemented, recoded or even displaced by what can be thought of as a
government of certain processes conceived as external to the institutions of
formal political authority. These processes might be economic, social, psychological or biological, or some combination of these. We shall do this in a
number of ways. First, we introduce the idea of bio-politics, i.e. a form of politics entailing the administration of the processes of life of populations.
Second, we examine in detail the notion of 'the governmentalization of the
state' as a way of thinking about the trajectory on which the government
through these processes is found and about the relationship between the
emergence and flourishing of government and the theory and practice of
sovereignty. In the next chapter, we sketch the elements of a genealogy of liberalism, and its relation to bio-politics and sovereignty. The argument of
these two chapters is that the governmentalization of the state is the broadest
condition of the emergence of liberal and social forms of rule for much of the
nineteenth and twentieth centuries. It is also what makes possible, perhaps
more surprisingly, certain aspects of non-liberal rule and authoritarian governmentality of the twentieth century, as we shall see in Chapter 7.

Bio-politics

From the end of the eighteenth century until perhaps quite recently, those
who criticized and sought to limit existing forms of government and those
who argued for its extension, coordination and centralization shared a
common conception of government. Government would be regarded as a
unitary, centralized and localized set of institutions that acted in a field that

was exterior to itself. Government would also cultivate, facilitate and work through the diverse processes that were to be found in this exterior domain. These processes would be conceived as vital, natural, organic, historical, economic, psychological, biological, cultural or social. They would cross and connect various conceptions of the object of government and various forms of knowledge. They could, to give two prominent examples, be 'bio-economic' or 'bio-sociological'. Most importantly they would be processes that followed from the matrix by which 'Man' was discovered as a living, working and social being. They would be processes which established the paradoxical position of life both as an autonomous domain and as an object and objective of systems of administration.

Liberalism might be used to denote those forms of rationality and techniques of government that, in recognizing the existence of these processes, sought to use them to limit the government of the state. Mirabeau's statement illustrates the view that government is not about the 'art of leading men' but about observing those natural and economic laws that provide security and subsistence and, beyond this, leaving men free. As his formulation suggests, liberalism views itself as constituted in relation to processes that are not of its making. The argument of this and the following chapter implies that this view is indeed in part right. It is right in the sense that liberalism is itself situated on a broader terrain of governmental invention. The liberal view is also, however, in part wrong. Liberalism conceives of this exteriority as composed of quasi-natural processes, including the natural history of societies. From the perspective of the analytics of government, these exterior processes are inseparable from the forms of knowledge and regimes of governmental practices in which they are discovered, represented, regulated and managed.

Here, following Foucault, I shall employ the term 'bio-politics' to designate a very broad terrain on and against which we can locate the liberal critique of too much government and its advocacy of what Benjamin Franklin called 'frugal government'.[2] Bio-politics is a politics concerning the administration of life, particularly as it appears at the level of populations. It is 'the endeavour, begun in the eighteenth century, to rationalize problems presented to governmental practice by the phenomena characteristic of a group of living human beings constituted as a population: health, sanitation, birth rate, longevity, race' (Foucault, 1997a: 73). It is concerned with matters of life and death, with birth and propagation, with health and illness, both physical and mental, and with the processes that sustain or retard the optimization of the life of a population. Bio-politics must then also concern the social, cultural, environmental, economic and geographic conditions under which humans live, procreate, become ill, maintain health or become healthy, and die. From this perspective bio-politics is concerned with the family, with housing, living and working conditions, with what we call 'lifestyle', with public health issues, patterns of migration, levels of economic growth and the standards of living. It is concerned with the bio-sphere in which humans dwell.

We might say that there is an internal and an external side to bio-politics (Lui-Bright, 1997). There is a social form of government concerned to govern the life and welfare of the populations that are assigned to certain states; and there is also a kind of international bio-politics that governs the movement, transitions, settlement and repatriation of various populations – including refugees, migrants, guest workers, tourists and students. This international bio-politics is a condition of the assignation of populations to states and thus of social government of any form.

This field of bio-politics, and its attempt to find an accommodation between the phenomena of population and 'bio-sociological' processes, will lead to complex organs of political coordination and centralization (Foucault, 1997b: 222–3). It is also here that we can locate the division of populations into sub-groups that contribute to or retard the general welfare and life of the population. It is this proclivity that has led to the discovery among the population of the criminal and dangerous classes, the feeble-minded and the imbecile, the invert and the degenerate, the unemployable and the abnormal, and has led to attempts to prevent, contain or eliminate them. It is here that Foucault locates the modern form of racism as a racism of the state in which the notion of race appears as a defence of the life and welfare of the population against internal and external enemies (Stoler, 1995: 84–8). It is here that the analytics of government is able to deliver its most profound insights into contemporary warfare as conducted at the level of, and in defence of, entire populations.

Bio-politics is a fundamental dimension, or even trajectory, of government from the eighteenth century concerned with the government of and through the processes and evolution of life. It constitutes as its objects and targets such entities as the population, the species and the race. In Foucault's narrative, however, the detailed administration of life by bio-political (and, it should be added, disciplinary) practices is not coextensive with the entire field of politics and government. There are at least two other dimensions of rule that are important here: *economic government*, which is internal to the field of government conceived as the art of conducting individuals and populations; and the theory and practices of *sovereignty*. Both provide liberalism with the means of criticizing and halting the effects of the generalization of the norm of the optimization of life.

Bio-politics then first meets quite distinct forms of rationality and knowledge concerned with the role of commerce in civil society. These take as their theoretical object the notion of the economy as a self-regulating system largely coincident with the boundaries of the nation. In doing so, political economy presents limits to the bio-political aim of the optimization of the life of the population. These limits are most clearly articulated by Malthus and his absolutely crucial discovery of a realm of scarcity and necessity in the relation between the processes that impel the growth of population and those natural ones that provide the subsistence for the increasing quantity of human life. The bio-economic reality discovered and enshrined in the work of the English political economists of the early nineteenth century will then be used to generate new norms of government that must be factored against the optimization of the life of the population.

This is the point at which liberalism comes into play. No less a government of and through processes than bio-politics, and no less dependent on a conception that these processes occur at the level of human populations, liberalism nevertheless is a key rationality within which bio-political problems and the means of their resolution appear. Liberalism has other sources, growing out of its critique of sovereignty and the democratization of the subject of right, that make its accommodation with bio-political problems and the government of 'bio-sociological processes' more difficult.[3] As Foucault puts it in regard to bio-political problems,

> 'Liberalism' enters the picture here, because it was in connection with liberalism that they began to have the look of a challenge. In a system anxious to have the respect of legal subjects and to ensure the free enterprise of individuals, how can the 'population' phenomenon, with its specific effects and problems, be taken into account? On behalf of what, and according to what rules, can it be managed? (1997a: 73)

We have earlier examined the view that liberalism could be understood as a critique of excessive government. Liberalism should be approached here as a critique not only of earlier forms of government, such as police and reason of state, but of existing and potential forms of bio-political government. This is to say that liberalism criticizes other possible forms that the government of processes might take. It might criticize those forms, for example, in which bio-political norms will be compromised by a lack of understanding of bio-economic norms. It might also criticize the detailed regulation of the biological processes of the species, and the tendencies toward state racism found in bio-politics, by an appeal to the framework of right – either legal or natural – that it will reinscribe from the theory and practice of sovereignty. If liberalism emerged less as a doctrine or form of the minimal state than as an ethos of review, this ethos needs to be situated in the rationalization of the field of bio-political problems. If it is always necessary to suspect that one is governing too much, this is because the imperatives of bio-political norms that lead to the creation of a coordinated and centralized administration of life need to be weighed against the norms of economic processes and the norms derived from the democratization of sovereign subject of right. This is why, for liberalism, the problem will be not a rejection of bio-political regulation but a way of managing it.

The question of the conflict-laden heterogeneity of the 'outside' of government also needs to be taken into account. Thus we will seek to account for two phenomena. The first is the way in which this outside sometimes gives rise to a bounded *unity* most often expressed in the notion of society. The second is how such a unity will attempt to resolve questions of heterogeneity, conflict and dispersion between different kinds of subject and different processes. We need to examine the relations between liberalism and society, between the distinctive liberal ethos of the critique and review of government and the development of a knowledge of society. It is necessary to present a framework by which we might understand the line of modification along which the 'right disposition of things' would be reconceived as a 'frugal government' which would be a government of economic processes. This line of modification is that of the 'governmentalization of the state'. Doing this also enables us to turn to a fuller account of liberalism as an art and rationality of government in relation to the themes of economy, security, law and civil society.

The broad thesis of this chapter is that the governmentalization of the state occurs according to a line of modification along which the household-ing and dispositional conception of government is supplemented, and to some degree displaced and reinscribed, by a government through particular and specifiable processes, at once opaque to rulers but rendered knowable by definite forms of knowledge. In this regard, liberal, social democratic, and even authoritarian and statist forms of rule can be understood as variations on the consequences of such a line of modification. Further, all 'modern' forms of the government of the state need to be understood as attempting to articulate a bio-politics aimed at enhancing the lives of a population through the application of the norm, with the elements of a transformed sovereignty that targets subjects within a territory and whose instrument is the law.

Sovereignty and the governmentalization of the state

One way of approaching the question of liberal government would be to view it as a formation that is made possible in part by a fundamental trajectory in the way in which governing is conceived. In his lecture on 'Governmentality', Foucault uses the somewhat enigmatic phrase 'the governmentalization of the state' (1991a: 103) to describe this line of modification. In Foucault's account, this is a multifaceted rather than unitary trajectory. It principally refers to the process whereby the art of government is separated from the theory and practice of sovereignty and whereby that theory and practice must reconcile itself with this burgeoning and proliferating art of government.

Foucault's lecture spends considerable time specifying the relation between sovereignty, discipline and government. It argues that, rather than viewing these as three successive types of society, they should be viewed as constituting a triangle, 'sovereignty–discipline–government, which has as its primary target the population and its essential mechanism the apparatuses of security' (1991a: 102). The problem space of rule, as it coalesces from the beginning of the nineteenth century and appears for the next two centuries, is thus one that is defined by three lineages. The first is that of sovereignty which, having first taken a juridical form, is democratized and anchored in the rights of the legal and political subject. The second is that of discipline which, having arisen in the practical techniques of the training of the body, becomes a generalized regulatory mechanism for the production of docile and useful subjects. The third is that of government which, having first arisen in the 'dispositional' problematic manifest in police and reason of state, becomes a government of the processes of life and labour found at the level of populations and in which the subject is revealed in its social, biological and economic form.

We can consider liberal and social approaches to government and, indeed, other non-liberal and illiberal forms of rule (see Chapters 6 and 7), as having this governmentalization of the state among their conditions of existence, and being located as different ways of problematizing and responding to this problem space of rule. In what follows, I disaggregate this 'governmentalization of state' into four discrete but overlapping components: the dissociation of government from sovereignty; the elaboration of practices and rationalities of government; the transformation of the exercise of sovereignty by government; and the emergence of a distinctively non-political sphere constituted by processes that can be represented as being outside government but also necessary to the fulfilment of governmental objectives. I shall now examine each of these elements through a reading of the developmental themes of Foucault's lecture on 'Governmentality'.

The separation of government from sovereignty

A narrative of the governmentalization of the state must begin with sovereignty. This is not only because the theory and practice of sovereignty lie behind our most common conceptions of politics and the state, but also because sovereignty is very broadly 'a mechanism of power that was effective under the feudal monarchy' (Foucault, 1980: 103). It is first necessary to show how an autonomous conception of government can emerge alongside the mechanisms of sovereignty. In Foucault's account, this separation of government from sovereignty entails the development of a notion of government as an activity, or an 'art', that is plural and immanent to the state. Alongside this there is the problematic of the sovereign–territory relation conceived as one in which the sovereign is external to and transcendent of the territory.

For Foucault, then, the government of the state is autonomous from the question of sovereignty in that it is separated from the activity and person of the sovereign. In this respect, Quentin Skinner concurs with Foucault's account. Skinner (1989: 102–12) locates the emergence of this sense of autonomy in the republican thinkers of Renaissance Italy, including Machiavelli. Skinner, however, considers another sense in which the government of the state is autonomous. The modern concept of the state, he argues,

> has a doubly impersonal character. We distinguish the state's authority from that of the ruler or magistrates entrusted with the exercise of its powers for the time being. But we also distinguish its authority from that of the whole society or community over which its powers are exercised. (1989: 112)

While Skinner finds the former distinction in the classical republican tradition, he finds the latter in the developing tradition of natural law absolutism.

Thus the aspirations of Hobbes, as much as Bodin, Suarez and Grotius, would include the more absolutist forms of government such as those which emerged from the early part of the seventeenth century. The government of the state becomes autonomous from different versions of sovereignty. It is autonomous from 'divine right' theories of rule and from the personage of the sovereign, as Foucault notes. But in reaction to notions of popular sovereignty, the government of the state is also treated as autonomous from individual citizens and the collective citizenry. Thus, Hobbes is concerned to show that while the constitution of the state depends on the agreements of individual citizens, the right of the state does not depend solely on such agreements. The state must be recognized as having its own rights and properties that cannot be reduced to the rights of citizens, either as individuals or as a collective (1989: 118).

The government of the state becomes autonomous from notions of sovereignty invested in the prince, by God, or in the people. This points to the polysemous character of sovereignty itself. The notion of sovereignty has its own history and effects: it is characterized by a power of life and death that was 'in reality the right to *take* life and *let* live' (Foucault, 1979: 136) or, more simply, the 'right to kill' (Tully, 1988: 17). Sovereignty undergoes its own transformation: in the juridical theories of sovereignty of the seventeenth and eighteenth centuries, such as those of Hobbes and Samuel von Pufendorf, we find a more limited account of the sovereign right of death as conditioned by the defence of the sovereign. From the seventeenth century, sovereignty will be conceived as the exercise of ultimate authority over a territory and the subjects who inhabit that territory. The end of sovereignty is, however, the continuation of sovereignty itself: it is caught in a kind of 'self-referring circularity' (Foucault, 1991a: 95). Thus Foucault argues that, if we take Pufendorf's definition of the end of sovereign authority as 'public utility' and seek to define the content of 'public utility', we find little more than that subjects obey laws, fulfil their expected tasks, and respect the political order.

This self-referential problem of sovereignty – for Foucault at least – is very close to the Machiavellian problem of the relation of prince to principality (as portrayed in the commentaries on Machiavelli). For Foucault, the critical literature of the seventeenth century, exemplified by Guillaume de La Perrière's *Miroir politique*, suggests that for Machiavelli the prince exists in a relation of externality and transcendence to his principality in that the territory is acquired by conquest or inheritance, and that the problem of governing has a particular goal: to cement this bond and protect it from internal and external dangers by manipulating relations of force.

It is clear that the notion of sovereignty is far from a universal and – like other concepts – must be understood in its historical variation according to specific regimes of practices and forms of rationality. Furthermore, it is important to keep in mind the way in which sovereignty as the state's concern for its own preservation might be a particular end of government (Hunter, 1998), and the way in which securing the sovereignty of states is an end of the art of international government, a point we return to below (Hindess, 1998a; Lui-Bright, 1997).

Let us summarize some of the major contrasts and relations between sovereignty and government. In Western European societies from the Middle Ages sovereignty is principally conceived as a transcendent form of authority exercised over subjects within a definite territory. Its principal instruments are laws, decrees and regulation backed up by coercive sanctions ultimately grounded in the right of death of the sovereign. By contrast, from at least the sixteenth century, a notion of government must take into account the nature of the things to be governed and their 'disposition'. As we have seen in the previous chapter, the term 'disposition' suggests something of the spatial and strategic arrangement of things and humans and the ordered possibilities of their movement within a particular territory.

Another way this contrast between sovereignty and government can be made is through the questions of life and death. The exercise of sovereignty works fundamentally through a right 'to kill and let live', to use Foucault's (1997b: 214) blunt turn of phrase, and has the sword as its symbol. Sovereignty is a 'deductive' exercise and relies on a technology of subtraction levied on its subjects (Foucault, 1979: 136). It subtracts products, money, wealth, goods, services, labour and blood. Sovereignty in this sense is a specific form of a rule over things. It seizes them, whether they are goods, time, bodies or ultimately life itself. The emergence of a form of rule that is distinct from sovereignty is also a rule over things but one that seeks to foster them, to increase the means of subsistence, to augment the wealth, strength and greatness of the state, to increase the happiness and prosperity of its inhabitants, and to multiply their numbers. In this sense, government follows a productive rather than a deductive logic. In German police science, as we have seen, the art of government will begin to thematize bio-political concerns for fostering the life of the population.

A good example of this contrast between the deductive exercise of sovereignty and the 'productive' arts of government is provided by Paul Veyne (1997: 151) when he contrasts the authority exercised by traffic police with that of a prince. The prince encountering traffic on a road imposes his own right of passage and leaves it at that. By contrast, the traffic cop channels the spontaneous movement of traffic so that it will flow smoothly and so that drivers may proceed in safety. There is a continuity to the work of a traffic cop and to his inanimate helpmates such as traffic lights, speed humps, roundabouts and stop signs that is not present in the event of the sovereign's appearance on the road. The former shapes, structures and guides flows and forces; while the latter is merely content to impose his will on the subjects. While some drivers might have to wait and thus feel at a temporary disadvantage, the system of traffic management is supposed to work for the overall welfare of all road users. On the other hand, the prince imposes his will over all his subjects, demands their obedience, and exercises his right. He issues an interdiction to his subjects to halt their activities and journeys so that he may claim his right.

There is one sphere in which the exercise of sovereignty and the development of an art of government are mutually conditioning – that of
international relations. Foucault (1991a: 104) mentions, but does not stress,
that the notion of a nominally separate state with territorial integrity subject
to non-interference by outside powers is itself a governmental product, and a
consequence of the 'external' dimension of doctrines of 'reason of state'.
Thus a close reading of the lecture on 'Governmentality' reveals that the
early modern literature on the government of the state is situated with reference to two international events: the 1648 treaties concluded at Westphalia
that inaugurated the modern system of sovereign states and the Congress of
Vienna of 1815 that re-established the territorial divisions of Europe at the
end of the Napoleonic Wars. The relation of the arts of government and sovereignty is not the replacement of one by the other but each acting as a
condition of the other. On the one hand, the existence of nominally independent sovereign states is a condition of forcing open those geopolitical
spaces upon which the arts of governing populations can operate (Dillon,
1995). On the other, a set of supranational agreements and the assignment of
populations to states are necessary conditions of the world inhabited by these
sovereign states (Hindess, 1988a).

The elaboration of government

The first aspect of the governmentalization of the state enables us to draw a
distinction between the exercise of government and that of sovereignty. The
second is the growth and proliferation of the rationalities and techniques of
government. But the second does not immediately follow from the first.
Mercantilism is a good illustration of this point.

Mercantilism introduces a set of governmental concerns and instruments
primarily concerned with turning the balance of trade to one's own advantage
and secondarily concerned with the growth and industriousness of the population (Dean, 1991: 28–32). Yet it remains tied up with the problem of
sovereignty conceived as the sovereign's might or greatness and with the augmentation of the royal or national treasury. The same point, as we have
suggested in the previous chapter, can be made for such forms of rationality
as cameralism, police science and reason of state. While these forms of rationality manifest a dispositional problematic such as that which Foucault
identifies in the anti-Machiavellian literature, they still remain tied to the
problem of sovereignty. Moreover, their primary and privileged instruments
are often those of sovereignty, i.e. laws and law-like regulations. Thus police
regulations were issued in the absence of any means of enforcement in
German territories. Further, where schemes for setting the poor to work were
proposed in England, the key agents were often from the judiciary – the local
magistrates and justices of the peace. Finally, mercantilism and its governmental cousins remain tied to a householding conception of œconomy and
the attempted derivation of the art of government from the art of governing
a family. This is certainly the case for political economy up to the time of

Adam Smith and evident in the writings of his near contemporary, Sir James Steuart (Tribe, 1978).

In order to attain some effective autonomy from sovereignty, the art of government must discover its own instruments and ways of reasoning that are distinct from patriarchalist models of the household and family, and do not simply entail the imposition of laws and use of subtractive mechanisms. In other words, it must find models that do not ultimately return to the rules of sovereignty. Again we must stress the importance of population as an object and objective of government. Population provides the key to overcoming the model of the family that was 'too thin, too weak and too insubstantial' and a framework based on sovereignty that was 'too large, too abstract and too rigid' (Foucault, 1991a: 98). It is the notion of population that makes possible the elaboration of distinctively governmental techniques and rationalities, as we have shown in the previous chapter.

The notion of population introduces several key things that will have broad effects on how the art of government is conceived, and also will enable its elaboration. First, it introduces a different conception of the governed. The members of a population are no longer subjects bound together in a territory who are obliged to submit to their sovereign. They are also, by the end of the eighteenth century, living, working and social beings, with their own customs, habits, histories and forms of labour and leisure. Second, a population is defined in relation to matters of life and death, health and illness, propagation and longevity, which can be known by statistical, demographic and epidemiological instruments. Knowledge of a population in this sense is concerned with the specification of variations around norms, themselves generated by statistical measures. Population itself is not simply a collection of living human beings but a kind of living entity with a history and a development, and with possibilities of pathology. In the *History of Sexuality* (1979: 139), Foucault uses the term 'species body' to designate this aspect of population and to distinguish a bio-politics of the population from an 'anatomo-politics' of the (individual) body. A third element of the notion of population follows from this view of it as a species body. It is a collective entity, the knowledge of which is irreducible to the knowledge that any of its members may have of themselves. It is also a collective with a history, customs, habits and so on that need to be taken into account. The population is not just a collection of living, working and speaking subjects; it is also a particular objective reality of which one can have knowledge. For example, one can ask – as indeed Malthus did (Dean, 1991: 144) – about the historical development of certain aspects of the population: its marriage customs, the number of marriages that are usually conjoined, at what ages, how many children are produced by these marriages, the customs that take place within the family, the price of labour and its variation, and the happiness of the working population at a given time. In short, one can know a population, and its industry, customs and history, as a collective entity that is not constituted by political or governmental institutions or frameworks. Perhaps this is one reason why liberal government not only governs through society as external to the institutions of formal political authority but also comes to regard that society as a discrete totality.[4] We return to this problem in the next chapter.

The elaboration of a notion of the population was a gradual process that was both technical and theoretical, relying on the development of statistics and census taking, and the techniques of epidemiology and demography perhaps even more than the theoretical innovations of political economists. What emerges is a dynamic totality and a source of instability and disequilibrium that is no longer reducible to the rather static model of the patriarchalist households within a kingdom, and their relation to the royal house. Thus, in order to break with a conception of government irrevocably tied to the theory of sovereignty, it is necessary for the art of government to leave behind the preoccupation with the kingdom as an extension of the royal household and the model of the government of the state based on the government of the family. One consequence of this is that the family becomes an element within the dynamic field of force that is the population. The family is a reality to be taken into account as an instrument and objective of government, rather than the very *a priori* of government itself.

Population is an absolutely key term in the elaboration of the art of government at the end of the eighteenth century. This is because it figures in and binds together two different trajectories. On the one hand, it provides the 'life-administering power' of bio-politics with an object. On the other, it provides liberalism as a critical rationality with a government-limiting critique. From the perspective of the public health movement, of those who sought the eradication of pauperism, criminality and degeneracy, and of those who addressed the question of the working, living and housing of the labouring populations in the first half of the nineteenth century, there appeared to be no internal limit to the exigencies of this administration of life which replaces the sovereign right of death with 'a power to foster life or disallow it' (Foucault, 1979: 137–8). By contrast, by the end of the eighteenth century, population finds its own constant, internal and ever-present limit in the resources necessary for its support. It is through population that the government of the living and of life will find its own limit in the endangering of the processes that produce the resources that support life.

The transformation of the exercise of sovereignty

The third aspect of the governmentalization of the state involves the manner in which governmental practices and forms of rationality begin to transform questions of sovereignty and its instruments. This might be approached on a number of fronts. First, the transformation of sovereignty provides the condition for the emergence of the liberal problematic of security. If the end of sovereignty refers ultimately to nothing but itself and its own continuation, those goals of government will be achieved by providing security to the economic, biological and social processes that are external to its mechanisms and to the forms of liberty on which they depend. This security through liberty also entails the question of how to secure the government of the state from the effects of a form of government which is a government through free persons (Hindess, 1997). As we shall see in the next chapter, the concerns over the possibility of the corruption of government by parties and factions, i.e. by the manner in which free individuals might act politically, is also a component of the liberal problem of security. In general, nevertheless, the art of government will try to enframe the economic and social processes external to political authority, and the liberties on which they depend, in mechanisms of security.

Second, there are transformations of the practice and theory of sovereignty itself that correspond to the development of the arts and rationalities of government. The legal form allows sovereignty to be 'an instrument and justification of the large scale administrative monarchies over and against localism' from the sixteenth to the eighteenth centuries (Foucault, 1980: 103). Sovereignty thus provides a set of instruments and a means of justification for the development of governmental mechanisms engendered by police science and mercantilism, and for the extension of disciplinary practices. At a theoretical level, sovereignty is recast at the same time in a juridical form that ties the exercise of sovereignty to the law, to notions of right, and to the legal subject. Foucault suggests that social contract theory can be understood as an attempt by the art of government to reconcile itself to the theory of sovereignty. He argues (Foucault, 1991a: 98, 101) that Hobbes sought to discover the 'ruling principles of an art of government' through a renewed theory of sovereignty based on a contract, and that Rousseau in *The Social Contract* can be understood as seeking a general principle of government which allows for a juridical principle of sovereignty and for the elements through which an art of government can be defined and characterized. Skinner (1989: 118–21) confirms this reading of Hobbes by noting how sovereignty arises from the contracts of particular persons but remains irreducible to the rights of citizens either individually or collectively. Thus, for Hobbes, there is always a disjunction between the right that is exercised by civil government and the source of that government in the contracts between particular individuals. Because of this disjunction, there must be a translation between the source of sovereignty and the exercise of government. Thus, he argues in *De Cive* (1983: 105), 'that right which every man had before to use his faculties to his own advantage, is now wholly translated on some certain man, or council, for the common benefit'.

Sovereignty begins to take on a new set of functions. It is no longer simply the effective mechanism of power it was under feudalism. The systems of sovereignty and the law 'have allowed a theory of right to be superimposed upon the mechanisms of discipline in such as way as to conceal its actual procedures, the element of domination in its techniques, and to guarantee to everyone, by virtue of the sovereignty of the State, the exercise of his proper sovereign rights' (Foucault, 1980: 105). The 'element of domination' that Foucault here identifies in discipline may also be found in the bio-political governmental regulation of the population. The more general argument would be that this element is concealed by the displacement of politics towards questions of sovereignty and the juridical subject of rights.

Moreover, the formation of the population and its members as bearers of a regulated and responsible freedom by both disciplinary and bio-political practices is itself a condition of the possibility of a democratization of sovereignty.

Law – as the characteristic instrument of sovereignty since the late Middle Ages – also undergoes transformation as a correlate of the trajectory of government. One might say that law is transformed from a juridical system concerned to codify and express the monarch's authority to an instrument of a normative order, which is part of complex apparatuses of normalizing practices (Ewald, 1990). As Foucault puts it: 'I do not mean to say that the law fades into the background or that the institutions of justice tend to disappear, but rather that the law operates more and more as a norm, and that the judicial institution is increasingly incorporated into a continuum of apparatuses (medical, administrative and so on) whose functions are for the most part regulatory' (1979: 144). We shall have more to say about this transformation of law and the relation between law, democratic sovereignty and liberal government in the next chapter.

The non-political and the political

The fourth and final aspect of the governmentalization of the state necessary to the appearance of liberal and social forms of government is the emergence of a distinction between political and non-political spheres, and the view that the political in some sense arises from and serves the non-political sphere. Perhaps the most fundamental way in which the non-political sphere has been conceived is by the concept of 'society'. This conception of society as a relatively pacified totality has both internal and external conditions. The external conditions crucially include those military and diplomatic arrangements that guarantee the existence of more or less autonomous states protected from outside interference. The history of the European state system and its characteristic instruments and the agreements that made up the Peace of Westphalia of 1648 may be understood in this light. The former, which ended the hostilities of the Thirty Years War, were agreements that effectively put an end to the dream of the reconstitution of the Roman Empire and the creation of a temporal order in harmony with the spiritual dominion of the Church. It is in this sense that we have already noted that reason of state contained an external element in that it subordinated religious disputation to the recognition that reality would now include a multiplicity of states. The population would henceforth follow the religion of the prince, the prince would forfeit his rights over a territory if he changed confessional faith, and no state could intervene in the internal affairs of another. The agreements of Westphalia thus mark the point at which wars between states in Europe would be waged for political, rather than religious, ends.

On the other hand, the transformation of the familialistic conception of governing through the notion of population begins to give positive shape to the non-political field that is external to government. The non-political sphere is construed as a quasi-autonomous and naturalistic reality constituted by processes that are irreducible to the will of the sovereign or its representatives. The economy is only one influential way of conceiving this reality as external to government, but so too is civil society, community, culture, or, as we have noted on several occasions, population. As Foucault suggested, the moment when government seeks a principle of its limitation in an outside which is not completely penetrable by its own mechanisms, is the moment when government has to deal not only 'with a territory, with a domain, and with its subjects, but . . . with a complex and independent reality that has its own laws and mechanisms of disturbance. This new reality is society' (1989a: 261).

We might now return to the conclusion of the previous chapter with a slightly different view. We might now say that in Western Europe between the sixteenth and eighteenth centuries, the dominance of the model of the family and the *oikos*, the subordination of the practice of government to the notion of sovereignty, and the use of law and regulations as the privileged instruments of government, all mean that the government of the state cannot escape the patriarchalist, dispositional problematic concerned with the 'government of things' in La Perrière's sense. However, with the emergence of a concept of population, with the discovery of the economy as an independent reality and practical domain of government, with the formation of society as the quasi-naturalistic totality beyond the reaches of the government and encompassing it, these polities pass a threshold in which the government of the numbers and households of the state will henceforth be modified, if not entirely displaced, by a government through economic, social, psychological and biological processes. The most fundamental set of formulas of government that will be founded on this government through such processes will be called liberalism, although this term is used broadly enough to encompass various political formations of the twentieth century including social liberalism and social democracy. To describe liberal government then is to analyse certain of the effects of this shift from a government of inhabitants, 'things' and households to a government through tendencies, laws, necessities and processes. In the following chapter I address the way in which this shift is played out in relation to issues of economy, security, law and society.

Notes

1 V. Mirabeau, *Philosophie Rurale*, as cited and translated by Keith Tribe (1995: 122).
2 I use the term 'bio-politics' despite the fact that it seems to have been largely overlooked by those who have taken up Foucault's notion of governmentality. The term provides a bridge between his pre-1976 deliberations and analyses on power (particularly in *Discipline and Punish* and *The History of Sexuality*) and his post-1977 deliberations on government. Foucault's conception of power from 1978 is radically different in at least two ways from that which he held until 1976. First, it employs the term 'government' to displace models of power drawn from both the language of war and the juridical theory of sovereignty. Second, it thematizes the notion of freedom as integral to the operation of power. However, it is also

important to recognize that this change of the theorization of power did not entail a radical break with all aspects of his earlier conception of power and his historical concepts. Power is still regarded as relational, strategic and productive. When in 1979 Foucault discusses liberalism, it is in a lecture course called 'The birth of bio-politics' (1997a: 73–9). Franklin's phrase is cited by Foucault in the summary of this lecture course (1997a: 77).

3   This term is used in Foucault's final lecture in 1976 (1997b: 223). It raises the question of the relation between the social and bio-politics. As a preliminary view, I would want to venture that the social is a particular region of bio-politics in so far as it addresses processes of dissolution and integration that stem from the social being of 'man', rather than his characteristics as a living organism or an economic being. In a broader view, the social as a field of knowledge could be understood as a consequence of one facet of medical knowledge, that concerning the morbidity and mortality of populations.

4   I owe the posing of this question to an unpublished paper by Christine Helliwell and Barry Hindess, 'Government and the marginalization of empire: on the image of a self-contained history of Western social thought'.

6 LIBERALISM

First, a central contention: that bio-politics is a necessary condition of liberalism, and that liberalism, as a critique and rationality of government, can be located along this line of modification we have called the governmentalization of the state. At one level, liberalism is a version of bio-politics; at another, it exists in a kind of permanent tension with bio-political imperatives. It is the idea of a government of the population and the imperatives that are derived from such an idea that both unites liberalism and bio-politics and makes liberalism a critique of the unlimited operation of bio-political imperatives. Because of this complex relation of liberalism and bio-politics, it would be a mistake to oppose classical liberalism to *social* forms of government. The discovery of society, itself only possible because of this bio-politics of the population, is a precondition for liberal government and a tool for its critique. What separates classical liberalism from, say, social democracy, is not that one recognizes that government must be anchored in society and its processes and the other does not, but rather the conception of society and the implications that flow from it.

A similar set of points can be made about discipline. Liberalism presents itself as a critique of excessive disciplinary power in the name of the rights and liberty of the individual. However, as we shall see, the generalization of discipline is a condition of liberal government and necessary to processes of the democratization of sovereignty.

The emergence of a liberal rationality of government is dependent on the discovery of the government of processes found in the population, the economy and society. It introduces the liberal problematic of security as the security of these 'non-political' processes on which government will depend, and it reconfigures the role of law. Law will be understood no longer simply as an instrument of sovereignty but as a component of the liberal technology of government. Against interpretations of liberalism as having a necessary relation to the 'rule of law', I argue here that the liberal technology of government, including law, has a much more fundamental affinity with norms. In this regard, a liberal rationality of government depends upon the emergence of a 'bio-political' domain.

In what follows I examine four major aspects through which we can elucidate the features of liberal government: economy, security, law and society.

Economy

Consider, first, the economy. Here we might distinguish a series of three 'events' in the emergence of a notion of the economy as a particular level of reality constituted by distinctively economic processes rather than as a sphere of positive action on the part of the sovereign. This series also charts the breakdown of the relation between a knowledge of the population and how to govern it found in reason of state and police science. I wish to argue that it is the third phase that is decisive in the establishment of liberalism as a form of government *through* rather than *of* the economy.

The first event is the discovery of the economy as a 'quasi-nature' that can nevertheless be represented and known by the sovereign. This is most clearly in evidence in the writings of the Physiocrats and in François Quesnay's *Tableau économique* (Tribe, 1987: 119–24; Gordon, 1991: 15; Foucault, 1997a: 76). In the writings of the Physiocrats, such as Mirabeau quoted at the beginning of the previous chapter, we find a conception of a natural order that is self-constituting and exists prior to any state of affairs established by government. Their conception of 'economic government' presupposes the existence of an order that is the source of wealth but which can be modified or tampered with, and the possibility of establishing an appropriate fiscal policy. While their principles disclose the operation of this natural order, the 'Table' is an abstract representation of the totality of exchanges between economic actors. Both the principles and the device of the Table are intended to enlighten the sovereign. By having the economy represented to him, the ruler can allow a system of liberty to prevail at the same time as he can monitor the activities within the economy. The *économistes*, as they were also known, presuppose the existence of the sovereign not as the constitutive framework of a discourse on wealth and trade – in the manner of mercantilism, for example – but as a kind of subject of economic knowledge of a set of processes that are no longer dependent upon its action.

The second point in the series is marked by Adam Smith's *The Wealth of Nations* and particularly for Foucault, his notion of the 'invisible hand' (Gordon, 1991: 15–8; Foucault, 1997a: 76). Foucault contrasts Quesnay's Table which aims 'to make visible (in the form of "evidence") the formation of the value and the circulation of wealth' with the invisible hand which 'presupposes the intrinsic invisibility between individual profit-seeking and the growth of collective wealth'. Against the attempt to render economic processes visible in the representational space of a Table, Smith's thesis can be understood as the 'benign opacity of economic processes'. The best outcome for the state is provided by the pursuit of individual self-interest in the exchanges of the market. The knowledge of how this outcome will be achieved is known neither to the economic subject nor by the government. Therefore, against police science, there is the impossibility of economic sovereignty, i.e. the impossibility of the sovereign determining all the economic exchanges of individuals to optimize wealth. Foucault thus calls political economy a 'lateral science' in a *tête-à-tête* with the art of government that it cannot constitute. Much of the liberal art of government is involved in the restructuring of the institutions of state and society in a manner consistent with, but not derived from, the protocols of political economy.

Gordon (1991: 16) terms the emergence of this economic reality, and its successive displacements, within governmental rationality a 'complex event' and adds that it cannot be understood as a moment of total discontinuity. We might note that there is substantial textual evidence for the view that the *Wealth of Nations* does not mark the emergence of an economic science, particularly in its final three books. Such evidence is encapsulated in the introduction to Book IV where Smith refers to 'Political Œconomy' as a 'branch of the science of a statesman or legislator' (1976: vol. 1, 428) with two objects: to enable the people to provide a plentiful revenue or subsistence for themselves, and to provide sufficient revenue for the public services. Smith's mode of conceptualization of the object of analysis still depends on the existence of a political and legislative framework and – despite the existence of a self-regulating system of exchanges animated by the liberty of self-interested subjects – ultimately invokes the presence of the sovereign (Tribe 1978: 100–45; 1981: 121–52). The final book concerns the 'revenue and expenses of the sovereign or commonwealth'. Moreover, the advocacy of the 'invisible hand' should be understood within the unity of moral, political and economic concerns.

The third point in the series that constitutes this complex event, however, could be marked by the development of English political economy, exemplified particularly by David Ricardo, in the early nineteenth century (Dean, 1991: 148–55). Here, the notion of the economy becomes a fundamental bio-economic reality, driven by the natural disequilibrium between subsistence and population discovered by Malthus. This is the case for Ricardo's differential theory of rent. Rather than a hidden hand that coordinates acts of individual self-interest in a process that is ultimately enframed within the protocols of sovereignty, the economy now concerns humankind's incessant struggle to bring more lands into cultivation, and to increase the productivity of its labour, so that it can defeat the natural and irreducible ontological scarcity it faces due to the laws of population.

The classical political economy of the early nineteenth century is contiguous with the broad bio-political field that is its condition in at least two ways. First, government will entail the making of regulations that need to take into account the natural and necessary processes that are exterior to it. Second, like bio-politics, it relies on processes that are to be found at the level of population as an organic, living entity. Where it differs from other versions of bio-politics is that it will not be content to derive norms of the optimal conditions for the population to expand and prosper. It will balance these considerations against another set of norms, those derived from the delicate, unstable disequilibrium between population and the resources necessary for its maintenance. The discovery of the ontological reality of scarcity means that the administration of life must take into account the means of production of the subsistence of that life.

Security

This series of transformations that lead to the emergence of the notion of the economy allows us to think about older conceptions of security and the correlative derivation of what might be called a liberal problematic of security. One might wish to argue that there is a complex set of continuities and modifications that are introduced by liberal government. A key example of the preservation of security as a principal end of government is found in Jeremy Bentham's *The Theory of Legislation* (1950). Bentham argues that there are four 'subordinate ends' of legislation under the ultimate end of utility or the 'greatest happiness of the greatest number'. These ends were to provide subsistence, to produce abundance, to favour equality, and to maintain security (1950: 96–7; Dean, 1991: 187–8). Security, including security of person, honour, property and condition, however, was lifted to the top of the hierarchy of government for it is the 'foundation of life' on which everything depends. Thus, we might consider in this context how Bentham thought about the relation between security and subsistence. In general, the provision of subsistence could only be provided for by the security of property in law and was not an activity of government. This is the case with one notable exception: the relief of the indigent poor. Subsistence must be provided for this category in order to prevent dangers to the security of the state, life and property. Of course, relief to the indigent should be granted in such a way as not to impede the mechanisms that produce abundance, the laws of the market, or individuals' willingness to enter the market – summed up in his principle of 'less eligibility'. Thus while the manner of poor relief must be consistent with the existence of the liberal economy, the fact of it follows from the concern for security.

This move allows quite a lot of room for detailed regulation. In Bentham's case, this includes the establishment of a National Charity Company and later a centralized form of administration, an Indigence Relief Ministry, and the recommendation of workhouses for the indigent in the form of pauper Panopticons (Dean, 1991: ch. 10). However, assistance to the indigent can be considered a mechanism of security that must be provided in such a way as to ensure the participation of labourers in the labour market and not to interfere with the 'natural' responsibility of male heads of households for the subsistence of their wives and children. In the first instance, then, regulation made in the service of security has to be structured in such a way as to lead indigent and other troublesome groups to exercise a responsible and disciplined freedom in the market and in the family.

In this regard, for Bentham, liberty is reduced to a branch of security. Governmental interventions in the name of security must seek to produce forms of liberty appropriate to the participation in the market. Thus the liberal problematic of security differs from a police conception of security in a first way. While the police conception makes the security of the state dependent upon the detailed regulation of 'men and things', the liberal problematic advises that security can be best attained by creating the conditions under which individuals can exercise various liberties. However, where the exercise of liberty might undermine the security of property or of the state, liberalism remains continuous with police in recommending detailed regulation of particular populations. We shall extend this theme in the following chapter. Unlike police, however, this detailed regulation must be made consistent with the natural laws of the economy and population.

However, the liberal problematic of security also differs from a police conception in another way. This second way is captured by Foucault's inversion of the relations between security and liberty. Where Bentham argues that liberty is a branch of security, Foucault turns this around to suggest that, for liberalism, liberty is also a condition of security (Gordon, 1991: 19–20). This means that to govern properly, to achieve security, it is necessary to respect the liberty of the governed so that the natural processes of the economy and the population might function effectively. Even though Bentham would be the last to underestimate the size of his pauper populations, there still remains a large part of the population that will already act rationally in the manner of Smith's *Homo œconomicus*. Thus the liberties of individuals as economic subjects with interests and as property owners is one part of a secure order.

There is a kind of circular relation between security and liberty. On the one hand, security entails the regulation of certain individuals and groups in order to lead them to choose to exercise their liberty in a disciplined and responsible manner. On the other, this responsible liberty is necessary to the security of those natural processes of economy and population which in turn secure the well-being of the state. The problem of *laissez-faire* then is not about the retreat from regulation but about 'the setting in place of mechanisms of security . . . whose function is to assure the security of those natural phenomena, economic processes, and the intrinsic processes of population; this is what becomes the basic objective of governmental rationality' (Foucault, 5 April 1978, cited in Gordon, 1991: 19).

Another aspect of this liberal problematic of security is developed by Hindess (1997). This aspect follows from Weber's definition of 'politically oriented action' as that which 'aims to exert influence on the government of a political organization; especially at the appropriation, redistribution or allocation of the powers of government' (1968: 55; Hindess, 1997: 261). When we distinguished between political rationality and governmental rationality, we saw that the former did not necessarily entail the practice of government itself. It might simply concern the promotion of the interests of a particular group or faction against the concern to govern on behalf of the population in the general interest of the state. Thus the government of the state can be undermined by its usurpation by a particular group. This is particularly acute when the government of the state operates through the action of free persons, as its does in its liberal forms. The problem of security therefore entails 'how to ensure that the politically oriented activities of the governed population do not disrupt the proper workings of various state agencies' (Hindess, 1997: 263). This question of how to properly regulate and limit the political activities of the governed is a key part of the liberal rationality of government. It is evident in David Hume's strictures against the 'founders of sects and factions' and their subversion of government, and in the writings of the American Federalists (1997: 263–5). One aspect of the liberal notion of security is how to secure the government against the depredations of faction, party and popular enthusiasms that might stem from the people. Just as people must exercise their economic freedom with proper discipline and responsibility, and be trained to do so by means of institutions such as workhouses or under the whip of hunger, so they must learn to exercise their political freedom responsibly – by means of institutional design or by limiting the scope of the activity of the state. We return to the point about institutional design below.

Liberalism thus retains the police concern with the order of the state but replaces its model of governed reality, from a 'visible grid of communication' of all forms of intercourse between humans in a spatial environment to the dense, opaque, autonomous processes of the population, civil society and its economy – processes that can only be known through forms of expertise. The liberal problematic of security is posed in relation to the operation of these processes and the responsible, disciplined and prudential subjects on which they depend. It is also posed as the establishment of those conditions under which the exercise of political and economic freedom will not endanger the operation of government itself.

Law and norm

The third and perhaps most revealing aspect of liberalism is the relation between liberalism and law. Law is transformed by liberalism in that its function as an instrument of the exercise of sovereignty becomes linked to a complex set of disciplinary and governmental apparatuses. Despite the proliferation of codes, constitutions and laws, liberalism has no necessary affinity with law. Liberalism – as a product and critique of bio-politics – has more in common with the norm than with law and transforms law into one component of a set of regulatory mechanisms concerned with the government of processes. The key questions about law for an analytics of government do not concern its general meaning, function or role in liberal-democratic societies. They concern, rather, its operation within any given regime of practices, the role it is assigned within specific programmes of government, the technology it is a part of, and the forms of subject it proposes to work through and upon.

A key example of this form of analysis of law is found in *The History of Sexuality* (1979). Here Foucault argues that the development of bio-power – or the power over life – has the effect of the 'growing importance assumed by the action of the norm, at the expense of the juridical system of the law' (1979: 144). Far from representing the view that law ceases to be important, Foucault's argument is that law is increasingly invested with norms and operates more and more as a norm. Judicial institutions become 'incorporated into a continuum of apparatuses (medical, administrative and so on) whose functions are for the most part regulatory' (1979: 144). In passing, it is well to note that this use of the term 'regulatory' connotes an association with the norm and normalizing powers. Foucault's argument that we have entered into a phase of 'juridical regression', despite the proliferation of the framing of constitutions, codes and the 'whole continual and clamorous legislative activity', is an assertion that the function of law as a coercive technique of sovereignty has been displaced and reinscribed in its role in normalizing power. Law cannot 'help but be armed', for Foucault (1979: 144), but this feature is increasingly encased in new normalizing and regulatory functions.

This account of the displacement of law by norm is elaborated by François Ewald (1990). He argues that a norm is a way for a group to provide itself – or be provided with – a common denominator without any recourse to a point of externality. Adolphe Quételet suggested a theory of the statistically determined 'average man' among a population (e.g. of average height) as a 'fictional entity' that is nevertheless 'society itself as it sees itself objectified in the mirror of probability and statistics' (1990: 145–6). Norms in themselves are counterfactual and self-referential: they operate as if there were such an average man, and they refer to nothing but the characteristics of the population so normalized. Moreover, these norms can be produced according to different logics, e.g. those of discipline, of probabilistic logic, and of the communicative logic of the technical norm.

If we consider the technical norm, argues Ewald (1990: 148), normalization is less concerned with establishing a model than with reaching an understanding regarding the choice of a model. The essential question is not the production of objects that can act as a standard but the establishment of procedures that will lead to a general agreement regarding the choice of norms and standards. In discourses of technical standardization all norms of terminology, of spatial measurement and of quality are interdependent, and this interdependence arises from the fact that what is normalized is not a world of things but language itself – its vocabulary, notation, writing, signs, locutions, its relation to numbers and diagrams, its syntax and so on. 'Normalization,' for Ewald's analysis of industrial standardization, 'is the institution of the perfect common language of pure communication required by industrial society' (1990: 151).

A norm, then, is not simply a value however arrived at, but a rule of judgement and a means of producing that rule (1990: 154). A norm creates an equivalence in that all are comparable in relation to it; but it also creates differences and inequalities in so far as it enables each to be individualized and hierarchically ordered in relation to it. The norm is thus intrinsic to the group that applies it to itself and hence is a form of regulation and stabilization that is independent of all philosophical or religious values. This means that the norm itself is 'post-metaphysical': it depends on values that are relative to the group and are revisable rather than absolutes. What is significant about the norm – and this perhaps distinguishes it from certain other values – is that it derives not from a general view of the cosmos, of being or of human nature, but from the characteristics or attributes of the things, activities, facts or populations to which it is to be applied.

The kind of law which is compatible with normalizing practices is one in which laws are produced with reference to the particular society it claims to regulate and not to a set of universal principles. For Ewald, this kind of law no longer emanates from the sovereign's will but from the collectivity without being willed by anyone in particular. It provides the group with sovereignty over itself but that sovereignty derives not from the social contract or from the general will but from the community's relation to a common standard. Ewald gives the example of the resolutions of the United Nations which become a means for evaluating conduct according to a set of agreed norms rather than a binding constraint. A rather more mundane example is traffic law – an example we mentioned in our contrast of sovereignty and government above. We might regard traffic laws as both coercively enforced constraints (through fines, licence confiscations, etc.) and a set of norms by which road users regulate their conduct (e.g. norms of the maximum speeds for safe driving on certain roads). While such laws still partake of a juridical system of law, i.e. law as an instrument of sovereignty, their function is to set and maintain norms for the regulation of conduct. The deployment of punitive instruments in this instance of course serves the most 'bio-political' of ends: the maintenance of the life and well-being of the population.

In light of this consideration of the norm and normalization we might understand Foucault's general orientation toward liberal democracy found in the cryptic summary of his lectures on government in 1978. Here he argues that there is no necessary relation between liberalism, the rule of law and representative democracy:

> Liberalism does not derive from juridical thought any more than it does from an economic analysis. It is not the idea of a political society founded on a contractual tie that gave birth to it; but in the search for a liberal technology of government, it appeared that regulation through the juridical form constituted a far more effective tool than the wisdom or moderation of the governors. Liberalism sought that regulation in 'the law', not through a legalism that would be natural to it but because the law defines forms of general intervention excluding particular, individual, or exceptional measures; and because the participation of the governed in the formulation of the law, in the parliamentary system, constitutes the most effective system of governmental economy. The 'state of right', the *Rechsstaat*, the rule of law, the organization of a 'truly representative' parliamentary system was, therefore, during the whole beginning of the nineteenth century, closely connected with liberalism, but . . . the democracies of the state of right were not necessarily liberal, nor was liberalism necessarily democratic or devoted to the forms of law. (Foucault, 1997a: 77)

There is no necessary, internal relation for Foucault between liberalism, law and representative democracy. Liberalism considered as a rationality and technology of government rather than as a political philosophy has a certain rationale for the adoption of the rule of law – its generality and exclusion of the particular – and for representative institutions – they permit the participation of the governed in the 'governmental economy'. Now let us note two things about this passage. First, it is the formal properties of law that lend it to being taken up by liberalism as an instrument of government.[1] Second, Foucault points to a circularity in this liberal rationality of government that can provide a 'non-sovereignty' version of representative democracy. Rather than saying that the governed should be the source of sovereignty because of their intrinsic rights and liberties as individuals or as members of a political community, he is suggesting that for liberalism the governed ought to participate in the election of governors because government already depends on the liberties and capacities of the governed exercised within an economy. Representative democracy, then, is merely one mechanism by which the exercise of political power can be limited and rationalized according to the exercise of freedom by the governed.

We should not, however, think that representative democratic institutions less than fundamentally helped to reshape liberal-democratic societies over the course of the twentieth century. The critical review of government and its officials by representative institutions opens a new space of politics. This is one of mobilization of those concerns and aspirations that are fostered by and come to compose social government (which we discuss below). The wants and desires shaped by interventions in health, education, and social provision are translated into the political programmes of mass labour and social-democratic parties. One of the effects of representative institutions has been to convert diverse social interventions into mass political demands.

On the other hand, representative democracy is also one means by which the participation of the governed in the operation of government can itself be limited and regulated. As Hindess notes, for the American Federalists 'one of the merits of representation . . . is precisely that it secures a form of popular government in which "the people, in their collective form" are excluded from any part in their government' (1997: 264). Representative institutions, in this sense, are a governmental response to the democratization of sovereignty, a way of managing the effects of faction among the people and ensuring the strict separation of the governed from their governors. The problem of the management of the exercise of political activities that might corrupt the operation of government is then displaced onto the elected representatives and those who control the administration of the institutions of government, such as public servants (1997: 265-6). Here representative institutions are one component in the problem of institutional design, which also includes the doctrine of the separation of powers and political non-interference in the judiciary and the broader principle of the rule of law.

Liberalism, then, has at least as much a historical bond with the norm as with the law. There are at least two senses in which this is the case. The first is that liberalism seeks to establish norms of good government. The most general norm of liberal government is that of the changing balance between governing too much and governing too little. Liberalism seeks to establish norms of government derived from the population in its concrete economic relations with the processes that lead to the production of the resources necessary for its sustenance and prosperity. It uses these norms of government to criticize earlier forms of the detailed regulation of the population found both in police and in reason of state. More significantly, it employs these norms to limit the bio-political imperative to create the optimal conditions of the life of the population.

The second sense in which liberalism has an affinity with the norm follows from what we have already considered about discipline. Foucault noted the duality of the political individual as a subject shaped through normalizing practices and as a citizen with rights and liberties. The relation of liberalism to government can be thought about through each of these perspectives on the political subject. Examined through the notion of the citizen, the question for liberalism is to define a form of state compatible with her or his rights and liberties and to establish a political form that allows the aggregation of citizens' diverse interests. Examined through the figure of the normalized subject, the problem becomes how to shape the liberty of the citizen in such a way as to ensure that she or he exercises freedom responsibly and in a disciplined fashion. Thus nineteenth-century liberalism is concerned not only with the development of representative institutions compatible with the individual citizen's rights but with ensuring that individuals as members of a population know how to exercise those rights properly. Liberalism is thus as much concerned with the appropriate normalizing practices to shape the exercise of citizens' political freedom as it is with guaranteeing their rights and liberties.

Liberalism does not jettison but transforms law and the 'juridical system of sovereignty'. It does this for a number of reasons. First, law was historically an instrument for the construction of large-scale administrative monarchies in the sixteenth and seventeenth centuries (Foucault, 1980: 103). It was thus a crucial means of overcoming localism and central to the establishment of constitutional nation-states. Second, law provides a general framework for governmental interventions which can ensure that such interventions set the rules for a form of government through the economy as a quasi-natural reality. Law, or so it is claimed, permits the operation of exchanges, free from corruption, nepotism and partiality. Third, law – and more generally the democratization of sovereignty – permits the participation of the governed in the governmental economy. The parliamentary form allows each citizen a choice of how best to ensure the workings of the laws of the economy, but not whether such laws should govern him or her. It also limits the involvement of the governed in the activity of their government and displaces the problem of the management of political activity onto a range of actors, including politicians, public servants and the judiciary. Fourth, law and juridical institutions and agents – particularly the courts – act as coordinating points for normalizing powers and governmental regulations. The juvenile justice system, family law and its administration, and even the criminal justice system themselves become invested with a multiplicity of agents (psychologists, psychiatrists, criminologists, social workers, doctors) and associated with a myriad of regulatory practices (counselling, therapy, rehabilitation, advice).

Finally, and perhaps most importantly, liberalism retains and transforms the institutions and practices of law as the instruments of review and mechanisms of accountability of government. It establishes various tribunals, commissions and inquiries that operationalize the language and procedures of law against abuses found in governmental mechanisms such as bureaucratic decision-making or in the exercise of regimes of discipline in various institutions from schools to asylums to prisons. Further, the language of rights and liberties consequent upon the juridification and democratization of sovereignty is the means by which liberalism seeks to check the appearance of authoritarian forms of government that follow from certain bio-political imperatives, as we shall see in the following chapter.

Our account of liberalism so far raises what will be a key problem of liberal governmentality: that of the dissonance between economic and juridical rationalities and the forms of subject they presuppose. This problem might be understood as having two aspects. These concern the relations of adjustment between, first, the totalizing unity of sovereignty–state–law and the non-totalizable multiplicity of economic exchanges; and, second, the legal subject of right and obligation and the economic subject of interest. The thought-space of liberalism establishes a complex domain of governmentality that situates juridical and economic subjectivity as relative moments. However it must do so by placing these within an overall aim of government, the maintenance of security. The notion of society is crucial to the attempted management of this governmental thought-space and to elaborating forms of government that are no longer, strictly speaking, liberal.

Society and social government

It is clear that the liberal rationality and technology of government which took shape in the latter part of the eighteenth century cannot be reduced to the formula of *laissez-faire* that gave birth to an ideal of minimal government. Liberalism had to deal with a complex problem-space of government in which the question of security is reconstituted as the security of those quasi-natural processes that are found within the population and the economy. Government thus concerns the management of those processes and discovering an optimal level of governmental regulation of them. Further, this problem-space has to deal with radically heterogeneous forms of the governed subject. On the one hand, the security of these quasi-natural processes depends on the capacity of rational and prudential subjects to exercise their liberty to pursue their interests within a market economy and to calculate the effects of marriage and family. On the other hand, the political structure within which such processes are secured is one that, for a variety of reasons, finds it necessary to employ the institutions and language of law and sovereignty, and indeed to give the exercise of sovereignty a representational form.

Thus the economic subject of interest has to be cultivated in a manner consistent with the political and legal subject of rights. How, then, can this problem-space be thought and acted upon? One key answer is found in the development of a notion of 'civil society' or, more simply, 'society'.

I want to note several features of this notion of society, which account for its shape and the manner in which it fits into the jigsaw puzzle of liberal government. The first feature is that 'society' acts as a container that is coincident with the nation. It places a boundary around the problems of the government of population within a territory. Society contains the dense and opaque autonomous processes of the economy and the population as well as the mechanisms for their government. It is also the 'real' existing space in which issues and problems generated by the legal-political sphere, including those of justice, are to be balanced against or reconciled with issues and problems raised in the economic sphere. Society and its processes are what must be secured. One of the consequences of this definition of the really existing space of society is that the problems and issues raised within the borders of the nation can be addressed in terms that are relatively isolated from matters external to those borders even when that nation is an actor in those external matters.

From a liberal point of view, society is an always and already existing natural reality. While there will be much debate over how the natural reality of society is connected to other natural realities, society itself will continue to have a natural existence and a natural history in that it is no longer regarded as an outcome of political or sovereign power or the product of actions or agreements between human beings. Among the writers of the eighteenth-century 'Scottish Enlightenment', for example, civil society is no longer a political or juridical society formed through a social contract or the exchange, transfer and surrender of natural rights. It is 'always-already there, the natural-historical form of human species life' (Burchell, 1991: 134). It is perhaps here, most importantly in the work of Adam Ferguson (Hill, 1996) and John Millar, that society appears in its own reality and humankind as a naturally social species. Even inequality, forms of authority and the ranks of society have to be explained in terms of the natural or acquired differences between individuals within society and the consequent difference in 'the capacity to influence others, to command their obedience in actions and gain their submission to one's views in counsel' (1991: 136). Juridical and political structures are merely a function of these naturally occurring social relations of authority.

The second point to note about this liberal conception of society is that it is a totality. Why should this be so? Population is a totality or unity in that the observable statistical regularities among a population are irreducible to the choices or actions of any of the members of the population. Moreover, these regularities act across all members of that population. A related point can be made about society. Society is that space where the actions and decisions of the members of a population are made and the form of society is just as irreducible to those actions and decisions as is the population. When Durkheim would come to his notion of social facts, conceiving of them as composing a reality *sui generis*, it would be by observing the statistical regularities revealed by rates of suicide within a population. There are two things to note about this. The first, from Foucault, is that the concern with those who make a determination to end their own lives was 'one of the first astonishments of a society in which political power had assigned itself the task of administering life' (1979: 139). The second is that this apparently most private of acts and choices is discovered or shown to obey regularities, unknown to each individual, that are only observable at the level of population. It is this latter characteristic that makes suicide a social fact. We come thus to infer the existence of society from the regularities observable in a population.

There is, however, another reason why society comes to be regarded as a totality. The problem of society arises from the liberal problematic of security and the concerns generated by the attempt to address the dissonance between different forms of subject. The problem that the notion of society proposes to answer is the problem of how we can attain security in a milieu constituted by radically heterogeneous forces, processes and types of subject, particularly those that are by their very nature dissolving, anarchic and fissiparous. The notion of society might break with the notion of a juridical or political society formed by the agreement of its members but it retains the Hobbesian problem of how order is possible and maintained. Order however is no longer something requiring the conscious consent or agreement of the members of society but is an autochthonous feature of social reality. When society itself becomes a kind of naturalized reality, order is transformed into questions of social solidarity, social reproduction and social structure. The Hobbesian problem of order, thought in terms of a contractual account of sovereignty, is overwritten by, but reinscribed within, the 'sociological' account of solidarity.

The third point, this time drawn from Foucault, is that society is conceived not simply as a unity coincident with the boundaries of the nation, but as a fractured totality, what he calls a 'self-rending unity' (Gordon, 1991: 22). This is the sociological content of the new liberal problematic of order. Society is a complex domain, one in which egoistic economic pursuits are found together with non-economic interests towards family, clan or nation, where self-interest is mixed with a certain amount of charitable altruism. It is a domain of cohesion and solidarity, but also of breakdown and dissolution. It is one in which we can discover both a uniform set of norms that act on all members of society and an arena fractured by political faction, by class, by religion, by gender. It is this character of society as a thought-space that allows liberalism to resituate the subject of interest (*Homo œconomicus*) as an abstract, ideal point within concrete and real relations of civil society, and to situate economic individuals in a social whole in which they will be made manageable.

This new object, society, is made up of the concrete exchanges of the economy, of the lives, infirmities, frailties and death of individuals, of the occupations, customs, habits, patterns of family life and modes of communication of the population, of the quest by the population for subsistence, and of the ensuing distribution of wealth. It is a domain of harmony and conflict, with its own historical forms of development, its own origins. Above all, civil society is the concrete thing that ultimately government must govern. It is subject to its own laws of population, production and so on and has, as it were, its own natural history. It is no longer simply an extension of the state. Liberalism, then, already contains the possibility of a *social government*, of a government that is anchored in the contending forces of modern societies.

This does not mean that liberalism was endowed from the start with a form of social citizenship that could reconcile the tensions between the claim of juridical and political equality of citizens and their economic inequality – as we noted in Chapter 2. Indeed, from the perspective of a liberal governmental economy, there was to be a certain normalization and inclusion of poverty, as witnessed by Patrick Colquhoun's famous statement that 'without a large proportion of poverty, there could be no riches, since riches are the offspring of labour, while labour can only result from a state of poverty . . . Poverty is therefore the most necessary component of society without which nations and communities could not exist in a state of civilization' (1806: 7). However, during the early part of the nineteenth century in Britain, for example, we witness a whole series of concerns emerging around the circumstances and consequence of poverty, rather than poverty itself. The normal poverty that was the source of wealth could be contrasted, in the first instance, with another kind of abnormal poverty, pauperism. Pauperism was a state of demoralization of the poor, removing their capacity for self-responsibility and leading the poor to prefer charity or poor relief to labour, encouraging their imprudent procreation and thus the increase of their numbers beyond the means to satisfy them, fostering criminality and independence from the control of the higher orders, and encouraging living conditions which would breed endemic and epidemic disease (Dean, 1991; Procacci, 1978).

The problem of pauperism, in so far as it preserved the natural and normalized status of poverty, was internal to the liberal governmental economy. However, by raising the question of the effects of such an economy, it opened up spaces in which the problems of poverty and inequality generated by it could be posed. In the case of a figure like Edwin Chadwick, for example, we can see how much of the reform and extension of national governmental administration he pioneered existed between these two poles. *The Poor Law Report of 1834* (Checkland and Checkland, 1974), to which he was a party, sought to maintain the separation of poverty and pauperism through the establishment of a centralized administrative superintendence of poor relief. Pauperism was to be normalized as poverty; and poverty was to be included in the liberal economy. The *Report on the Sanitary Conditions of the Labouring Population* (Chadwick, 1965), of which he was the author, by contrast, rests on a recognition that there are material conditions of existence of the labouring population that account for the propensity to disease and pauperism and the fostering of epidemics. If, for T. H. Marshall (1963), the 1834 Poor Law opposes social rights to civil and political rights, the sanitary reforms suggest that the right to proper housing and sanitation is a condition for the poor to participate in a liberal economy. Moreover, because through epidemics the effects of the urban conditions of the labouring populations are felt among all ranks of society, the problem of poverty will necessarily be one of how the poor are to be *included* within society.

These are not the only contexts in which this question of the condition of the labouring population will be posed and in which we find the emergence of what, by the second third of the nineteenth century in Britain and France, becomes known as the 'social question'. The problem of child labour and, after the legal restriction of it, the new open space of the upbringing and education of children, that of domestic hygiene and the habitation of the urban masses, and that of the position of women as both 'natural' dependants upon their husbands and as relays of medical and educational norms within the family, were among the key spaces in which this social question would be posed and contested during the nineteenth century (Donzelot, 1979). These were also the types of problems that would lead to the inscription of this moral and social territory into thought (Rose, 1998: 59). The development of statistics, commissions of inquiry, reports, censuses and surveys into issues of poverty, illness, mortality, crime, alcoholism and suicide give to the social a kind of 'positivity', i.e. a reality with its own regularities, laws and characteristics.

The emergence of the social in the nineteenth century, as a field of problematization, knowledge and inscription, raises important issues for an analytics of government, including the status of social government 'after' the welfare state. In Donzelot's influential account, we should note that the emergence of the social facilitates the development of a 'scientific' discipline and practice of philanthropy. In other words, the social is not first or necessarily tied to a centralized bureaucratic apparatus such as that embodied in the ideal of a 'welfare state'. This is because the social is an attempt to resolve two types of problem that are generated by the liberal critique of police or what Donzelot calls the 'liberal definition of the state' (1979: 53–8).

It is no longer possible to govern directly the lives of individuals and groups because first, a fundamental discontinuity has been introduced between the state and the family, and second, prudential government must govern through the forms and processes found within the economy. Both the relation between the state and the family and that between the state and the economy are juridically constituted as versions of the public–private dichotomy. In both cases, we witness the delineation of a sphere of private authority and autonomy, of the factory owner or private entrepreneur and of the father and head of household. Each of these forms of authority gives rise to a host of concerns. The liberal economy raises a whole field of new problems – of poverty and pauperism, of urban life and the conditions of the labouring classes, of the arbitrary authority of factory owners, and later of the discovery of business cycles and cyclical unemployment. The juridical definition of the family, on the other hand, poses the question of how to render it autonomous from the state so that it becomes both the site for the promotion of its members and also a field of intervention. The problem of the family, then, is under what circumstances and with what agencies it will be possible to intervene to deal with problems of child neglect or abuse, domestic economy and hygiene, educational needs and personal morality.

In both cases, the problem is solved through philanthropy and its interventions. In the case of the question of the impoverishment of the workers due to the liberal economy, philanthropic interventions are organized around the problem of assistance or relief. Assistance, however, will not be the mere giving of alms, but a question of 'economic morality'. The philanthropic rationality thus proceeds in a quite different way. It says, in effect, that in a society of juridical and civil equals, there are no grounds for a right to assistance but nor are there grounds to issue commands. Instead, the poor will be granted assistance on the condition that they accept advice and expertise – particularly on the virtues of saving. By the discourse of savings, the poor and the poor family could retain autonomy in relation to a punitive centralized and institutional form of poor relief. Philanthropy would also work through members of the family, particularly women, to introduce norms of domestic hygiene, education, childrearing and child labour, and thus offer children and women certain increased autonomy against the juridically and economically constituted patriarchal authority of the male head of household. Only where liberal society threatened to slide into its opposite, would hygienists 'urge the state to intervene in the private law by applying the norm' (Donzelot, 1979: 57).

The liberal economy of government then not only prepares the way for a government of society and the production of knowledge of it. It establishes it as a necessity. The knowledge bases of society – from social economy, social physics and social statistics to criminology, educational psychology, sociology and beyond to feminism – become the 'dialogical partners' (Weir, 1996) of liberalism's process of self-critique, self-review and self-renewal. There is thus a kind of structure to the space of dissent, advice and expertise that is possible within liberal government. Social economy and social statistics can show that the economy is only self-regulating within certain parameters, that it results in urban misery, is subject to business cycles creating unemployment, and so on (Procacci, 1978). Experts on population, public health and social hygiene show that certain individuals imprudently procreate, that certain families are deficient in relation to norms of hygiene, domestic economy and health, and in the upbringing and education of their children. Still others demonstrate that certain individuals and groups do not possess the capacities to act as responsible citizens, that they form dogmatical opinions, wild enthusiasms and factions (Hindess, 1997), that some do not have the mental capacities or knowledge to make informed decisions, and that others are beyond rehabilitation and possess an intrinsic criminality (Pasquino, 1980).

One way of understanding the sheer heterogeneity and diversity of the social would be to examine key phrases in which 'social' acts as a qualifier, and which respond to particular problematizations of the liberal governmental regime. From the mid nineteenth century we see the emergence of a whole range of problematizations *within* the overall economy of this liberal governmental and institutional regime that have a kind of loose kinship. These occur about such concerns and themes as:

1   the *social question*: the health, living and urban conditions of the labour-
    ing classes, the elimination of pauperism and other social, political and
    moral evils (Procacci, 1993)
2   *social promotion*: the upbringing, health, sexuality and education of chil-
    dren, the position of women as housewives and mothers, and the family
    as a vehicle for social and economic aspirations (Donzelot, 1979)
3   *social defence*: the defence of society by 'neutralizing' and eliminating the
    'dangerous classes', the incorrigible delinquent, the recidivist, *Homo
    criminalis*, etc. (Foucault, 1997b; Pasquino, 1980)
4   *social security*: securing society in matters of the economic and military
    efficiency of national population
5   *social insurance*: the security of the population in relation to age, sickness,
    infirmity, unemployment and injury (Ewald, 1991; Defert, 1991).

These tasks are undertaken by agencies and figures whose expertise is established in relation to such problems. Witness the emergence of the statistical
societies and the sanitary reform movement, the general practitioner, the
social worker, the professional police officer, the child psychologist, the career
public servant and so on. They are elaborated within a range of new institutional or recently reformed institutional spaces: public (state) schools, juvenile
courts, government departments, police stations, unemployment exchanges,
wage-fixing tribunals, baby health and family planning clinics and so on.

    These problems, agencies and authorities possess neither a necessary
coherence nor unity. However, from the late nineteenth to the mid twentieth
centuries, a common vocabulary was formed that sought a general codification of these problems as issues entailing the whole of society. This
vocabulary sought to discover the means of translating the particular, the personal and the private into the general, the public and the social. It sought to
locate the law, and the juridical subject of right and responsibility, as but one
region within the wider, concrete and more fundamental evolution of society.
It gave rise to a range of disciplines that more or less successfully established
themselves within universities and research institutions. These included public
health, sociology, welfare economics, social administration, social work and
social policy. Such disciplines made it possible to understand all these previous developments as part of a unified process that would culminate in a
specific form of the operation of national governments: the 'welfare state',
which was more an ethos or an ethical ideal than a set of completed or established institutions.

    There is a key point to note about the social, liberalism and democracy.
The critical function of liberalism opens the possibility for this myriad of
social concerns to be raised and for the establishment of forms of knowledge regarding them. These social concerns in turn form and reform the

aspirations of individuals, families and almost the entire population. However, it is the contingent combination of this mass social promotion with the development of representative institutions that translates social aspiration into political demand and party platforms. It is these programmes, above all, that elaborate the ideal of a welfare state. One of the key conditions for the emergence of this ideal is therefore this contingent combination of the effects of social government with representative institutions.

We return to this theme of social government, particularly in relation to questions of risk and social insurance in Chapter 9. But social insurance as a way of managing the risk of fracture and dissolution within industrial society is only one problematic of national government in the twentieth century. Another bio-political way of managing risk will look to heredity rather than environment, will accent the racial rather than social aspect of populations, and will draw upon aspects of sovereignty quite different from those of liberalism. It may seem somewhat surprising that various authoritarian forms of governmentality are assembled from elements of the trajectories of sovereignty and bio-politics. As much as liberal and social democracy, the authoritarian forms of rule of the twentieth century can be mapped onto the trajectory of the governmentalization of the state.

Note

1. This account of law is not therefore concerned with either (1) the legitimacy of law which Max Weber, for example, finds in its formal properties, or (2) law as a source of the legitimacy of particular regimes. For Foucault, law is approached not as a source of legitimacy in modern societies, but as an instrument of rule.

7 AUTHORITARIAN GOVERNMENTALITY

Massacres have become vital. (Michel Foucault, 1979: 137)

With the outbreak of war, and the issue of the order calling for the sys-tematic murder of those deemed 'unworthy of life', the crucial step is taken from the racist utopian dream to its realization in the 'Final Solution'. (Detlev J. K. Peukert, 1993: 245)

The literature on governmentality has stressed the study of rule in liberal democracies. This concern is understandable given that the substantive prob-lems that are addressed in this literature are largely those found within the territorial boundaries of liberal-democratic states. How can the study of gov-ernment illuminate questions of non-liberal and authoritarian rule both inside and outside these liberal democracies? What resources do we have for beginning to consider questions of liberal rule through non-liberal means, such as might be found in forms of colonial government? Moreover, how are we to understand the prevalence of motifs of race in liberal democracies and the rise of neo-conservatism as well as neo-liberalism? And what tools do we possess for thinking about the technologies and rationalities of authoritarian forms of rule *per se* such as in the case of Nazi Germany or contemporary China? In this chapter we investigate some openings about how we might begin to think about this cluster of problems. The broad argument is that 'authoritarian governmentality', like liberal and social forms of rule, is made up of elements assembled from bio-politics and sovereignty.[1] Further, like lib-eral and social forms of rule, authoritarian governmentality can also be located on the trajectory of the governmentalization of the state. This term encompasses those practices and rationalities immanent to liberal govern-ment itself, which are applied to certain populations held to be without the attributes of responsible freedom. More directly, it refers to non-liberal and explicitly authoritarian types of rule that seek to operate through obedient rather than free subjects, or, at a minimum, endeavour to neutralize opposi-tion to authority. We thus start with the illiberality of liberalism and then move on to non-liberal rule.

The illiberality of liberal government

In Chapter 4 we alluded to Foucault's enigmatic statement that 'Our societies have proved to be really demonic since they happen to combine those two games – the city–citizen game and the shepherd–flock game – in what we call modern states' (1988c: 71). We are now in a position to comprehend more fully what is condensed in this phrase.

Liberalism is a particular form of articulation of the 'shepherd–flock game' and the 'city-citizen' game, of a pastoral power that takes the form of a bio-politics of the administration of life and a form of sovereignty that deploys the law and rights to limit, to offer guarantees, to make safe and, above all, to legitimate and justify the operations of bio-political programmes and disciplinary practices. Liberalism, however, can never fully check the 'demonic' possibilities contained within this volatile mix, as evident in recent revelations about the way in which liberal-democratic states (like those in Scandanavia) have, in the course of the twentieth century, practised forced sterilization in the name of a eugenic utopia on certain of their populations. Even more pervasive has been the tendency within certain states (Australia, Canada), having ceased to attempt actual genocide, to commit forms of cultural genocide upon indigenous people within their borders in the name of their own well-being, such as in the case of the removal of children from their parents and families. While the bio-political imperative does not account for all that bedevils liberal-democratic states, it is remarkable how much of what is done of an illiberal character is done with the best of bio-political intentions.

Let us then consider the issue of the illiberality and apparent authoritarianism of liberal forms of government. Much of the literature of governmentality has stressed the way in which the explicit and programmatic character of liberal government appeals to a notion of the subject active in its own government and presupposes certain types of free subject in the operation of particular programmes of conduct. There are two different ways in which we can approach the illiberality of that 'free subject'. The first and most obvious way concerns those practices and rationalities that divide populations and exclude certain categories from the status of the autonomous and rational person. The second is the way in which the free subject of liberalism is divided against him or herself in so far as the condition of mature and responsible use of freedom entails a domination of aspects of the self. This dual character of liberal government is neatly summed up by Foucault's notion of 'dividing practices' in which:

> The subject is either divided inside himself or divided from others. This process objectivizes him. Examples are the mad and the sane, the sick and the healthy, the criminals and the 'good boys'. (1982: 208)

I shall consider shortly some episodes – both 'liberal' and 'authoritarian' – in the history of the government of those held not to display the attributes of responsibility and autonomy. First, however, let us consider the sense in which the liberal subject is divided against itself. Mariana Valverde (1996), in an analysis of the writings of John Stuart Mill, has identified a form of ethical and moral 'despotism' at the core of his notions of the juridical and political subject. Mill argues that the doctrine of liberty only applies to 'human beings in the maturity of their faculties', thus excluding children, young persons of minority legal status, and barbarians. For the latter 'despotism is a legitimate mode of government' provided that the end is their improvement. Valverde argues that it is possible then to justify good despots in the case of those subjects, particularly if that despotism would be used to improve people. A key way in which liberal government can resolve the apparent tension between despotic means and liberal ends is the term 'habit':

> Habit is an extremely useful category of and for governance because it mediates between consciousness and unconsciousness and desire and compulsion. Compelled to eat our vegetables as children, as adults we come to experience a meal without vegetables as undesirable and even unnatural. As adults, we often compel ourselves to re-form, re-build our habits, by engaging in a self-despotism (e.g. throwing way all cigarettes or alcohol in the house so as not to 'tempt' the part of the self that is despotically ruled by the 'higher' self) that, we hope, will result in the permanent transformation of desire, so that eventually the lower self will not even want to smoke or drink. (1996: 362; see also, Valverde, 1998b)

Valverde's argument draws attention to the fact that a form of 'despotism' is at the heart of liberal government prior to any division between those capable of bearing the freedoms and responsibilities of mature subjectivity and those who are not. But as she notes this division also supposes that the unimproved subject is capable of improvement. For Mill the improvement of English national culture means that women can attain self-government. Similarly, a liberal approach to education must assume that most children will be capable of being trained in those habits that will lead them to the state of maturity and reason. One could argue that in these cases the forms of despotism required are relatively benign in that they take the form of cultural development, training and instruction. However, even in Mill's schema, there is the possibility of a justification for authoritarian types of rule. This is particularly the case for unimproved nations, like Africa, or those with knowledge but which are degenerate and static, like China, lacking any possibility of self-improvement. Thus 'their almost only hope of making any steps in advance depends on the chances of a good despot' (Mill, cited in Valverde, 1996: 361). Liberal rule is completely consistent, in this schema, with authoritarian rule of colonial societies and, by extension today, with post-colonial rule of societies in which populations are yet to attain the maturity required of the liberal subject.

We can also note, from this example, the sense in which practices of improvement can be used to divide populations on the basis of those who avail themselves of the opportunity for improvement and those who do not. Thus the illiterate might be excluded from the franchise for Mill not because of their illiteracy as such, but rather because they exhibit the 'wilful failure to avail oneself of public education where available' (Valverde, 1996: 363).

Mill's position, as Valverde notes, is not that of Bentham, whom he accuses of a cultural universalization of utilitarianism and not considering the possibility of law as an instrument of national culture. Nor, despite the racially specific version of its notion of improvement, is Mill's position concerned with the possibility of the degeneration of the English race itself, a feature of social imperialist thought, Fabian socialism and eugenics at the end of the century. His version of liberalism stands as a kind of high point of optimism about the possibility of improvement of the English nation by relatively benign means between the much harsher regime advocated by Bentham at the beginning of the nineteenth century and the theme of the degeneration of the race at its end. These are much clearer examples of the second aspect of these dividing practices, the way in which liberal forms of thought and political rationality contemplate the treatment of certain of those without the attributes of juridical and political responsibility, and especially those who are deemed to be forever without the possibility of achieving responsible autonomy.

Within liberal forms of government, at least, there is a long history of people who, for one reason or another, are deemed not to possess or to display the attributes (e.g. autonomy, responsibility) required of the juridical and political subject of rights and who are therefore subjected to all sorts of disciplinary, bio-political and even sovereign interventions. The list of those so subjected would include at various times those furnished with the status of the indigent, the degenerate, the feeble-minded, the aboriginal, the homosexual, the delinquent, the dangerous or even, and much more generally, the minor. At least a part of the history of feminism could be read as a struggle against the exclusion of women, particularly as wives, from the status of juridical and political subject.

We can distinguish three different points in a series of non-liberal forms of political rationality: those non-liberal forms of thought and practice that are a component of liberal rationalities; those non-liberal forms of thought that gain a certain legitimacy within liberal democracies; and non-liberal forms of rule proper. Mill's argument concerning the role of 'good despots' for those nations without the spring of spontaneous improvement is a case of a liberal theoretical endorsement of non-liberal forms of rule. At the technical and practical level, Bentham's pauper management scheme and the nineteenth-century workhouse provide another illustration of the first case (Dean, 1991). The principle of 'less eligibility', formulated by Bentham, was – in the words of *The Poor Law Report of 1834* – to ensure that the situation of the pauper 'on the whole shall not be made really or apparently so eligible as the situation of the independent labourer of the lowest class' (Checkland and Checkland, 1974: 335). The administrative principle of less eligibility effects a division between the population that subsists through the exchange of labour and those who depend on relief, social assistance or charity for that subsistence. In Bentham's dream of a centralized administration of pauperism, the fact of falling into the latter category alone makes it possible for paupers to be subject to a regime of confinement, forced labour, strict disciplinary routines, human experimentation, systems of punishment for petty infractions, sexual abstinence and the wearing of uniforms. While this gothic construction is nothing like the general mixed English workhouse of the nineteenth century, both demonstrate the compatibility between a liberal governmental economy and exceedingly illiberal and non-liberal forms of rule.

It is remarkable how regularly the division is made in varieties of liberal rationality and associated human sciences between those who are capable of bearing the freedoms and responsibilities of a citizen and those who, for whatever reason, are deemed not to possess the characteristics necessary for such a task. The latter are thus liable to a range of disciplinary, sovereign and other interventions, including ones that we might recognize as 'social', e.g the introduction of labour exchanges and other decasualization measures. In the last decades of the nineteenth century, social investigators and reformers such as Charles Booth and William Beveridge sought to make a new division between the unemployable and the employable:

> From Booth to Beveridge, the schemes of de-casualization had as their objective the re-establishment by administrative means of the boundary between the employable and the unemployable. They sought to bring to the former the beneficent and education discipline of regular employment while exposing the latter for the harsh but necessary remedy their condition demanded. (Rose, 1985: 51)

While Booth in his *Life and Labour of the People in London* (1889–1897) distinguished between eight classes of the population located on a hierarchical continuum, the key point of problematization concerned the relation between the bottom class A – of occasional labourers, loafers and semi-criminals – and those immediately above them, especially class B, the casual earners. As Rose (1985: 50–1) notes, while this latter class might pull itself up the population hierarchy through industriousness, the almost irresistible pull was in the other direction. Similarly, Beveridge argued that 'it is essential to maintain a distinction between those who, however irregularly employed, are yet members, though inferior members, of the industrial army and those who are mere parasites, incapable of performing any useful service whatever' (1985: 51–2). Both Booth and Beveridge argued for the separation of the unemployables, the residuum, from the rest of the labouring population whether in labour colonies or in public institutions. The latter, however, added a further reason for this separation:

> For Booth, the rationale of the removal of the casual support to colonies was that this would do away with the demoralising casual labour market, remove a source of social vice, and eliminate a competitive pressure upon the respectable and employable poor. Beveridge had added a further imperative – the unemployables were to be denied the right to reproduce. (1985: 52)

What has changed since the earlier configuration marked by the pauper/poverty distinction drawn by Bentham and Edwin Chadwick and the injunctions of Malthus concerning the relation between poor relief and the imprudent propagation of the population? There are evident similarities: the fundamental division between those who enjoy full participation in the labour market, civil freedom and responsible fatherhood, and those who should not, remains remarkably unchanged. However, a number of things have changed. It is now recognized that there are institutional conditions that can ensure participation in the labour market, including the elimination of the demoralizing casual labour market and the establishment of labour exchanges. Civil freedom now entails more than the wage contract and extends to the franchise. Finally, in the case of Beveridge, preventive measures are advocated to ensure that the unemployable do not procreate. This goes beyond the Malthusian proscription of those forms of poor relief that might encourage the indigent to procreate without regard to the necessary means of subsistence.

The central change that occurs between the early-nineteenth-century Bentham/Malthus figuration around pauperism and the late-nineteenth-century rationality of Booth and Beveridge is the successive transformation of the notion of 'demoralization'. In the former, the demoralizing effects of pauperism had been conceived in terms of a model of pestilence in which it was necessary to act on those conditions – conceived as moral, physical and social – that turn the labouring poor into the indigent. Given conditions where the life of the pauper, the idle or the criminal appeared more eligible than that of the labouring population, there would always be a risk of the spread of the contagion. This kind of model could be used for all types of intervention into the health of towns, sanitary reforms, factory reform, the reform of the Poor Laws, and even the establishment of a preventive police. During the nineteenth century, however, the themes of the corruption of morals and its deleterious effects on the labouring population come to be taken over and subsumed by the theme of degeneracy. The demoralization of the labouring population in towns becomes tied to the degeneration of the race.

With Morel in 1857, degenerations become deviations from normal human type, which were transmissible by heredity and which deteriorated progressively toward extinction (Rose, 1985: 56–7). In its initial formulation, degeneracy does not issue in deleterious evolutionary consequence and may serve the useful function of eliminating unhealthy variations. With its notions of 'constitution' as the important matrix through which such deviations are acquired and inherited, this theory of degeneracy does not allow a strict distinction between innate characteristics of heredity and the characteristics acquired through the environment. It was left to Francis Galton, the founder of eugenics, to reverse the relation between degeneracy and reproduction so that those who were most degenerate were also likely to breed the most and to attribute degeneracy purely to heredity. Employing 'Darwinian' categories of species as the differentiated unity of a breeding population, and mathematical and statistical notions of the norm as a way of explaining the mechanism of heredity, the notion of degeneracy was able to be re-posed at the level of the degeneration of the population as a whole (1985: 64–5). The deleterious effects of social ills upon the population were not simply those that stemmed from the struggle for subsistence, as with Malthus, but those that stemmed from the limitation of the population and its effects upon the variation and selection of characteristics. Thus the decline of the birth rate at the end of the nineteenth century could be explained by the limitation of family size among the upper part of the nation, as Alfred Marshall put it in 1890 (1985: 62), i.e. by the fit, the prudent, the well-off and the healthy. This gave the poor, the ill educated, the unfit, and the physically and mentally feeble, a reproductive advantage.

With eugenics, and its injunctions on the management of breeding in human populations, we arrive at a bio-politics that cannot be contained within the limits of a liberal rationality. Or, to put it more precisely, some of the consequences of a social policy based on eugenics could not be easily reformulated in liberal terms. Thus while it might be possible to consider proposals such as cheap housing and allowances to encourage the fit – or those with 'civic worth', to cite Galton – in terms of the operations of an autonomous responsible self-acting subject, this would not be the case for measures to survey and confine the feeble-minded and the habitual criminal so that they would not reproduce.

Bentham had once called the pauper host 'that part of the national livestock which has no feathers and walks on two legs' and was concerned with the regulation of sexual relations even between husbands and wives in his pauper Panopticons (Bentham, 1843: 366–7; Dean, 1991: 180–7). The image of stock, however, was not viewed as a part of a selective breeding programme. And despite Malthus's proscription against improvident procreation, he did not theorize the effects of differential procreative prudence upon the population as a whole. Eugenics, however, resituates the statistical knowledge of the population, with its notions of norm, variation and deviation, together with a biological theory of evolution, within the framework of a system of alliance, lineage and descent in which the operative terms are stock, constitution, heredity, nobility and ancestry. That its political and social programmes were not immediately realized, that it continued to meet hostility and resistance, should not distract us from its range of effects. As Rose (1985: 82–3) argues, it provided the conditions for the emergence of a science of mental measurement by posing the question of mental deficiency and feeble-mindedness in a particular way. It allowed the posing of the question of mental deficiency and efficiency in such a way as to make an individual psychology possible. And, most importantly here, it provided one dimension of the struggles over the formation of social policy, and opened up the notion of environment and strategies based on the regulation of environmental conditions that would compose the opposed and alternative strategy of hygienists.

Liberalism always contains the possibility of non-liberal interventions into the lives of those who do not possess the attributes required to play the city–citizen game. It also regularly expresses the fear that the absence of responsible autonomy could spread to ever-larger sections of the population. In this sense there is nothing particularly new or different about eugenics. What the case of eugenics does demonstrate, however, is the way in which knowledge of populations and individuals cannot simply be regarded as a product of liberal conceptions of government or that such knowledge will give rise to social and political programmes of a liberal character. Liberalism, as I have suggested, depends on an articulation of a bio-politics of the population with a democratization of sovereignty and in that sense is one resolution of the city–citizen game and the shepherd–flock game. In the complex trajectories of juridical-political power of sovereignty and of pastoral power, and the transformation of the elements that compose them, we find renewed articulations of sovereignty and bio-politics. As a political programme, eugenics rearticulates bio-political conceptions of population, norm and even sexuality with the language of alliance and lineage. In doing so, it ends up defining a kind of thought-space in which debates and struggles over the concepts, objects, methods and strategies of politics will be fought out in the early twentieth century. It is a component in the opening of a space for a new definition of social interventions and insurance against social risks. It provides a language that will be taken and engaged with even by those who will oppose its policy prescriptions. Of critical importance is the flexible and variable language of 'efficiency' of populations which allows a connection to be made between the internal quality of a particular population and the external competition between populations. A bio-politics of the population and of race, in the language of those who advocated imperialism, in Fabian socialism and in eugenics, links internal questions of the quality of the national population to questions of its fitness in relation to other national populations.

Bio-politics, race and non-liberal rule

There are, of course, plenty of examples of the exercise of sovereignty in the twentieth century that have practised a decidedly non-liberal form and programme of national government in relation to both their own populations and those of other states. Does this mean that the form of government of such states is assembled from elements that are radically different from the ones that we have discussed here? Does this mean that state socialism and National Socialism, for example, could not be subject to an analysis of the arts of government? The answer to both these questions, I believe, is no. The general argument of this chapter is that the exercise of the government of modern states can be understood as different articulations of forms of pastoral power with forms of sovereignty. Liberalism, as we have just seen, makes that articulation in a specific way. Other types of rule are no less distinctive assemblages of elements of a bio-politics concerned with the detailed administration of life and of a sovereign power that reserves the right of death to itself.

Consider again the contrastive terms in which Foucault views bio-politics and sovereignty. The final chapter in the first volume of the *History of Sexuality* contrasts sovereignty and bio-politics and is called 'Right of death and power over life'. The initial terms of the contrast between the two registers of government is between one that could employ power to put subjects to death, even if this right to kill was conditioned by the defence of the sovereign, and one that was concerned with the fostering of life. Nevertheless, each part of the contrast can be further broken down. The right of death can also be understood as 'the right to take life or let live'; the power over life as the power 'to foster life or disallow it'. Thus the contrast concerns the way in which the different forms of power treat matters of life and death. Thus bio-politics reinscribes the earlier right of death and places it within a new and different form. It is no longer so much the right of the sovereign to put to death its enemies but the right to disqualify the life of those who are a threat to the life of the population, to disallow those deemed 'unworthy of life'.

This allows us first to consider what might be thought of as the dark side of bio-politics. In Foucault's (1979: 136–7) account, bio-politics does not put an end to the practice of war. It provides it with new and more sophisticated killing machines. These machines allow killing itself to be re-posed at the level of entire populations. Wars become genocidal in the twentieth century. The same state that takes on itself the duty to enhance the life of the population also exercises the power of death over whole populations. Atomic weapons are the ultimate weapons of this process of the power to put whole populations to death. We might also consider here the aptly named biological and chemical weapons that seek to exterminate populations by visiting plagues upon them or polluting the biosphere in which they live to the point at which life is no longer sustainable. Nor does the birth of bio-politics put an end to the killing of one's own populations. Rather it intensifies that killing – whether by an 'ethnic cleansing' that visits holocausts upon whole groups or by the mass slaughters of classes and groups conducted in the name of the utopia to be achieved.

At the level of the individual, perhaps the most striking example of the dark side of bio-politics is torture (Rejali, 1994). Torture, such as that practised in Iran during the twentieth century, employs medical and psychological techniques and disciplines, including electrical shock treatment, to 'open the private concerns of bodies to public control' (1994: 63). It employs a knowledge of the body and the life of the individual as, for example, in the use of a 'pressure device' on the skull calibrated according to the knowledge at which the bones break (1994: 71). Death marks the failure of such torture: 'one finds in modern punishments the principle of the operation; the imperative to maintain life at all costs' (1994: 72). The psychological effects of torture are 'among the most serious and valued' (1994: 74), inducing dissociation of the prisoner from his body, memories and self-characterizations. Finally, torture is pastoral in that the torturer takes the role of the individual who can liberate the prisoner if he cooperates and fixes upon a particular course of action.

There is a certain restraint in sovereign power. The right of death is only occasionally exercised as the right to kill. More often sovereign power is manifest in the *refraining* from the right to kill. The bio-political imperative knows no such restraint. Power is exercised at the level of life and of populations and hence wars will be waged at that level, on behalf of each and all. This point brings us to the heart of Foucault's provocative thesis about bio-politics: that there is an intimate connection between the exercise of a life-administering power and the commission of genocide: 'If genocide is indeed the dream of modern powers, this is not because of a recent return of the ancient right to kill: it is because power is situated and exercised at the level of life, the species, the race, and the large-scale phenomena of population' (1979: 137). In an expression that deserves more notice, Foucault proposes that: 'massacres become vital'. We might add, following Rejali, that 'tortures become vital'.

There is thus a kind of perverse homogeneity between the power over life and the power to take life characteristic of bio-power. The emergence of a bio-political racism in the nineteenth and twentieth centuries can be approached as a trajectory in which this homogeneity threatens to turn into a necessity. This racism can be approached as a fundamental mechanism of power that is inscribed in the bio-political domain (Stoler, 1995: 84–5). For Foucault, the primary function of this form of racism is to establish a division between those who must live and those who must die, and to distinguish the superior from the inferior, the fit from the unfit. The series, 'population, evolution and race' is not simply a way of thinking about the superiority of the 'white races', or of justifying colonialism, but also a way of thinking about how to treat the degenerates and the abnormals within one's own population and prevent the further degeneration of the race. The notion and techniques of population had given rise, at the end of the nineteenth century, to a new linkage between population, the internal organization of states, and the competition between states.

The second and most important function of this bio-political racism in the nineteenth century for Foucault is that 'it establishes a positive relation between the right to kill and the assurance of life' (Stoler, 1995: 84). The life of the population, its vigour, its health, its capacity to survive, become necessarily linked to the elimination of internal and external threats. This power to disallow life is perhaps best encapsulated in the injunctions of the eugenic project: identify those who are degenerate, abnormal, feeble-minded or of an inferior race, and subject them to forced sterilization; encourage those who are superior, fit and intelligent to propagate. But this last example does not necessarily establish a positive justification for the right to kill, only the right to disallow life.

If we are to begin to understand the type of racism engaged in by Nazism, however, we need to take into account another kind of denouement between the bio-political management of population and the exercise of sovereignty. This version of sovereignty is no longer the transformed and democratized form of sovereignty founded on the liberty of the juridical subject, as it is for liberalism, but a sovereignty that takes up and transforms a further element of sovereignty, its 'symbolics of blood' (Foucault, 1979: 148).

For Foucault, sovereignty is grounded in blood – as a reality and as a symbol – just as one might say that sexuality becomes the key field upon which bio-political management of populations is articulated. When power was exercised through repression and deduction, through a law over which hangs the sword, when it was exercised upon the scaffold, by the torturer and the executioner, and when relations between households and families were forged through alliance, 'blood was *a reality with a symbolic function*'. By contrast, for bio-politics with its themes of health, vigour, fitness, vitality, progeny, survival and race, 'power spoke *of* sexuality and *to* sexuality' (1979: 147, original emphasis).

The novelty of National Socialism was the way it articulated 'the oneiric exaltation of blood', of fatherland and of the triumph of the race, in an immensely cynical and naïve fashion, with the paroxysms of a disciplinary power concerned with the detailed administration of the life of the population and the regulation of sexuality, family, marriage, education and so on (1979: 149–50). Nazism generalized bio-power without the limit critique posed by the juridical subject of right but it could not do away with sovereignty. Instead it established a set of permanent interventions into the conduct of the individual within the population and articulated this with the 'mythical concern for blood and the triumph of the race'. Thus the shepherd–flock game and the city–citizen game are transmuted into the eugenic ordering of biological existence and articulated upon the themes of the purity of blood and the myth of the fatherland.

In such an articulation of these elements of sovereign and bio-political forms of power, the relation between the administration of life and the right to kill entire populations is no longer simply one of a dreadful homogeneity. It has become a necessary one. The administration of life comes to require a blood-bath. It is not simply that power – and therefore war – will be exercised at the level of entire populations. It is that the act of disqualifying the right to life of other races becomes necessary for the fostering of the life of the race. Moreover, the elimination of other races is only one face of the purification of one's own race (Foucault, 1997b: 231). The other part is to expose the latter to a universal and absolute danger, to expose it to the risk of death and total destruction. For Foucault, with the Nazi state we have an 'absolutely racist state, an absolutely murderous state and an absolutely suicidal state', one that prescribes the Final Solution for other races (of which the Jews are the symbol and the manifestation) and the absolute suicide of the race (1997b: 232).

Foucault's analysis of the political rationality of National Socialism finds confirmation in the work of recent German historians on at least one point, that of the fundamental role of the human sciences in the atrocities of that regime (Peters, 1995). The late Detlev Peukert drew upon studies of psychiatry under National Socialism, the history of compulsory sterilization programmes, genetics, eugenics, medicine, social policy and education, and his own work on social-welfare education, to argue that 'what was new about the "Final Solution" in world-historical terms was the fact that it resulted from the fatal racist dynamism present within the human and social sciences' (1993: 236). Again we witness a fundamental division of the population, on this occasion made on a particular qualitative distinction between 'value' and 'non-value', and a treatment of the *Volkskörper* or body of the nation that consisted in 'selection' and 'eradication'. Peukert argues that twentieth-century medical and human sciences are confronted by what he calls a 'logodicy' that tries to resolve the dilemma between the rationalist dream of the perfectibility of humankind and the empirical existence of human finitude, of illness, suffering and death. One resolution of this dilemma is the projection of the rationalist project away from the finite individual onto a potential immortal body. In the German case, what Foucault called the 'species body' of the population is mapped onto the body of the *Volk* or race. The bio-political imperative is rearticulated with a kind of mythicized version of sovereignty. Like Foucault, Peukert argues that the logic of National Socialism, with its concern for the nurture and improvement of the immortal *Volkskörper*, had a double significance: heroic death on one side and eradication on the other (1993: 242).

National Socialism is one contingent, historical trajectory of the development of the bio-political dimension of the social, medical, psychological and human sciences that occurs under a particular set of historical circumstances. One should not underestimate the factors operative in German society, the historical legacy of war and revolutionary movements, the nature of the German polity, and the economic crises of the early twentieth century. Nevertheless, Peukert and Foucault would both agree that the kind of state racism practised by the Nazis, that would lead to the Final Solution, was quite different from traditional anti-Semitism in so far as it took the form of a 'biological politics', as the German historians call it, that drew upon the full resources of the human, social and behavioural sciences.

In this regard, Peukert's retrieval of the process by which the human sciences move from a concern with 'mass well-being' to acting as the instrument of 'mass annihilation' remains extremely interesting. In the case of 'social-welfare education' he identifies a number of phases (1993: 243–5). First, there was the formulation of the problem of the control of youth in the late nineteenth century within a progressivist discourse in which every child has a right to physical, mental and social fitness. This was followed by a phase of routinization and a crisis of confidence exemplified by the failure of legal schemes of detention or protection of those who are 'unfit' or 'ineducable'. The third phase, coinciding with the final years of the Weimar Republic, has disturbing overtones for our own period. Here there were a series of scandals in young people's homes and a debate about the limits of educability coupled with welfare-state retrenchment. This debate introduced a new cost–benefits trade-off with services allocated on the basis of immediate return and with the criterion of 'value' brought into the calculative framework. Value at this stage may or may not be determined on the basis of race or genetics, but the 'ineducable' were excluded in 1932 from reform-school education. After 1933 those who opposed the racial version of determining value were forced into silence, compulsory sterilization of the genetically unhealthy was practised, and concentration camps for the racially inferior were established. However, even this programme faced a crisis of confidence: the utopian goals came up against their limits and the catalogue of deviance became greater and more detailed. The positive racism of youth-welfare provision now met the negative radicalization of a policy of eradication of those who, in the language of the order that represents the crucial step in the Final Solution, are deemed 'unworthy of life' (*lebensunwertes Leben*). The bio-political government of life had arrived at the point at which it decides whose lives are worth living. With the technology of murder up and running, the social and human sciences 'are engaged in a parallel process of theoretical and institutional generalization that is aimed at an all-embracing racist restructuring of social policy, of educational policy, and of health and welfare policy' (Peukert, 1993: 245). The term *Gemeinschaftsfremde*, community alien, came to embrace failures, ne'er-do-wells, parasites, good-for-nothings, troublemakers and those with criminal tendencies, and threatened all these with detention, imprisonment or death.

The phrase 'those unworthy of life' is striking because it so clearly resonates with the bio-political attempt to govern life. We should be clear that there was nothing necessary in the path of National Socialism and that there were crucial steps in the conversion of knowledge and services concerned with the care of the needy into a technology of mass annihilation. However, given that many, if not all, of the forms of knowledge and technologies of government (including the concentration camp) were the product of polities characterized at least broadly by liberal forms of rule, it does suggest that there is no room for complacency and that the liberal critique of bio-politics cannot offer the kind of guarantees it claims to. Foucault is right to provoke us with the idea that the assurance of life is connected with the death command and to claim that 'the coexistence in political structures of large destructive mechanisms and institutions oriented toward the care of individual life is something puzzling and needs some investigation' (1988b: 147). Mass slaughters may not necessarily or logically follow from the forms of political rationality and types of knowledge we employ, but they do not arise from a sphere that is opposed to that rationality and knowledge. It is crucial to realize, as Peukert argues in his book *Inside Nazi Germany* (1989: 208), that racism was a social policy, that is, a policy that was concerned with the elimination of all those who deviated from an ever more detailed set of norms and the reshaping of society into a 'people of German blood and Nordic race; four-square in body and soul'.

What Peukert cannot address is the rationality of what he conceives as the irrational component of Nazism. While he understands the role of the human sciences in the formation of Nazi biological politics, he tends to consign the themes of blood, race, and *Volk* to an irrational sublimation contained within them rather than viewing them, as Foucault does, as rearticulated elements of sovereign power. This brings us to the central distinctiveness of Foucault's comments. National Socialism is not regarded as the pinnacle of the total administration of life undertaken with the help of the human sciences and bio-political technologies, as it might be by the Frankfurt School and their descendants. The key point for Foucault is that National Socialism is regarded as a particular articulation of specific elements of bio-politics, and its knowledge of populations and individuals, and sovereignty. It is not simply the logic of the bureaucratic application of the human sciences that is at issue but the reinscription of racial discourse within a bio-politics of the population and its linkage with themes of sovereign identity, autonomy and political community. A political discourse that divides populations on the basis of race has certain fairly obvious political dangers. However, one that makes the welfare and life of a racialized population the basis for national sovereignty and political community could be viewed as more clearly 'demonic'.[2]

Unfortunately, this story of bio-political racism does not end with Nazism. Foucault also insists that the possibilities of state racism are found in many versions of the articulation of bio-politics and sovereignty, including many varieties of socialism (1997b: 233–4; Stoler, 1995: 96–7). The problem with socialism for Foucault is that it has a kind of state racism inscribed in its premises and that, even if it has sometimes criticized bio-power, it has not re-examined the foundations and modes of functioning of racism. When socialism analyses its own emergence as a result of economic transformation, it does not have a need for an immediate recourse to these racist motifs. When it insists on the necessity of struggle to socialist transformation, a struggle that is against the enemies within the capitalist state, Foucault argues, it necessarily revives the theme of racism. Moreover, when socialism takes upon itself the task of managing, multiplying and fostering life, of limiting chances and risks, and of governing biological processes, it ends up practising a form of racism which is not properly ethnic but evolutionary and biological.[3] The enemies within the state on which this racism will be practised are the mentally ill, the criminal and political adversaries and – with say China's one-child policy – imprudent parents and their potential offspring (Sigley, 1996). In the latter case, we find a form of government that combines market-based norms and bio-political interventions into the intimate life of the population in a non-liberal manner in order to realize the objective of the quantity and quality of the population necessary for the socialist plan.

This kind of evolutionary and eugenic racism is one that can be practised against one's own population in the name of optimizing its quantity and quality. Thus the Chinese government 'claims that, not only is it possible to know in detail the object to be governed, but, further, it is possible to predict the precise outcome of any possible intervention' (1996: 473). This kind of rule is non-liberal in that, first, it does not use any version of the liberal subject to limit or try to offer guarantees for or make safe population programmes, and, second, it seeks to unite market-style economic norms with bio-political ones. Thus national authorities assign numerical targets, and provincial authorities translate these into birth quotas that are distributed among prefectures and counties, which in turn divide the quota out to communes, townships and so on. The policy is implemented at the micro-level of brigades, or street or lane committees and their sub-groups (1996: 474–5). The latter are responsible for 'one hundred or so households . . . to keep records of their family plans, contraceptive use and monthly cycles'. This detailed chain of command uses such instruments as local meetings of married couples, certificates of permission to become pregnant, allowances for couples of single children, and harsh fines for those conceiving without a certificate and those with more than one child.

The Chinese policy thus inscribes sovereign elements (of decree, interdiction, punishment and reward) within a detailed bio-political intervention into the intimate lives of its population. It does this not in the name of the fatherland, blood and racial purity, but in terms of the targets envisaged by the plan. On one point, it is clear that Chinese policy is non-liberal in that it does not rely on the choices, aspirations or capacities of the individual subject. This does not stop it having some similarity with early liberal policies, particularly Malthusian informed poor policies. In both cases, the process of economic liberalization and the recommendation of prudential procreation are linked. One tries to privatize the costs of imprudent propagation onto individuals, families and their offspring; the other tries to prevent burdens upon the developmental dreams of the socialist state.

The study of governmentality is yet to open up the extensive discussion of authoritarian and non-liberal governmentality. Foucault's analysis of National Socialism is a striking contribution to this problem for a number of reasons. First, it shows that this case of what, to put it mildly, might be thought of as a non-liberal or authoritarian form of rule is composed, like liberal rule, of bio-political and sovereign elements. It also places National Socialism, like liberalism, within the development of a government of bio-political processes. This does not mean that we should efface the differences between liberal and non-liberal rule. Nor is the analysis an attempt to undermine our critical distinctions between such forms. What it does illustrate, however, are the dangers inherent in bio-political rule and in the articulation of the shepherd–flock and city–citizen games that Foucault held as central to modern politics. The continuities between authoritarian and liberal governmentality, together with the recovery of the illiberal components of liberalism, remind us of the dangers of not calling into question the self-understanding of liberalism as a limited government acting through a knowledge of the processes of life yet, at the same time, safeguarding the rights of the political and juridical subject.

The more general argument advanced here is that modern politics cannot escape the articulation of a productive bio-political government of processes based on population, life, procreation and sexuality with the deductive logic of sovereignty based on the territory, death and blood. It follows that given we continue to live in a system of modern states, we must face up to forms of bio-political racism, i.e. a racism that follows not simply from discrimination, scapegoating or institutions, but from the elements by which we are compelled to think about and imagine states and their populations and seek to govern them. This is as true for the liberal art of government as for non-liberal rule. The former's emphasis on governing through freedom means that it always contains a division between those who are capable of bearing the responsibilities and freedoms of mature citizenship and those who are not. For the latter, this will often mean despotic provision for their special needs with the aim of rendering them autonomous by fostering capacities of responsibility and self-governance. Under certain conditions, however, frustrations with such programmes of improvement may lead to forms of knowledge and political rationality that identify certain groups as without value and beyond improvement. Liberal regimes of government can thus slide from the 'good despot' for the improvable to sovereign interventions to confine, to contain, to coerce and to eliminate, if only by prevention, those deemed without value. It is true, perhaps, that many of our worst nightmares tend to be realized when these elements of sovereignty and bio-political rule are articulated somewhat differently from the way they are in liberalism. This should offer no reason for complacency even for those who find themselves marked as the mature subjects within the boundaries contained by liberal-democratic constitutionalism, let alone those who currently remain in need of a 'good despot' within and outside these boundaries. It offers even less room for complacency for those who find themselves occupying the position of the 'good despot'.

The emergence of government as separate from the question of sovereignty first took the form of a dispositional problematic that sought a detailed regulation of humans as members of households and inhabitants within a kingdom and then flourished as a government through certain processes. On the basis of the government of economic, vital and social processes, two great strategies for the government of risk emerged at the beginning of the twentieth century. In order to manage the risks and dangers associated with an industrial economy (and with a government of the state that would be an economic government), national government would be faced with two distinct, but related, registers in which to operate, which depended on the separation of the factors of environment and heredity at the end of the nineteenth century. The first strategy of 'social government' would mobilize a knowledge of the differential occurrence of the risks among a population of living in an industrial society and seek to protect in advance each individual citizen against the differential quantity of risk he or she might bear. The key technology of such a strategy to act upon the social environment of living individuals was social insurance, although this would be allied with health, education and welfare provision for populations, and social work, psychological and other rehabilitation measures for the adjustment of individuals. The other great strategy of 'racial hygiene' would be to mobilize a knowledge of heredity and seek to prevent the propagation of those individuals and groups who would be most exposed to risk and to the manifestation of danger. The methods of such a strategy would be eugenic and its objective would be to increase the fitness and efficiency of the population.

Liberalism in the twentieth century stands astride these two great strategies in its search for a norm of good government that respects both economic processes and the bio-political imperative for the optimization of the life of the population. It fosters the social by conceiving of the government of the state as securing the processes that constitute a society separate from the state, and by the gradual recognition, in myriad arenas, of the effects of economic government. Social interventions are necessary not only to offset the effects of economic government but also to install a form of social citizenship that is compatible with the requirements of the industrial economy. However, liberalism also remains in a position of review of such social interventions, constantly anxious that with each step of their progress they might undermine the economic processes they were meant to secure.

Liberal government, however, also stands among the conditions of possibility of forms of authoritarian governmentality of the twentieth century. This is partially because liberalism is itself interlaced with forms of despotism for those who are deemed not (or not yet) to possess the attributes required of the autonomous and responsible subject. By allowing the possibility of despotism for certain individuals and populations, liberalism fostered the development of non-liberal forms of governmentality from Bentham's workhouse to eugenic programmes for sterilization of certain populations. Authoritarian governmentality is thus an element in liberal forms of rule as well as a genre of political rationalities unto itself.

Non-liberal forms of rule can be distinguished from liberal forms of government in that they do not accept a conception of limited government characterized by the rule of law that would secure the rights of individual citizens. Such a distinction should not prevent us from noticing two ways in which non-liberal forms of rule are similar to liberal government. The first is that non-liberal and liberal forms of rule must find ways of articulating elements of sovereignty and bio-politics. This is a condition of all forms of government of the state in the twentieth century. Second, both liberal and non-liberal forms of rule propose to operate through the processes that are constitutive of a population, particularly the bio-political imperative of the optimization of the processes of life. That liberal and non-liberal forms must combine elements of the same broad rationalities of rule, however, should not blind us to the different elements of sovereignty and bio-politics they accentuate and the different ways they articulate them. Race, blood and fatherland represent one articulation of these elements; population, law and nation quite another.

Finally, we can underline the sense in which twentieth-century authoritarian governmentality shares certain features with liberal government by contrasting it with the ideal of 'good police' in the eighteenth century. While both seek the detailed regulation of the subjects of rule, the warrant for that regulation in twentieth-century authoritarianism is found in forms of scientific knowledge of the opaque processes that constitute a population, rather than in the transparency and visibility of the things to be governed. While authoritarian and police forms of rule are alike in that the life of a population is linked to the strength of the state, it is only in the twentieth century that fostering the life of the population comes to depend on disallowing the life of those deemed unworthy of life. And where police used the techniques of sovereignty to exercise the right of death, authoritarian rule will link the exercise of sovereignty and its instruments of death with a power over life exercised at the level of populations and races.

Authoritarian governmentality, together with social government, is one of the two great strategies for the control of the risk manifest in the populations of industrial societies characteristic of the now concluding century. It is the transformation of the government of risk that indicates a new trajectory on which the governmentalization of the state meets a governmentalization of the mechanisms of government themselves.

Notes

1 I am indebted to Simon Philpott for broaching this question of 'authoritarian governmentality'. For his use of the term as a framework for understanding Indonesian politics, see Philpott (1997, especially Ch. 4).
2 I have not the space here to discuss the similarities and differences between Zygmunt Bauman's (1989) important account of the Holocaust and the present understanding of the specific character of Nazi racism as a rationality of extermination. Bauman's account concurs with the one presented here in so far as it presents the Holocaust as something that must be understood as endogenous to Western civilization and its processes of rationalization rather than as an aberrant psychological, social or political pathology. Moreover, to the extent that his account stresses the collapse or non-emergence of democracy, it indicates the failure of the democratization of sovereignty as a fundamental precondition of Nazi rule, a theme which echoes those of Hannah Arendt's famous book, *The Origins of Totalitarianism* (1958). Foucault's brief remarks seem to add to or qualify Bauman's account in two ways. They first offer the possibility of a closer specification of the kind of rationality and technology that makes possible a racialized politics and policy by demonstrating its bio-political character. Such a view enables us to get a clearer understanding of the role of the human sciences in such a politics. They also suggest that Nazi politics articulates this biological politics with alternative traditions and frameworks of sovereignty such as those of fatherland, *Volk* and blood. It is not simply the imperative of the totalistic administration of life which accounts for the mentality of Nazi rule, but the way the bio-political discourses and sovereign themes are resinscribed and modified within one another.
3 Note that Foucault's point here extends one made by Hannah Arendt (1958: 313). 'Practically speaking,' she states 'it will make little difference whether totalitarian movements adopt the pattern of Nazism or Bolshevism, organize the masses in the name of race or class, pretend to follow the laws of life and nature or of dialectics and economics.' Bio-political state racism can be justified in terms of the goal of the evolution to an ideal society or optimizing the quality of the population as much as the evolution of the race. The practice of state racism upon populations retarding social and political evolution does not necessarily always speak the language of race.

8 NEO-LIBERALISM AND ADVANCED LIBERAL GOVERNMENT

In the final two chapters we begin the task of offering a diagnosis of the transformations of governmentality at the end of the twentieth century. In the next chapter, I shall suggest that the shifts in liberal mentalities and regimes of government are among the first events in a new trajectory that takes off from and recodes the government through economic, social and vital processes. Along this new line, as we shall argue, the government through processes is increasingly displaced by a government of government, a 'reflexive government'.

An analytics of government, however, works from concrete analysis rather than general hypothesis. The present chapter commences this task. It extends Foucault's own attempts, discussed in Chapter 2, at grasping the multiplicity and complexity of rule in contemporary liberal democracies. It does this in two ways. It first focuses on several aspects of neo-liberal rationalities of government, including the notion of society, the shaping of freedom, and the aims of neo-liberal reform. The remedies suggested entail a breaching of older divisions between state and civil society, and a kind of 'folding back' of the objectives of government upon themselves. The paradigmatic case of this is the construction of 'quasi' or 'artificial' markets as a solution to the excessive expenditure, rigidity, bureaucracy and dependency of the welfare state. This investigation of neo-liberal rationalities reveals them to be reflexive to the extent to which the objectives of policy also become their means.

Second, this chapter examines the elements that are assembled in governing advanced liberal democracies. We shall see that advanced liberal government endeavours not only to work through the various forms of freedom and agency of individuals and collectives but also to deploy indirect means for the surveillance and regulation of that agency. Advanced liberal practices are thus reflexive to the extent that they are concerned to promote and then govern through forms of 'indigenous government' of individuals, organizations and collectives (O'Malley, 1998).

In the course of the following discussion, we shall use the term 'neo-liberalism' to refer to specific styles of the general mentality of rule, and to distinguish that mentality from others such as communitarianism and neo-conservatism. Advanced liberalism will designate the broader realm of the various assemblages of rationalities, technologies and agencies that constitute the characteristic ways of governing in contemporary liberal democracies. Such a distinction enables us to consider how neo-liberal rationalities exist in complex interrelations with neo-conservatism and populist, anti-governmental reaction, as well as with debates on morality and community. While neo-liberalism might be characterized as the dominant contemporary rationality of government, it is found within a field of contestation in which there are multiple rationalities of government and a plurality of varieties of neo-liberalism.[1]

Society, freedom and reform

It is clear that, since the 1960s and 1970s, the ways in which we think about, criticize, review and seek to reform government in advanced liberal democracies have undergone something of a sea change. One way of approaching this change would be to consider the question of the relationship between government and the notion of society. In most advanced liberal democracies after World War II the ideal of the welfare state, if not the operation of welfarist government, succeeded in representing the function and objectives of government in terms of a specific relation between state and society. Government was understood as an activity undertaken by the national welfare state acting as a unified body upon and in defence of a unitary domain, society. The purposes of this government were conceived as enframing society within mechanisms of security by which the state would care for the welfare of the population 'from the cradle to the grave'. The claim made for 'Keynesian' techniques of social intervention – adjustments to fiscal and monetary policy, direct state investments – was that they established a form of security in which the health of society and the health of the economy became mutually reinforcing over the course of the economic cycle. For Donzelot (1991), these techniques were an attempt to regulate economic and social *time* (the time of the business cycle and the time of effective demand) by the manipulation of variables such as unemployment and inflation. The paradoxical consequence of the linking of the social with a centralized bureaucratic and fiscal apparatus was that society loses its identity: the idea of a civil sphere beyond the state that is a constant source of energies, dynamism and renewal threatens to collapse under the weight of its administration.

The ideal of a welfare state was an assemblage of unstable and heterogeneous elements. The Keynesian feedback loop between the economic and the social is only the most obvious. It is the one that will be exploited by 'neo-liberal' and 'monetarist' arguments concerning the inflationary political cycle of the welfare state and the ungovernability of liberal democracies. There is also the attempt (explored in Chapter 4) to fuse the care of the population – inherited from the Christian universalism of souls by way of nineteenth-century scientific philanthropy – with the notions of citizenship, an irrevocably exclusionary status, within the liberal regime of security. Yet again, there are the difficulties inherent in an art of government that seeks to operate through and adjust the competing demands of the social subject with its needs, the prudential subject with its responsibilities, the economic subject with its interests, and the juridical subject with its rights. The social was always then a 'hybrid' assemblage of unstable elements, as Deleuze (1979: xv) noted, an 'artefact' in Paul Hirst's (1981) terms. This instability was exacerbated by the attempt to instrumentalize the social into a mechanism of national economic government. It is perhaps not surprising that theories of government would find a point of renewal in their constitutive resources: the person as individual, people in their associations, and conceptions of the responsible autonomy of citizens. Here I propose to investigate neo-liberalism through three themes: that of individual versus social obligation, various conceptions of freedom and autonomy, and its multiplicity.

'There is no such thing as society'

Consider in this regard Margaret Thatcher's comments reported in a 1987 interview which are perhaps among the most infamous examples of general neo-liberal rationality:

> I think we've been through a period where too many people have been given to understand that if they have a problem, it's the government's job to cope with it. 'I have a problem. I'll get a grant.' 'I'm homeless, the government must house me.' They're casting their problem on society. And, you know, there is no such thing as society. There are individual men and women, and there are families. And no government can do anything except through people, and people must look to themselves first. It is our duty to look after ourselves, and then to look after our neighbour. (1987: 10)

How should we understand the then incumbent political leader's turn of phrase? Part homily, part political rhetoric, these statements nevertheless make it possible to draw out some aspects of one version of the neo-liberal critique of 'too much' government. Clearly something has happened to the notion of society as a problematic of national government and a principle for its self-limitation and review. What is at stake is not the ontological status of society, but the way in which 'society' functions in a mentality of national government. This is borne out by Thatcher's later attempt at self-clarification:

> My meaning, clear at the time but subsequently distorted beyond recognition, was that society was not an abstraction, separate from the men and women who composed it, but a living structure of individuals, families, neighbours and voluntary associations . . . The error to which I was objecting was the confusion of society with the helper of first resort . . . Society for me was not an excuse, it was a source of obligation. (Thatcher, 1993: 626)[2]

The position encapsulated in the statement 'there is no such thing as society' is thus about the rejection of a certain relation between citizens as individuals and in their associations, and society as incarnated in the national state. It would be mistaken to imagine that such statements stand in evidence of the 'end of the social' or 'death of the social', to revive a trope found in a particular kind of cultural critique (Baudrillard, 1983). Such a trope suggests a finality and rupture that is not borne out by contemporary governmental and political rationalities. In an empirical sense, there are still social workers, systems of social security, and even a proliferation of social policy specialists. Notwithstanding F.A. Hayek's (1976) arguments, various authorities might even claim to be acting in the name of something called 'social justice'. Moreover, advanced liberal forms of national government encompass a range of possibilities. In at least one version, we can expect an attempt to reconfigure social expertise and the objectives of social government. This is quite clear in debates about the decline or relative strength of trust and associational relations in civic life that are allied with the term 'social capital' (e.g. Putnam, 1996). The 'social' remains as a domain of knowledge, intervention, practices and institutions, even if it has been or is in the process of being reconfigured. Various national governments and transnational associations at particular political conjunctures, moreover, will take up and utilize this domain of social government for various purposes.

Another view of the salience of Thatcher's statement 'there is no such thing as society' is that it has entered the lexicon of contemporary politics as an object of ridicule or at least of a distancing. It now often stands as an index of the 'failure' of a certain type of political programme and a means by which 'alternative' political programmes can argue for the necessity of certain types of social intervention of national government (e.g. Etzioni, 1996: 11). However, when we consider the content of these 'alternatives', it is precisely the image of society as a 'living structure of individuals, families, neighbours and voluntary associations', as Thatcher put it, that is evoked. From the perspective of the end of the twentieth century, Mrs Thatcher's comment does not mark a decisive break in the discourse of politics. Rather, it announces the now barely contestable proposal that a certain art of national government becomes available when society is regarded less as a source of needs that are individually distributed and collectively borne and more as a source of energies contained within individuals' exercise of freedom and self-responsibility. A key corollary of the exercise of that freedom is voluntary association or – as it is known in various forms of political discourse – 'community'. The distance between Thatcher's statement and the theorists of social capital, who emphasize levels of trust and civic participation, or the advocates of 'communitarianism', who seek to 'reaffirm shared values', is not as great as might be first imagined or either party might allow.[3]

What Thatcher's statement does indicate is one sense in which a national government of society is no longer necessary. If society is to be viewed as a source of energies consequent upon autonomous action and association, it is at best something to be facilitated and cultivated rather than a problematic and unstable domain to be regulated. It is possible, then, to bypass the sociological problematic of the fragility of the conflict-ridden unity of society. Such a problematic conceived of society as the locus of bonds of solidarity that need to be enframed in mechanisms of security. The welfare state is one conception of such mechanisms, enforcing solidarity and preventing dissolution by the provision for the needs of the national population, ensuring the rights and liberties of socially responsible citizens and neutralizing the threat of social dangers. A rejection of the sociological problematic leaves little point to the mechanisms of social insurance and security unless they can be transformed into ones that foster the energies and activities of individuals and collectives. One might note that a consequence of this evasion of the sociological problematic is that some of the energies and forms of autonomy so unleashed might be unpalatable to advocates of neo-liberalism, such as the rise of neo-conservative and sometimes overtly racist political and social movements. The way in which traditional conservative parties governed their religious fundamentalist and racist constituencies is in danger of collapse. The rise of theological conservatism and anti-government populism parallels the embrace of neo-liberal policies by mainstream parties.

While it may be possible to conceive of a government that is no longer the government of society, the rise of these movements suggests there is a certain cost in the attempt to do so. For the moment, however, we shall bracket off our scepticism about this project and try to make intelligible the conditions and consequences of contemporary liberalism. How can any version of liberalism – or any rationality of national government – bypass 'society'? The general answer to this question is that the liberal problematic of security is undergoing a change from the security of social, economic and demographic processes to the security of governmental mechanisms – a point we develop in the next chapter. The manner in which this shift has occurred during the last two decades of the twentieth century is through a displacement of social policy by cultural transformation and the movement beyond a 'welfarist' social regime. In order to understand the ramifications of this, we must consider another issue to which Thatcher's statement alerts us, that of the responsibility and autonomy of free subjects in their voluntary associations.

A *responsible and disciplined autonomy*

One might want first to consider a critical history of the recent ways in which the notion of 'freedom' has been articulated in various forms of political reason. Such a history might also consider a sense in which the notion of 'freedom' has come to be taken over and turned to ends quite different from, if not exactly contrary to, those for which it was earlier intended.

Such a history could start with a number of forms of thought that had their origins in the 1960s and which, at first glance, are as far from Thatcherite language as possible. First, there was what might be called a number of critiques of the welfare state that might be broadly located on the Left and were associated with the movements of social and cultural emancipation. The welfare state was understood as a paternalist mechanism of social control, relying on a uniform provision that is bureaucratic, hierarchical, sometimes coercive and oppressive, and often unresponsive to the needs and differences of individuals and communities. One could track this critique through a complex theoretical and practical lineage in the 1970s. Programmes of community action and community development deployed notions and practices of 'empowerment' and 'participation' against these ills of the state (Cruikshank, 1994). The recent history of community as a 'technology of citizenship' is hardly a discovery of 1990s communitarians. During the same period, it seemed that Marxist and feminist theories of the welfare state never tired of showing that it functioned to reproduce not only capitalist social relations but patriarchal divisions of labour and forms of dependency for women (Gough, 1979; Wilson, 1977).

These critiques of the welfare state were allied with the critique of professions and expertise (e.g. Illich et al., 1977). The professions were said to be unaccountable systems of exclusion, delegitimating local, folk and alternative forms of knowledge and de-skilling the population of its existing capacities and local knowledge. Feminism, in particular, argued for a new way of approaching issues of women's health against a male-dominated medical profession (e.g. Ehrenreich and English, 1979). The latter was shown to objectify and discipline women's bodies in a patriarchal manner, exclude women as healers, and achieve dominance over female occupations such as nursing. What is at stake here is not merely professional accountability but a radical appropriation of control over one's own body and a reassertion of autonomy and rights of self-determination within the doctor–patient or, more generally, professional–client relationship. The feminist critique of the medical profession is perhaps an exemplar of multiple critiques of the formation of needs within the welfare state. As Yeatman (1994: 106–10) has shown, the critique of professional domination thus makes way for a 'politics of need formation' in which various clienteles of the welfare state – e.g. those with disabilities, the users of mental health services, and their carers – reveal that the construction of need is 'irreducibly multiple', appropriate the language of self-determination, and claim 'user's rights'. A consequence of this is that a 'politics of voice and representation' seeks to displace a welfare state held to be paternalistic. One outcome of the critique of professional expertise and knowledge has been to make the application and use of expert knowledge dependent upon the 'choice' of those formerly regarded as clients of services. This prepares for the conception of quality service provision as 'customer-focused' and for the widespread tendency to reconfigure formerly public provision as markets in services and expertise over which the consumer is sovereign.

The critiques both of state and of professional domination thus meet up with a more fundamental line along which we might trace a cultural renewal of notions of freedom and emancipation and the elaboration of a set of techniques and practices on the basis of this renewal. This trajectory might begin with 'counter-cultural movements' of the 1960s, the mass experimentation in drugs among the young, the importation of 'Eastern' religions, cults, healing practices, yoga, meditation, martial arts and so on. It might also encompass another line moving from the 'sexual revolution', through 'sexual politics', to the questioning of sexuality and sexual identity. We might think of this as a kind of rediscovery, within certain societies that like to consider themselves Western, of a culture of the self and its actualization. These movements, whether cultural or political, also start to rethink the ways in which it is possible to act as a part of a collective and on oneself. We find here a whole series of techniques for self-actualization that will prove polyvalent in their application: techniques of consciousness raising, empowerment, self-esteem, alternative pedagogy, the rhetoric of voice and representation, and so on.

Far from being marginal to our main concerns, all of these developments intersect with neo-liberal critiques of the welfare state in the new valorization of the self-actualized subject. It is often noted that these developments are the targets of conservative cultural criticism in the hands of thinkers such as Daniel Bell (1979). What is less often noted is the way in which these movements and their critiques of the welfare state in the name of autonomy came to be remapped onto the critiques of excessive government of neo-liberal thought. Where the political and cultural movements sought a utopian vision of the emancipated self, however, the neo-liberal critiques of the welfare state sought to redeploy the 'free subject' as a technical instrument in the achievement of governmental purposes and objectives. Contemporary liberal rule rediscovers freedom as a technical modality, and is able to translate (even if only roughly) the concerns of social and cultural movements into its own vocabulary and a set of practical formulas for the review, rationalization and renewal of governmental practice. The notion of freedom and the free conduct of individuals once again becomes the principle by which government is to be rationalized and reformed. However, this principle itself is subject to a series of successive displacements. The displacements reveal a conception of freedom that moves away from the emancipatory aspirations of social movements toward the virtuous, disciplined and responsible autonomy of the citizenry desired by neo-conservatives.

Neo-liberalism – if we can use the term broadly to describe a range of (but not all) contemporary mentalities of rule – introduces a quite distinctive conception of freedom. As Graham Burchell (1996: 24) has remarked, freedom is no longer the freedom of the 'system of natural liberty' of Adam Smith and the Scottish Enlightenment but freedom as 'artefact' of F.A. Hayek. Hayek's position is germane because it extends and introduces a further set of nuances into our earlier accounts of forms of neo-liberalism. For Hayek, however, freedom is somewhat different from the 'constructivist' artefact that Foucault discovered in the ordoliberals (discussed in Chapter 2):

Man has not developed in freedom. The member of the little band to which he had had to stick in order to survive was anything but free. *Freedom is an artefact of civilization* that released man from the trammels of the small group, the momentary moods of which even the leader had to obey. Freedom was made possible by the gradual evolution of *the discipline of civilization which is at the same time the*

> *discipline of freedom.* It protects him by impersonal abstract rules against arbitrary violence of others and enables each individual to try to build for himself a protected domain with which nobody else is allowed to interfere and within which he can use his own knowledge for his own purposes. We owe our freedom to restraints of freedom. (1979: 163, original emphasis)

For neo-liberalism, freedom is no longer a natural attribute of *Homo œconomicus,* the rational subject of interest. It is an artefact. Yet Hayek's position is important because it alerts us to the different ways in which it can be an artefact. For the German post-war ordoliberals such as Alexander von Rüstow, freedom is something to be contrived by a 'vital policy' that promotes the conditions of the free, entrepreneurial conduct of economically rational individuals (Gordon, 1991: 40–1). Hayek, however, offers a critique of this kind of approach when he conceives of culture as an intermediate and key layer between nature and reason. Any account of the ethos of contemporary neo-liberalism, particularly in the English-speaking world, must heed the consequences of this kind of critique.

Freedom for Hayek is a product neither of nature nor of governmental policy and its institutions but of cultural evolution conceived as the development of civilization and its discipline. The introduction of this theme of cultural evolution allows his argument to outflank the either/or logic implied in the opposition between the natural and the artificial conceived as the processes of biological selection and the rational designs of government (Hayek, 1979: 155). He conceives nature, culture and rational design as three separate processes, each of which gives rise to 'rules of conduct'. These rules are stratified: at base, the 'instinctive' drives; above these, 'traditions' restraining the first; and finally, the 'thin layer of deliberately adopted or modified rules' (1979: 159–60). So drives, traditions and consciously adopted rules operate within the respective spheres of nature, culture and reason.

In the course of cultural evolution, Hayek argues, rules of conduct are selected that help human groups adapt to their social environment, prosper and expand. The development of civilization is thus dependent on the capacity to learn and pass on these rules of conduct. Cultural evolution is a kind of ongoing learning process. These rules change in the course of the transition to an 'abstract and open' society in which relations among strangers are governed by abstract rules (forming the basis of law) and impersonal signals (such as those provided by prices) (1979: 162). Such cultural rules of conduct are learnt not from rationally constructed institutions but from the 'spontaneous social orders' of the market, language, morals and law. An important consequence follows. Reason does not lead to civilization; it is its effect. Reason is the consequence of those learnt rules of conduct by which humans become intelligent and it is by submitting to their discipline that humans can become free (1979: 163). This is one point at which neo-liberalism meets both neo-conservatism and the concern of communitarianism for the 'moral order'. In response to the claim that freedom involves a kind of romantic notion of self-fulfilment, Hayek shows that freedom depends upon the disciplining effects of social orders that have developed through cultural evolution. It is by observing the rules of conduct learnt in the course of that evolution – around the market and the family, in particular – that we learn how to practise our freedom.

The specificity of Hayek's conception of freedom is that it is both *negative*, in that it is freedom from coercion by the arbitrary will of others, and *anti-naturalist*, in that its conditions are not found in the natural state of humankind. Hayek is thus able to criticize what he calls the 'constructivism' of the type Foucault finds in the ordoliberals and which, coming from a very different political stance, might best be represented by Karl Polanyi's *The Great Transformation* (1957), which showed how the historical establishment of markets in labour, money and land requires active legal and governmental reform. Hayek (1976: 17–24) himself provides a rather different genealogy of the 'constructivist fallacy' in Bentham and 'utilitarianism'. Indeed, it is here, as Elie Halévy (1928) showed, that one finds the problem of the relation between the natural harmony of interests found in the market and the artificial harmonization of interests by government.

Liberal and neo-liberal notions of freedom are tied to the question of the market. Here again Hayek's difference from both early liberalism and other neo-liberalisms is instructive. For early liberalism, the market is a quasi-natural reality whose laws must be respected by government. The state must make regulations that allow the natural and necessary regulations of the market to operate and the interests of the rational and free subject to be pursued. For the *Ordoliberalen*, by contrast, the central problem is how to contrive the conditions under which entrepreneurial and competitive conduct can be allowed to come into play and the market can hence operate. Yet again it is the differences between neo-liberalisms that are important. With the ordoliberals the market appears not as a set of natural relations but as an 'artificial game of competitive freedom' undertaken under the legal guarantees and limits established by an institutional and juridical officialdom (Gordon, 1991: 41). In this sense the ordoliberals, like Polanyi's 'institutionalist' thesis, view the functioning of the market and the construction of freedom as dependent on the active interventions of the liberal state and the organization of a coherent public institutional and legal framework.

For Hayek, by contrast, the market is neither a natural sphere of the relations between exchanging individuals nor an artificial contrivance of appropriate policies but a spontaneous social order governed by customary rules selected by a complex cultural learning process. He uses the German word *Bildung* to designate a social order that is not a consciously designed institution but is established in the course of its own development. The question of the political conditions of the market is one of developing the appropriate constitutional framework according to the 'rule of law'. This means that government exercises coercion and restraint of individuals only in accordance with the rules learnt from the process of cultural evolution, or, as he puts it, 'the recognized rules of just conduct designed to define and protect the domain of all individuals' (Hayek, 1979: 109). The rule of law means that government is limited to applying universal rules announced in advance to an unknown number of cases and in an unknown number of future instances. One consequence of this is that it is not possible to make laws which discriminate in favour of or against any particular class of individuals and so avoid parliaments and laws becoming the 'playball of group interests' (1979: 99). Another is that it creates the conditions by which the cultural rules of conduct contained within the spontaneous orders of the market – and indeed of morals, language and law itself – can be reinforced and not abandoned or transgressed. Hayek thus agrees with the ordoliberals on the need for definite political and legal conditions of the market. However, for Hayek these are to be secured by a constitutional framework that limits governmental regulation by a conception of the rule of law that is derived from the rules of conduct arrived at in the process of cultural evolution.

If freedom is subject to successive displacements in neo-liberalism, so too are key terms that form the diagram of the 'free subject' such as 'interests' and 'choice'. In eighteenth-century economic liberalism, interests are conceived as the purposes that economic individuals can represent to themselves and pursue within the market. Moreover, these individual interests are brought into harmony by means of their pursuit in the exchanges of the market. For neo-liberalism, interests are no longer something which simply occur to economic individuals in their pursuit of pleasure and avoidance of pain. Rather, the play and interplay of interests require particular institutional, cultural or economic conditions. Again this can take a number of versions. The first version is the constructivist one instanced in von Rüstow's vision in which all aspects of life are to be reshaped according to the ethos of the enterprise. Another is found in the Chicago School's claim that it is possible to direct and predict behaviour by means of an indefinite extension of market rationality. In the latter case, the individual will learn that freedom consists in not simply regarding oneself as an enterprise but becoming an entrepreneur of oneself and all the innate and acquired skills, talents and capacities that comprise 'human capital' (Gordon, 1991: 43–4). In both these cases, interests come into play when the environment is manipulated to allow interested behaviour to flourish, whether by adopting the ethos of enterprise or by becoming an entrepreneur of a stock of human capital. Finally, there is Hayek's approach. Here the spontaneous order of the market can only properly operate if individuals are free in the sense that they are permitted to use their own knowledge for their own purposes (Hayek, 1976: 8). This requires a constitutional framework in which abstract rules are made which do not favour or disfavour particular interests. Here interests are at once immanent to the spontaneous order of the market (and are thus bio-cultural in their origins) and the source of danger to the 'general interest' in that they give rise to interest groups. These groups threaten to use government for particularized ends rather than as an abstract and impersonal set of means. In this sense the 'general welfare' is to be defined not as the securing of particular needs in response to the demands of interest groups but as making it possible for individuals and small groups to pursue their own interests.

Finally, contemporary rule effects a series of displacements in the notion of *choice*. This is evident in Foucault's own analysis of the American neo-liberals' use of the term as representing a 'reactivation' and a 'radical inversion' of the economic agent of the Scottish Enlightenment (Gordon, 1991: 43). It is also the case with a range of theories: rational choice theory, public choice theory, agency theory, the new institutional economics. Choice is no longer the rational response of the economic actor to the calculation of one's natural interest. It becomes a fundamental human faculty that can be made calculable and manipulated by working on the environment and spaces within which it is exercised. Choice thus becomes a calculable element within the economically rationalizing and optimizing behaviours of professionals, workers, consumers, clients and service providers. This is its radical inversion, one that operates at the intersecting of economic rationality and behaviourism. However, it overrides and outflanks all arguments concerning social determination and stands as a principle which can 'sweep aside the anthropological categories and frameworks of the human and social sciences' (1991: 43). If one should object that the determination of conduct by the embedding of market rationality in all spheres is just as much a danger as state totalitarianism (Dean, 1994a: 193), the neo-liberal economist might respond that the difference lies in the former allowing the play of individual choice. It is not so much a denial that there can be such things as collective beliefs and desires; rather, these things exist only in so far as they are mediated by individual choice.

The relation between these multiple neo-liberal critiques of government and advanced liberal forms of rule brings another layer of complexity to any account of our experience of the political today. In the next section, we shall turn to the features of advanced liberal government. I want to conclude this discussion of neo-liberalism as a form of critique and a mentality of rule by spelling out and exemplifying one of the principal implications of this discussion, that there is more than one type of neo-liberalism – a theme already touched upon in Chapter 2 – and by further opening up the question of the relation between neo-liberalism and neo-conservatism.

Styles of neo-liberalism and neo-conservatism

All variants of neo-liberalism not only assume the importance of the market; they essentialize it. This means they regard the market as something that can be analysed 'in terms of an inner essence or principle which produces necessary effects by the mere fact of its presence' (Hindess, 1987: 149). However, they differ in the manner in which the operation of the market is to be secured and its essence realized. At the level of national governments, labour and social democratic parties undertake activist policies to coordinate and facilitate the institutions and agencies necessary for the operation of the market and the productions of types of subjects required by it. They thus take a path somewhat similar to the ordoliberals of the post-war German Federal Republic in that they foresee a necessary organizing role for the national state in establishing the market as a game of competitive freedom.

Conservative parties, at least in the English-speaking world, have followed an approach that could be characterized as both consistent with Hayek while deploying and multiplying the 'governmental constructivism' of the *Ordoliberalen*. Here we witness a retraction of public provision in the name of fiscal prudence and increased national savings. The relation between this retraction and the *Bildung* of the market is twofold. On the one hand, macro-economic policies follow from the rules of sound financial conduct taught by the market. On the other, the operation of the market is restored to its role of educator in the sound rules of conduct. But this species of neo-liberalism adds a twist not really contained within the Hayekian story. It is less of a corollary to Hayek than a kind of *folding* of the objectives of neo-liberalism upon liberal rule itself. It is at this point that governmental constructivism comes into play. If the market teaches the manner in which we should guide our own conduct, then the way in which we gain access to guidance regarding our conduct will be through the construction of markets.

Consider the changing forms of support for the unemployed in Australia as an example of how the construction of markets can be approached as an educative exercise (Dean, 1995; 1998a). This could be read as a kind of case study of the different ethical investments of this terrain of advanced liberal government. Under the Labor incumbency of 1983–96, the national state introduced case-management approaches to unemployment, and coordinated access to job-search assistance, employment exchange services, training, job-creation schemes and even subsidized jobs. The unemployed person entered into a contract with a national state that promised access to benefits and services, including the guarantee of a job for the long-term unemployed, in return for compliance with the demand that the unemployed practise their 'freedom' in a certain way, that is, as active job seekers. The national state in effect said: 'if you make yourself into an active job seeker, we will support you and provide access to those services and expertise that will make you job-ready'. To put this another way, the state is constituted by a promise: 'we will assist you to practise your freedom, as long as you practise it our way'.

In August 1996, the new conservative (Liberal–National) Australian government moved quickly on the question of unemployment. This government rescinded the notion of a job guarantee, and 'cashed out' most publicly funded job-creation and job-subsidy schemes. In doing so, the conservative government hoped to establish a fully competitive market in what it calls 'employment placement enterprises' (Dean, 1998a). Like the policies of the Labor government, the new policies and plans accepted the need for the unemployed to work on themselves, with the assistance of self-help facilities, case managers, job-search training, job clubs and training programmes, in order to make themselves ready and available to take up opportunities in the labour market. Indeed the language of the 'job seeker' and 'active' labour market programmes was retained. Both sets of policies share market-oriented objectives. However, under the conservatives, the national state shifted from organizing and facilitating access to services and expertise to establishing and coordinating markets in such services and expertise. Now the government's own agencies were reconstituted as competitors in such a market. The contract between the state and the job seeker is replaced by a myriad of contracts between the job seeker and the competing 'employment placement enterprises'. The ethos here is not so much 'you can practise your freedom as long as you choose to do it our way', as it was under Labor. Now the ethos is better characterized as 'if you require guidance and training in the practice of freedom you must first exercise your freedom as a consumer of employment services to gain access to such guidance and training'. We thus have a kind of circular paradox in which it is necessary to exercise freedom – as a consumer – in order to gain the support and guidance that will allow you to exercise freedom – as a worker.[4]

The ethos of this form of neo-liberalism is one of a kind of double-play or reduplication, or a folding back of its objectives upon itself, or, to use the language we shall shortly adopt, a form of reflexive government. The general objectives of government are consistent with Hayek but its particular tactics are a kind of governmental constructivism. The market is now reconstituted as a global entity seriously compromising the capacities of national governments. As such, it directs the conduct of government in terms of macro-economic policy, fiscal and monetary policies, etc., so that we might learn to govern our conduct as individuals, and as public and private authorities and agencies. This is clearly consistent with Hayek. Yet, at the same time this variant of neo-liberalism seeks to contrive and actively construct markets where they do not exist. Thus it is no longer a question of establishing a social framework for the operation of the competitive market (as, in their different ways, both the *Ordoliberalen* and Australian Labor were doing). Nor is it a matter of utilizing businesses and private and community agencies in the service of social and political objectives. Instead, it involves the reconfiguration of the framework of social government as a set of markets in services, provision and expertise, and a reconstruction of the unemployed as consumers within these markets. One way of activating the elements of contemporary liberal rule – as in the experience under Labor in Australia – pays homage to the values, rationality, and rules of conduct of the market but keeps them at arm's length as something exterior to its own exercise. Another way, more in keeping with the dominant strand of neo-liberalism in the English-speaking world, breaches the line between state and society in order to allow the value and rules of markets to reform all spheres.

This is why the headline rhetoric of the two forms of neo-liberalism are so different. Left-of-centre parties appear more likely to represent their objectives in terms of 'active citizenship' and the 'active society', notions which encompass but go beyond participation in the market to include participation in other social spheres, including leisure, domestic work, family caring and politics itself. They are likely to keep some distance from the more radical dimensions of the promotion of what in Britain in the 1980s became known as the 'enterprise culture' (Heelas and Morris, 1992). The aims of cultural reform of this latter kind are to revive and extend the norms and values associated with the market including those of 'responsibility, initiative, competitiveness and risk-taking, and industrious effort', to use the list of one of its major political architects (Young, 1992: 33).

Yet it is precisely this notion of a reform that can no longer be political (given the retraction of the responsibilities of formal political authority) and social (and its associations with the welfare state) that most clearly articulates what is novel about neo-liberalism in the greater part of the English-speaking world in recent decades. The central mechanism that follows a neo-liberal critique of the welfare state is cultural reform. This is first evidenced in the lineage of targets of conservative cultural critique since the 1970s: the critique of modernism and acquisitive consumerism; the attack on the 'counter-culture'; the analysis of the dependency culture and its underclass fostered by the welfare state, particularly in the USA; and the clarion call for a revival of an enterprise culture in Britain. Neo-liberal cultural critique would have little significance if cultural reform were not conceived as central to implanting the norms and values of the market and the forms of conduct to be derived from it in all spheres, including the institutions and instruments of government themselves.

It is at this point we can begin to see why Hayek's arguments represent a powerful version of neo-liberalism as a way of thinking about government. Mrs Thatcher's statement that 'there is no such thing as society' could be viewed as a corollary of Hayek's conception of freedom as arising from the course of cultural evolution that has selected the values and rules of the market. Hayek succeeds in providing an anti-naturalistic conception of freedom that bypasses processes of *social* reform and which restricts *political* reform to imposing limits on the action of government. Yet, as we have seen, reform is cultural not simply because this neo-liberalism has run out of alternatives. It is cultural because what is at issue are the values and rules of conduct that have been developed in the course of the evolution of spontaneous social orders. This is why the ethos of neo-liberalism is at once conservative and radical. It is conservative in its revival and restoration of the values (or 'virtues') and rules of conduct associated with these orders, particularly those of the market. And it is radical because, by the process of reduplication and folding back, it multiplies and ramifies these values and rules into ever-new spheres including its own instruments and agencies.

Neo-liberalism, in this form at least, is a response to a kind of 'political reproduction' problem that is posed by neo-conservatives in the United States and embodied in the Republican Contract with America (Cruikshank, 1998). This is the problem of how to govern through the autonomy of the governed when they are no longer virtuous. It takes a contemporary form when the citizenry is corrupted by, to list a few neo-conservative targets: 'rent-seeking' politicians and bureaucrats; misguided and dangerous ideas (such as those perpetrated by the 'counter-culture'); schools that fail to teach the three Rs and personal responsibility; permissive morality and easy divorce laws; and dependency-fostering social provision, such as the programmes of the Great Society. Neo-liberalism and neo-conservatism share this same diagnosis of the problem of the corruption of the people and the need to lead them to accept their responsibilities and become a virtuous citizenry again. Neo-conservatism often adopts sovereign instruments to enforce marriage and heterosexual relations, fight illegal immigration (and restrict legal immigration), enforce minimum labour and 'workfare' programmes, and demand punishment rather than rehabilitation of criminal offenders (1998: 152). Neo-liberalism, in contrast, looks to a kind of cultural revolution that will restore the responsible autonomy of the citizenry. This revolution is made possible by returning to the values associated with the course of evolution of civilization. However, we should be careful not to draw too strict a line between the two, given the emphasis on a 'culture war' by the neo-conservatives in the USA, conducted against the 'counter-culture', multiculturalism, and the decentring of sexuality and familial relations.

Neo-liberalism, like neo-conservatism, calls for radical cultural renewal. This, at least in one highly influential version, could be said to constitute its ethos. In this version, it rejects the possibility of a rational knowledge of society and its deployment in the direction of public policy. If Thatcher dismisses the political salience of society, Hayek can argue that 'there seems to me still to exist no more justification for a theoretical discipline of sociology than there would be for a theoretical discipline of naturology' (1979: 173). We are at the nadir of a trajectory of social government that might be said to reach its zenith with the relation between *solidarisme* as a doctrine of state and Emile Durkheim's notion of society (Donzelot, 1991). Durkheim's (1992: 51) conception of the state as the 'organ of social thought' in which 'its principal function is to think' now appears as the polar opposite of a neo-liberal position that rejects the possibility of both a theoretical knowledge of society and any centrally directing intelligence.

Hayek's philosophy makes intelligible the goals of contemporary neo-liberalism as no less than the deployment of the culturally acquired rules of conduct to safeguard our civilization and the freedom it secures. In its invocation of virtues associated with the spontaneous social orders of market and family, neo-liberalism is clearly consistent with neo-conservatism. The clearest difference would be the different conceptions of the means of eliciting these virtues. Here neo-conservatism only has exhortation, sovereign measures and a 'statist' imposition of morality that often runs counter to its anti-political impulses. Contemporary liberalism, by contrast, operationalizes culturally acquired virtues by reforming ever-new spheres so they are accountable to the imperatives of learnt rules of conduct, including and especially the institutions of national government themselves. When public authority must act, it must be sure that it does so in conformity with the rules of conduct associated with markets. For example, according to one influential US text 'reinventing government' is about making it 'entrepreneurial' (Osborne and Gaebler, 1993). In Australia, the public employment service is replaced by a network of employment placement enterprises, in which the public agency is now in competition with private and community enterprises. Because change can no longer be a rationally directed process of social reform, for neo-liberalism it must be conducted according to cultural values, rules and norms. So far these rules and values have best been condensed into the cultural form of 'enterprise' and the 'consumer'.

We are becoming clearer about the experience of the present from which our critical history of government and liberalism is undertaken. This is a present in which at least one version of our governmental reason has found a way, for the first time in 200 years, to bypass 'society'. Of crucial importance in this is the emergence of a form of government that entails a reduplication of the objectives of government upon itself – what we shall call in Chapter 9 a reflexive government.

Advanced liberal government

The genealogy of liberal government has thus returned to its own present in revealing the singularity of certain versions of neo-liberalism to the extent that they break with the notion of 'society' as the field of operation of the government of the state. We should remember, however, that this is an event within a specific rationality of government, of a particular and limited diagram of the task of national government. We should be wary of regarding it as a fundamental rupture within modes of governing.

The idea of a government of society is no doubt utopian. The idea of a liberal government without society no less so. Liberal government without society would seem to present us with a radical impossibility. The very distinction of liberal government from a police conception of order was that 'society' would form an outside and boundary of government that must be respected and that was no longer permeable by the regulations of police (Foucault, 1989a: 261). Moreover, we have adduced several reasons (in Chapter 6) why this outside should be understood as a totality: the task of government becomes identified with the bounded space of national territory; society is discovered in the statistical regularities among the population inhabiting this territory; and the conception of a self-fracturing unity is fundamental to the liberal problematic of security. How, then, can we return to a government without society and not return to a 'totalitarian' conception of the governed order as completely transparent and amenable to government (such as found in early modern conceptions of police) or as a domain in which resistance is to be permanently neutralized and eradicated (as in twentieth-century authoritarian government)? How can liberalism enunciate a principle of self-limitation and an outside that is no longer 'society'?

It might be argued that the self-determining or free subject has replaced society as the principle of self-limitation of government. Such a view would suggest that contemporary liberalism guards against governing 'too much' by appealing to the rights and liberties of individuals. A useful way of thinking about liberalism as a regime of government, however, is to consider the multiple ways it works through and attempts to construct a world of autonomous individuals, of 'free subjects'. The latter phrase makes clear the full ambivalence of liberalism regarding the self-determining individual. This is a subject whose freedom is a condition of subjection. The exercise of authority presupposes the existence of a free subject of need, desire, rights, interests and choice. However its subjection is also a condition of freedom: in order to act freely, the subject must first be shaped, guided and moulded into one capable of responsibly exercising that freedom through systems of domination. Subjection and subjectification are laid upon one another. Each is a condition of the other. At one moment, they might be made identical (e.g. in disciplinary practices within the school, for example). At others, they are separated and made relatively autonomous (e.g. in practices of self-help and self-development, in the taking up of physical exercise) so that the relations of subjection involved are obscure and distant. Advanced liberal practices of rule are 'practices of liberty' in the sense that they continually associate and dissociate subjection and subjectification, domination and the fabrication of subjectivities. On the one hand they contract, consult, negotiate, create partnerships, even empower and activate forms of agency, liberty and the choices of individuals, consumers, professionals, households, neighbourhoods and communities. On the other, they set norms, standards, benchmarks, performance indicators, quality controls and best practice standards, to monitor, measure and render calculable the performance of these various agencies. The position of 'freedom' in advanced liberal regimes of government is exceedingly ambivalent: it can act as a principle of philosophical critique of government while at the same time be an artefact of multiple practices of government.

If we were to locate the principle of self-limitation of advanced liberal government in the free subject, even allowing for all the ambivalence of such a term, our answer would be true but partial. This free subject is a situated one. It is found first within 'a *living structure* of individuals, families, neighbours and voluntary associations' as Margaret Thatcher put it. It is found within its relationships to family, community and culture. It is situated in organic networks of affect, identification and care. It is also situated within 'artificial' but no less real networks of identification based on lifestyle choice, habitation, profession and career path, patterns of consumption, and voluntary association. Finally, it is institutionally and organizationally located. The free subject is found in the workplace, the community organization, the school, the home and the shopping mall. It is here that its choices will be made sovereign and its decisions will be calculating. It is here also that its activities will be monitored and its performance made calculable.

The conditions under which liberalism has dispensed with society are found in the forms, rationalities and practices of rule that might be encompassed by the term 'advanced liberal government'. This style of rule is composite, plural and multiform. It is reducible neither to philosophical principles nor to a political ideology. Of crucial importance is the way it operates through a multiplicity of these practices of liberty, i.e. practices concerned with structuring, shaping, predicting and making calculable the operation of our freedom, and of working off and through diagrams of free subjects constituted by forms of governmental and political reasoning.

There are several features of these new regimes of government that are important to emphasize here: the 'new prudentialism'; the deployment of technologies of agency and technologies of performance; and what might be called a contemporary form of pluralism. In the following account I have drawn upon and attempted to integrate many studies of governmentality and sought to develop and systematize overviews of ways of governing in advanced liberal democracies.

The new prudentialism

There is a certain affinity between advanced liberal government and the rationalities and technologies of risk. Risk is a polyvalent and polysemous vocabulary and set of practices and it would be premature to reduce the different risk rationalities and technologies to one another. In the following chapter, in the course of engaging with Ulrich Beck's *Risk Society*, I shall distinguish between certain types of risk rationality. For the purposes of the present discussion the point of coupling of risk technologies with contemporary formulas of rule might be described, after Pat O'Malley (1992), as the 'new prudentialism'. Here, we witness the multiple 'responsibilization' of individuals, families, households, and communities for their own risks – of physical and mental ill-health, of unemployment, of poverty in old age, of poor educational performance, of becoming victims of crime. Competition between public (state) schools, private health insurance and superannuation schemes, community policing and 'neighbourhood watch' schemes, and so on, are all instances of contriving practices of liberty in which the responsibilities for risk minimization become a feature of the choices that are made by individuals, households and communities as consumers, clients and users of services.

The new prudentialism differs from older, nineteenth-century forms of prudentialism in a number of ways. It first of all multiplies the domains to be monitored and prudently managed. Early nineteenth-century Malthusianism added procreative prudence and independence from poor relief to earlier injunctions to industry, frugality in domestic economy, and sobriety (Dean, 1991). Today the active citizen must add the monitoring of their risks of physical and mental ill-health, of sexually acquired disease, of dependency (on drugs, alcohol, nicotine, welfare or in personal relationships), of being a victim of crime, of a lack of adequate resources in retirement, of their own and their children's education, of low self-esteem and so on. Further, what is calculated is not the dangerousness of certain activities (e.g. gambling, drinking, poor hygiene), places (the alehouse, ghettos) and populations (the dangerous classes) but the risks that traverse each and every member of the population and which it is their individual and collective duty to control. Dangerousness is a qualitative judgement based on observable symptoms or empirical occurrences. Risk is both qualitative and quantitative; it is indicated by observable symptoms or by invisible abstract correlation of factors. It does not divide populations by a single division (the dangerous classes versus the labouring classes) so much as follow the warp and weft of risk within a population. There are only 'at-risk' groups, or high- and low-risk groups. Some spaces and neighbourhoods, times of day and night, are inherently risky. Some are more risky than others. Risk is a continuum rather than a clear break. Risk, in this sense, never completely evaporates. It can be minimized, localized and avoided, but never dissipated. There are, it is true, sub-populations to be targeted, but the entire population remains the primary locus of risk.

I do not mean to suggest that risk is irrevocably the opposite of dangerousness or other divisions of the population. In fact, one might suggest that the divisions of risk track the pathways already established in the identification of danger, and that the categories of 'high risk' are often conflated with divisions of social class. In this respect, the vocabulary of risk might better be thought of as reinscribing and recoding earlier languages of stratification, disadvantage and marginalization. However, the consequences that follow from the vocabulary of risk are rather different from earlier ones: strategies of harm minimization in relation to drug use are distinct from sovereign interventions to proscribe dangerous drugs; measures of health promotion for smokers or obesity may effectively target 'working class' men but they do so to erase risky behaviours, not redress disadvantage.

One can identify an emergent division between *active citizens* (capable of managing their own risk) and *targeted populations* (disadvantaged groups, the 'at risk', the high risk) who require intervention in the management of risks. The crucial thing, however, is to realize that these are liminal categories marking a fluid threshold rather than a strict divide. One of the consequences of the language of risk is that the entire population can be the locus of a vulnerability that can also single out specific populations, in a way that the language of danger, class or disadvantage cannot. Moreover, the new prudentialism suggests, if not a new, at least an additional role for professions as calculators, managers and tutors of risk, taking on educative, estimative and preventive functions (Rose, 1996a). The calculations of risk are intertwined with two different types of technology. One is deployed from below. The other, as it were, is utilized from above.

The technologies of agency

These are technologies of government that seek to enhance or deploy our possibilities of agency. There are two broad types of technologies of agency. The first comprises the extra-juridical and quasi-juridical proliferation of contract evidenced in the 'contracting-out' of formerly public services to private and community agencies, agreements made by unemployed persons, learning contracts of schoolchildren, performance contracts between ministers and senior public servants, enterprise agreements and so on. This proliferation of contract has been termed the 'new contractualism' (Yeatman,

1998). One of the key features of the logic of contractualization is that once its ethos of negotiated intersubjectivity is accepted, then all criticism becomes simply a means to retooling and expanding the logic of contract.

The technologies of agency also comprise what Barbara Cruikshank (1993; 1994) has called 'technologies of citizenship' – the multiple techniques of self-esteem, of empowerment and of consultation and negotiation that are used in activities as diverse as community development, social and environmental impact studies, health promotion campaigns, teaching at all levels, community policing, the combating of various kinds of dependency and so on. Technologies of agency also include the instruments of 'voice' and 'representation' by which the claims of user groups can enter into the negotiation over needs (Yeatman, 1994: 110). These technologies of citizenship engage us as active and free citizens, as informed and responsible consumers, as members of self-managing communities and organizations, as actors in democratizing social movements, and as agents capable of taking control of our own risks. All this is only dimly grasped in social scientists' relentless talk about recovering agency, grounding our commitments in a theory of the subject, in the celebration of resistance, and in the new idolization of social movements. This is not to cancel out agency but to seek to show how it is produced, how it is inserted in a system of purposes, and how it might overrun the limits established for it by a particular programme or even the strategic purposes of a regime of government.

Two points can be made here. First, these technologies of agency often come into play when certain individuals, groups and communities become what I have called targeted populations, i.e. populations that manifest high risk, or are composed of individuals deemed at risk. Victims of crime, smokers, abused children, gay men, intravenous drug users, the unemployed, indigenous people and so on are all subject to these technologies of agency, the object being to transform their status, to make them active citizens capable, as individuals and communities, of managing their own risk. Second, the two types of technologies of agency can be combined, e.g. in the government of the unemployed (Dean, 1995). The long-term unemployed enter into agreements to subject themselves to technologies of citizenship (e.g. counselling to improve self-esteem, training to increase labour market skills, etc.). The advantage of this particular assemblage over earlier techniques of empowerment is that the contract (often underwritten with sovereign sanctions, e.g. the cutting-off of allowances, low grades, etc.) acts as a kind of 'obligatory passage point' (Callon, 1986) through which individuals are required to agree to a range of normalizing, therapeutic and training measures designed to empower them, enhance their self-esteem, optimize their skills and entrepreneurship and so on.

The technologies of performance

We are also witnessing a swarming of what I would like to call technologies of performance. These are the plural technologies of government designed to penetrate the enclosures of expertise fostered under the welfare state and to subsume the substantive domains of expertise (of the doctor, the nurse, the social worker, the school principal, the professor) to new formal calculative regimes (Rose and Miller, 1992). Here, the devolution of budgets, the setting of performance indicators, 'benchmarking', the establishment of 'quasi-markets' in expertise and service provision, the 'corporatization' and 'privatization' of formerly public services, and the contracting-out of services, are all more or less technical means for locking the moral and political requirements of the shaping of conduct into the optimization of performance. These technologies of performance, then, are utilized from above, as an indirect means of regulating agencies, of transforming professionals into 'calculating individuals' within 'calculable spaces', subject to particular 'calculative regimes', to use Peter Miller's (1992) language. Of great importance here is the explosion of audit first noted and analysed by Michael Power (1994). These technologies of performance present themselves as techniques of restoring trust (i.e. accountability, transparency and democratic control) in the activities of firms, service providers, public services and professionals. As such, they presuppose a culture of mistrust in professions and institutions that they themselves contribute to, produce and intensify.

This distinction between technologies of agency and technologies of performance allows us to examine two different but related strategies for the transformation of expertise and the regulation of the activities of professionals, service providers, technicians, experts, etc. The first one allows performance to dominate over agency and is, in this sense, utilized from 'above'. It is a particular strategy of what Miller and Rose have called 'government at a distance' (1990; Rose and Miller, 1992). By deploying the technologies of agency, in particular the contract, this strategy seeks to establish institutional spaces – government departments, community organizations, service deliverers – as self-managing local centres. On the other hand, these local centres are to be self-regulated and made accountable by the new technologies of performance that establish them as centres of calculation and subsume the substantive domains of expertise to new forms of formal rationality. It is a strategy that seeks to make these local centres into independent centres of budgetary calculation, 'budget units' or 'cost centres', in which the regulation of services and the management of budgets is undertaken by the polymorphism of the audit and various kinds of accounting.

Professionals are also regulated by a strategy that is deployed from below as it were. Here the language of sovereignty and its instruments are used. This takes the form of the enshrinement of the rights of consumers or users in the internal regulation of government departments and the service providers (whether private for-profit bodies or in the non-profit 'third sector') with which they contract (Yeatman, 1994: 107). Needs formation is no longer a matter of the scientifically informed production of truth by professionals employed under the welfare state; it is allowed to enter into a space of negotiated settlement conducted in the name of user rights. From below, the agency and voice of users and carers enter into contestation with professional practice and knowledge. From above, the rights of consumers and users become the criteria for the evaluation of performance of professionals and a technique by which authorities can be open to a rich source of innovation and critical information about changing demographics, markets and environments.

A *contemporary pluralism*

Finally, I want to draw attention to the way in which all of this has led to a new kind of pluralism or what Rose (1996a) has called a new 'politics of community'. The targeted populations, through technologies of agency, can be empowered by, or enter into partnership with, professionals, bureaucrats and service providers. With the help of the markets in services, agencies and expertise, they are enjoined to manage their own communities, e.g. as gay men, ethnic groups, drug users, users of mental health services, victims of abuse and domestic violence, perpetrators of the same, and victims of violent crime. In place of a unified welfare state, we have a series of fragmented and discontinuous agencies. These may be public, quasi-autonomous, for profit, or from the rapidly expanding community or 'third sector'. All of these are agencies and specialists for dealing with targeted groups. They employ technologies of agency to transform 'at-risk' and 'high-risk' groups into active citizens. These citizens are to become self-managing, to enter into political participation, and to demand action from governments. The eliciting of the participation of the 'gay community' in the fight against HIV/AIDS is perhaps a signal instance (Bartos, 1994; Ballard, 1998). So too might be the way the victim status and the 'refusal of victimhood' have become a necessary component of our practices surrounding crime and punishment.

Community is quite evidently a key term in what I have just described. However, it is crucial to recognize that it is not the primary unit of contemporary pluralism. Community, as much as the autonomous citizen, is a resultant of a detailed work of political construction. It is an attempt to stabilize and normalize particular sets of relations and practices and to establish relatively continuous regimes of authority. It works on the much more open and fluid identifications that characterize contemporary forms of sociality, which Maffesoli (1990; 1991) has termed 'aggregations'.

Indeed, nothing illustrates the dream of the 'death of society' and the governmental construction of community and its agency better than the sphere of criminal justice. There has been an extraordinary political reinstatement of victims of crime. The criminal is no longer the victim of environment, social conditions or heredity, to be punished and rehabilitated and returned to the society after paying his or her 'debt'. We have seen a kind of metamorphosis of *Homo criminalis* discovered a century earlier by criminology (Pasquino, 1980). Now, however, criminal behaviour is simply a manifestation of a level of risk that exists within populations. *Homo criminalis* is an element within each and all, to be removed and contained, to be eliminated and neutralized, even, if possible, *before* its manifestation in crime.

The victim of crime, however, now takes centre-stage. These victims need counselling and help (e.g. post-traumatic stress counselling). They have failed to manage their own risk as individuals, as households and as neighbourhoods (O'Malley, 1992). Thus they need to be empowered, form support groups, acquire a political voice, reclaim risky times and spaces (e.g. in feminist 'reclaim the night' marches, and in the use of private security firms, surveillance cameras, secure housing developments, 'neighbourhood watch' schemes). The agency of victims is then mobilized to demand harsher penalties through such measures as 'truth in sentencing', 'three strikes legislation', and even, in the USA particularly, capital punishment. Our practices of punishment are no longer in the service of a social restitution in which justice is decided and regulated by the executive and juridical arms of the state. Rather, they are a contest between a criminal manifesting danger and a community at risk demanding a new form of retribution and a new type of social defence. The 'state' acts as a neutralized and neutralizing referee in this contest. At least in this case, if not in others (e.g. the fight against AIDS), the refusal of victimhood has become central to the political mobilization of the status of victims.

We have thus been enjoined to think of ourselves as self-managing individuals and communities, enterprising persons and active citizens, and as members of a whole range of what Durkheim would have called 'intermediate groups' – households, families, work teams, associations, consumer groups and above all communities – rather than as members of a social and political community coincident with the national state. Now, however, these groups no longer mediate between society and the individual but represent a plurality of agents that are put into play in diverse strategies of government. Government, if one likes, has become more multiple, diffuse, facilitative and empowering. It is also, however, strangely more disciplinary, stringent and punitive. The national state takes on less a directive and distributive role, and more a coordinative, arbitratory and preventive one.

A post-welfarist regime of the social

In this chapter we have sought to offer a preliminary diagnosis of what marks the novelty of our present. Rather than accede to the hubris of 'meta-histories of promise' or the postmodernist dance of 'signs, speed and spectacles' discussed in Chapter 2, an analytics of government engages contemporary liberal rule as a general rationality or mentality on the one hand, and as a particular regime or assemblage of government on the other. From the perspective of the former, at least one variant of neo-liberalism can now conceive of government, perhaps for the first time in two centuries, as no longer a government of society. This is not without consequences or costs, and often forces a fundamental realignment of traditional conservative forces. This style of neo-liberalism ceases to be a government of society in that it no longer conceives its task in terms of a division between state and society or of a public sector opposed to a private one. The ideal here is to bridge these older divisions so that the structures and values of the market are folded back onto what were formerly areas of public provision and to reconfigure the latter as a series of quasi-markets in services and expertise. The market has ceased to be a kind of 'fenced-off nature reserve' kept at arm's length from the sphere of public service; instead, the contrivance of markets becomes the technical means for the reformation of all types of provision (e.g. Burchell, 1994). To be sure, the point of doing this is to prevent excessive government by ensuring the most efficient use of resources. But it is also, and perhaps more importantly, to reform institutional and individual conduct so that both come to embody the values and orientations of the market, expressed in notions of the enterprise and the consumer.

The goal of neo-liberal critique of the welfare state is a displacement of social policy and social government by the task of cultural reformation. Where neo-conservatism uses exhortation, sometimes religious, and sovereign instruments in its 'culture wars' to fight the effects of dependency, addiction and the 'counter-culture', neo-liberalism tries to render this objective of cultural reform practicable by means of a form of governmental constructivism. For example, it is no longer enough to provide services and expertise to assist the unemployed to exercise their freedom on the labour market; access to such services and expertise must take the form of a market so that the unemployed can *learn* to exercise their freedom on such a market as a consumer. If the market is the embodiment of rules of conduct that guarantee freedom, then the reconfiguration of the social must take the form of markets. This will underwrite the cultural reformation. This is what I mean by the folding back of the objectives of government upon themselves. It is the first example of what we mean by reflexive government. Reflexive government is hence not the addition of more reflection to the way in which we govern and are governed, but the turning of the ends of government upon themselves and the transit of the conception of the governmental domain from processes exterior to political authority to the instruments of government themselves.

From the perspective of the analysis of forms of contemporary rationalities of government, there are indications that it is now possible to consider the task of national government to be to govern without governing society. This may take the form of the proposition that a theoretical knowledge of society is impossible, after Hayek, or the dictum that rather than depend on society people must rely on themselves, in the manner of Mrs Thatcher. More fundamentally, it registers the displacement we have just noted in which the task of national government is less to govern social and economic processes external to itself than to secure the institutions and mechanisms of social and economic government themselves. Part of the security of such mechanisms is to ensure that they take a form which is consistent with the objectives of government and which promotes individual and institutional conduct that is consistent with those objectives. Hence we find ourselves in a world in which the problematization of the inefficiency, bureaucracy, rigidity, unaccountability and dependency said to be characteristic of the welfare state leads to solutions that entail the contrivance of markets and the development of a governmental consumerism.

From the perspective of advanced liberal regimes of government, we witness the utilization of two distinct, yet intertwined technologies: technologies of agency, which seek to enhance and improve our capacities for participation, agreement and action; and technologies of performance, in which these capacities are made calculable and comparable so that they might be optimized. If the former allow the transmission of flows of information from the bottom, and the formation of more or less durable identities, agencies and wills, the latter make possible the indirect regulation and surveillance of these entities. These two technologies are part of a strategy in which our moral and political conduct is put into play as elements within systems of governmental purposes (Dean, 1996b).

Together these technologies forge a new linkage between the regulation of conduct and the technical requirements of the optimization of performance. These technologies form components of the assemblage of current governmental practices together with the polymorphous rationality of risk. This assemblage is a condition of and conditioned by a form of pluralism that acts upon our loose forms of identification and obligation to construct certain types of durable entities (e.g. communities, households, regions) which discover themselves as social and political actors in partnership with markets in services and expertise.

We are working our way toward something of a diagnosis of the transformation of the rationalities and practices of rule in our present. It is not too big a jump, however, to suggest that the ethos of the welfare state has been displaced by one of 'performance government' and that we have witnessed, not the death of the social, but the emergence of a post-welfarist regime of the social. With a welfarist version of the social, a unitary apparatus sought to act through and upon 'the social' to secure society. With the new regime, multiple agencies seek to put our actions into play so that they might be acted upon and rendered calculable and comparable, and so that we might optimize our capacities for performance as various types of persons and aggregations. Here the 'social' and its agencies (social workers, nurses, counsellors, community bodies, government departments, educational authorities, even social movements and support groups) become our partners and facilitators, as well as being tutors in the multiple forms of risk. The 'social' is no longer the diverse sector that is subject to the ineluctable logic of bureaucratic rationalization under the aegis of the welfare state. Rather, the social is reconfigured as a series of 'quasi-markets' in the provision of services and expertise by a range of publicly funded, non-profit and private for-profit, organizations and bodies. The problematic of security is shifting from that of securing the economic and social processes external to the state, and the forms of 'natural liberty' on which they depend, to one of constructing centres of agency and activity, of making them durable, and of implanting continuous relations of authority. These centres are then placed under the discrete and indirect surveillance of regulatory authorities in order to normalize, stabilize, and optimize activities, identities and power relations.

We have already suggested that the control of risks of the governmental economy of liberalism gave rise to two great strategies of government in the twentieth century, both of which take off from forms of knowledge of the population. The first tries to govern the population in such a way as to optimize the life of some, while disallowing the life of others, by acting upon biological processes of heredity. The second endeavours to act upon the social environment in such a way as to make safe or compensate for the harms to the life of a population generated by industrial society. Among the most privileged instruments of such a strategy is the technology of social insurance. That these two strategies of the assurance of life have given way to new, dispersed forms of the government of risk indicates the emergence of something new in the trajectory of the arts of government.

We have begun our diagnosis of the contours of governmental change at the end of the twentieth century. Neo-liberal rationalities of government offer liberal democracies their first example of a new style of government – one characterized by a 'folding back' of the objectives of government upon its means. My hypothesis is that just as early liberalism represented the first event in a series of the governmentalization of the state, so neo-liberalism represents the first event in a new series of the governmentalization of government. The rediscovery of community and the development of a general communitarian rationality, the notion of an ethical government or a government that consolidates and works through a common morality, suggest others. In order to explore further this new series, we shall follow these themes of the pluralization, individualization and dispersion of risk and the emergence of reflexive government in the following chapter.

Notes

1 The use of the term 'advanced liberalism' to designate the assemblage of rationalities and technologies of contemporary liberal rule was first introduced into the lexicon of the literature on governmentality by Rose (1993), who drew upon the characterization of the 'advanced psychiatric society' in Castel et al. (1982). The present author is responsible for the broad distinction employed here between neo-liberalism and advanced liberalism. Although neo-liberalism might be a dominant mentality of contemporary government, we have witnessed the rise of a range of alternatives from communitarianism (Etzioni, 1996) to neo- and even theo-conservatism that define themselves in opposition to it (Cruikshank, 1998).
2 I thank Pat O'Malley for this reference.
3 I am referring to the writings of Robert D. Putnam (1996) and Amitai Etzioni (1995; 1996), both of whom appear to have been influential in labour and left-liberal circles in the UK and the USA. In the latter case, Thatcher is placed next to Jeremy Bentham on the axis of society-as-fiction individualism (Etzioni, 1996: 11). However, Etzioni does not attempt to provide an account of society and offers a definition of community from which Mrs Thatcher and other 'neo-liberals' are hardly likely to demur. Community is a 'web of affect-laden relationships' and 'a

measure of commitment to shared values, norms, and meanings, and a shared history and identity' (1996: 127). The fuss about Victorian 'virtues' associated with the Conservative Prime Minister, and her commendation of voluntary work and association (see Thatcher, 1985), suggest a broad measure of agreement with the communitarian programme as laid out by Etzioni.

4   There are still those who are not capable of exercising such a form of freedom because of their youth, lack of motivation or lack of attachment to the work ethic. From the perspective of conservative policies, it is legitimate for this population, or at least a segment of it, to be forced to work. In March 1997, the new conservative (Liberal–National) government introduced the self-explanatory Social Security Legislation Amendment (Work for the Dole) Bill 1997 into parliament. It was later passed.

9 RISK AND REFLEXIVE GOVERNMENT

The story of government in the twentieth century might be understood as an attempt to find a mode of government able to offer an assurance of the life of the population. In Nazism we find the most radical attempt at the assurance of the life of the race by first disallowing and then eliminating the life of others. Nazism stands at the terrible endpoint of a trajectory which seeks to minimize harm, and control the risks to a population (including those posed by other populations), by acting upon its mechanisms of heredity to improve its fitness and efficiency. It is perhaps the most clear, but not the only, example of Foucault's suggestion that our societies have proved truly demonic in their attempts to articulate elements of sovereignty with those of bio-politics. However, it is the case that many liberal states have found other techniques for the assurance of the life of the population and the aversion of the risks associated with unemployment, poverty, ill-health, old age, sickness, accidents and so on. Without underplaying the sheer incidence of racial intolerance, systemic discrimination and racial murder within liberal-democratic countries in the twentieth century, and without denying the degree to which liberal and social-democratic states have witnessed practices akin to a 'negative eugenics' (the prevention of procreation among certain populations), it is true that most forms of liberal government have applied rather different techniques to the management of the risk associated with twentieth-century life. Social government or the government of the various risks posed to populations took a form that is quite distinct from the racial social policies we examined in Chapter 7.

This chapter addresses risk as a governmental rationality, particularly as it is incarnated in the technology of social insurance. This provides us with a key perspective on the transformation of forms of social government in the twentieth century. It also allows us to begin to chart something of a nascent shift in the trajectory of government: the manner in which the government of processes, which reinscribed and encased the dispositional and householding government of the state, is now itself subject to another line of modification. The governmentalization of the state is now joined by a new and significant process: the govermentalization of government. The government through processes is itself being redefined by a government of government or a 'reflexive government', to use (and slightly modify) a concept coined and first employed by Samantha Ashenden (1996).

To orient ourselves to the field marked out by risk rationality, by the social and by reflexive government, we shall here first examine the influential sociological theses of Ulrich Beck on 'risk society'. I shall suggest that the sociological account of risk society and the analytics of governmental practices of risk have something to learn from one another. The second section uses François Ewald's analysis of insurance practices to begin to draw out the implications of social insurance for the emergence of social government and associated notions of solidarity and society. This again raises the question of the rise and possible fall of the social in the twentieth century. In a final section, we consider the notion of 'reflexive government'. Here I suggest that Beck provides us with a figure of thought that might be usefully adapted to the concerns of an analytics of government. Beck writes of reflexive modernization, meaning nothing more than the modernization of modernity, and in doing so hopes to avoid the sterile debates over modernism and postmodernism. While not acceding to this diagnosis – or the problematic of modernity in which it is located – we can usefully introduce the notion of 'reflexive government' or the governmentalization of government into the lexicon of an analytics of government. This notion indicates a process that entails a shift of the liberal and social problematics of security from the security of social and economic processes to the security of governmental mechanisms.

Two approaches to risk

> Nothing is a risk in itself; there is no risk in reality. But on the other hand, anything *can* be a risk; it all depends on how one analyses the danger, considers the event. (Ewald, 1991: 199, original emphasis)

There is no such thing as risk in reality. This is the starting point with regard to the series that defines risk. Risk is a way – or rather, a set of different ways – of ordering reality, of rendering it into a calculable form. It is a way of representing events in a certain form so they might be made governable in particular ways, with particular techniques and for particular goals. It is a component of diverse forms of calculative rationality for governing the conduct of individuals, collectivities and populations. It is thus not possible to speak of incalculable risks, or of risks that escape our modes of calculation, and even less possible to speak of a social order in which risk is largely calculable and contrast it with one in which risk has become largely incalculable.

A second proposition that follows from the first: the significance of risk lies not with risk *itself* but with what risk gets attached to. Risk, to put it in Kantian terms, is a category of our understanding rather than intuition or sensibility (cf. Ewald, 1991: 199). If the task of critique is to investigate the historical conditions of true knowledge, then the critique of risk will investigate the different modes of calculation of risk and the moral and political technologies within which such calculations are to be found. Most importantly, it will investigate the regimes of practices in which risk is imbricated and the political programmes and social imaginaries that deploy risk and its techniques and draw their inspiration from it. What is important about risk is not risk itself. Rather it is: the forms of knowledge that make it thinkable, such as statistics, sociology, epidemiology, management and accounting; the techniques that discover it, from the calculus of probabilities to the interview; the technologies that seek to govern it, including risk screening, case management, social insurance and situational crime prevention; and the political rationalities and programmes that deploy it, from those that dreamt of a welfare state to those that imagine an advanced liberal society of prudential individuals and communities.

This leads us to another point. If what is significant about risk is its connection with all these things, then our analysis of risk must rid itself of the opposition between the calculable and the incalculable in order to understand those practices, techniques and rationalities that seek to make the incalculable calculable, and the different ways they do so. This central point will be made by comparing two forms of analysis of risk, a contemporary sociological one derived from the influential writings of Ulrich Beck, and the analytics of government that we have been following in the present book. In the first, risk is viewed within a general schema and narrative of phases of modernity and as a feature of the ontological condition of humans within current social forms. In the second, risk is analysed as a component of assemblages of practices, techniques and rationalities concerned with how we govern. In the sociological account, risk forms an axial principle that characterizes types of society and the processes they are undergoing. According to an analytics of government, risk is a calculative rationality that is tethered to assorted techniques for the regulation, management and shaping of human conduct in the service of specific ends and with definite, but to some extent unforeseen, effects. In the sociological account, we can talk of a 'risk society' in a realist sense, that is, as an actually existing global entity – or at least a global entity nascent within processes of modernization. In an analytics of government, notions of risk can be made intelligible as specific representations that render reality in such a form as to make it amenable to types of action and intervention. As we suggested in Chapter 8, it is possible that the proliferation of rationalities of risk has become linked to the end of the problematic of society as a general way of thinking about the field of political action and governmental interventions. Thus one of the leading practitioners of the governmental approach has ventured to raise the question of 'the death of the social' (Rose, 1996a).[1]

The sociological account of risk society and the governmental account of risk as calculative rationality have something to offer our understanding of the fate of the social and each has something to learn from the other. Beck's sociology can learn from the emphasis on the analysis of the particular practices, techniques and rationalities through which risk becomes constructed as a governable entity. Yet Beck's sociology reveals certain limitations in existing applications of the analytics of government. To emphasize the specificity of particular practices and rationalities of risk would seem to deny the possibility of offering any general understanding of the processes of the transformation of contemporary governmental practices. In this respect, Beck provides us with a 'thought-figure' that might be usefully adapted to governmental concerns. Reflexive government means that the central target and objective of national government becomes the reform of the performance of the existing governmental institutions and techniques, that such reform entails a folding back of the objectives of government upon its means, and that government is made operable through the activation of the energies and capacities of existing agencies and institutions. While liberal government has sought to rationalize and reform existing mechanisms of government, it did this so that such institutions would not unduly interfere with the economic and other processes on which effective government depended and through which it operated. If reflexive government works through forms of liberty it is not because such liberty is necessary to the working of processes external to the institutions of government, but because various kinds of responsible autonomy and choice allow the most effective operation of institutions and practices. The distinguishing feature of reflexive government is that the point of the reform of the institutions and mechanisms of government is to secure them in the face of processes that are deemed beyond governmental control, of which the governmental rationality of economic globalization is paradigmatic. As far as the social is concerned, reflexive government means the rejection of a welfarist regime and its reconfiguration as a series of markets in services and provision that relies upon the rational choices and calculations of individuals within various collectivities and forms of indigenous government. The hypothesis of 'reflexive government', moreover, does not imply that government has ceased to try to change society. Quite the contrary.

Risk and reflexive modernization

First, however, let us briefly recall certain aspects of Beck's well-known account of risk and its presuppositions and some of the more general features of the literature on governmentality. The sociological account of risk is concerned to displace what might be called 'post-ism', i.e. the view we are living in a period that can be best characterized by what it displaces, postmodernity, post-industrialism, *post-histoire* and so forth (Beck, 1988: 86; 1992b: 9). It attempts to give a positive account of the present, or at least of what is novel in the present, and to situate that positive account in relation to previous accounts of modernization and modernity. However, the sociological account shares with modernization theory the view that it is indeed possible to give a general characterization of that present, and that earlier modernization theories derived from Marx and Max Weber were more or less adequate to a previous phase of industrial society, failing only to grasp the extent to which the legitimation of progress in industrial capitalism was secured by an instrumental rationality that claimed to control the risks it produced. Beck argues that:

> In advanced modernity the social production of wealth is systematically accompanied by the social production of risks. Accordingly, the problems and conflicts relating to distribution in a society of scarcity overlap with the problems and conflicts that arise from the production, definition, and distribution of techno-scientifically produced risks. (1992b: 19)

So begins *Risk Society*. According to Beck, there are two phases of modernization. The first phase – classical modernization – brought about industrial society, facing a premodern society that is described as traditional. In premodern societies, risk as such does not exist. According to Beck, we can talk of hazards but not risks in a world in which the fundamental threats to human existence are ones that result from natural and unpredictable disasters such as plagues, famines, earthquakes, floods and other acts of God (Beck, 1992a: 98). The first phase of modernization demystifies the traditional ranks and hierarchies and the fixed identities that accompany them and also transforms the relations between humans and nature. Social and personal identities come to be formed in relation to the spheres of the production and distribution of wealth and of reproduction. These identities are thus ones of class with its own cultures and traditions and of gender formed in the nuclear family with its divisions of labour. Wealth production is driven by a will to control and manipulate nature under the imperatives of economic growth. This control of nature is effected through the understanding of science and its application in technology. Science and technology thus replace religion in the legitimation of industrial society. The control of nature is a component of an Enlightenment narrative of progress. However, industrial technology also generates risks that, according to this Enlightenment narrative, can be made controllable by an instrumental rationality. Scientific knowledge of diverse types (i.e. the natural, social and human sciences) is enlisted in the establishment of a calculus of risk that results in making the unforeseen hazards of industrial society compatible with this Enlightenment narrative. Modernity promises not the elimination of the hazards of industrial technology and production but the calculation and therefore just distribution of the risks involved. Thus insurance, particularly social insurance, represents a 'social compact against industrially produced hazards and damages' which lies at the core of the consensus on progress (1992a: 100).

For Beck, unlike earlier theorists, the second contemporary stage of modernization faces not a world of traditional mores, beliefs and hierarchies but industrial society itself, its science and technology, and its politics and culture. Modernity now exists in an agonistic relation to an earlier modernity, industrial society. Hence this stage of modernization is 'reflexive modernization', a modernization of modernity. Beck discusses reflexive modernization as a 'creative (self-)destruction' of the epoch of industrial society, a 'radicalization of modernity' without revolution or even necessarily with the mandatory crisis and systems failures, and an undercutting of the features of that epoch (1994: 2–3). What is appealing about this notion of reflexive modernization is not simply its bypassing of now sterile debates or its theoretical elegance;

it is that it begins to identify a line of emergence that is unintended but involves contests over the status of knowledge. These contestations make the future an open horizon. Reflexivity is hence sharply distinguished from reflection. To speak of reflexivity is thus not to say that society has become more reflective or thoughtful or necessarily better informed about decision-making. Rather, it is to say that modernity finds itself in a state of 'self-confrontation with the effects of risk society that cannot be assimilated in the system of industrial society' (1994: 5). Beck enjoins us to participate in a reflection on reflexive modernization, but it is clear that reflexivity can proceed with or without reflection. The former is not necessarily entailed in the latter.

Here 'risk' figures as the key term. Under industrial society, according to Beck, the production of risks is subordinate to the production of wealth to the extent that risks are taken to be the predictable and limited but necessary side-effects of technical and economic progress. Risks are a matter for the experts and thus for scientific legitimation. However, the risks associated with nuclear power and chemical and biotechnological production begin to have 'global' effects and become subject to public debate that encompasses the problematization of scientific knowledge. What we might understand as issues of ecological crisis, and the contestations between citizen initiatives and formal authority, are at the heart of the new risk society. Because these risks cannot be contained within the boundaries of the old nation or avoided by simply having access to property and wealth, the logic of their distribution is supranational and different from that of class or status. I take up this theme of the 'globalization' of risk in the next part of this chapter.

The nascent risk society is not simply characterized, however, by a transformation of the 'axial principle' of industrial modernity but also unleashes a range of social, cultural and political dynamics which I shall not go into here. These include the individualization of social inequality and identity, the emergence of citizens' movements that arise from a new consciousness of risk, and the loss of the scientific monopoly on truth and science's aura of unchallengeability. Of particular salience here is the emergence of a 'sub-politics' in which citizens' initiatives and social movements put onto the agenda the ethical, political and environmental effects of the transformations in scientific knowledge and its application in technological domains.

Beck's methodological approach to risk rests upon three major presuppositions. The first is the *totalizing* assumption that risk should be approached within a narrative of the modernization process that brings about a 'risk society'. Following from this is the assumption of the *uniformity* of risk so that it is possible to make a general and abstract characterization of risk in a given type of society, i.e. that risk has fundamentally the same characteristics in all spheres. Despite his dissent from the assumption of the untroubled efficacy of scientific knowledge, and his emphasis on truth contestation and fragmentation, Beck follows the Weber/Frankfurt School view to the extent that all kinds of reason compose a hegemonic form of instrumental rationality (*Zweckrationalität*) – with often demonic effects. In a discussion of genetic engineering, for example, Beck notes the over-generality of

Horkheimer and Adorno's account of Nazism, but still insists that genetic engineering 'must be understood to issue from the Enlightenment as applied to technology' (1995: 29). This kind of totalization leads, among other things, to a view that insists that the choice/consumerist aspect of current genetic (and other pre-natal) screening is largely illusory and that screening for hereditary disease is 'objectively eugenics'. Among other things, this approach seems to beg the question of why the new genetics takes a liberal, pro-choice tack rather than an authoritarian, state-imposed one.

Finally, there is the *realist* assumption that the reason why risk is a feature of quotidian existence in this risk society, and a component of individual and collective experience and identities, is that real riskiness has increased so much that it has outrun the mechanisms of its calculation and control.[2] By this I mean not that Beck fails to recognize the socially produced and culturally constructed nature of risk but rather that he wants to treat risk ontologically. Thus we can talk of the reality of industrial risk society because it has produced massive, physical, incalculable and illimitable hazards for which it can no longer provide precaution.

The point here is not that these assumptions are mistaken but that they are relatively unhelpful for the analysis of risk. However, it is not difficult to displace all three and to reveal an alternative perspective on the question of risk. Instead of a totalizing approach of risk, it is easy to show the virtue of focusing on the concrete and empirical and analysing specific types of risk rationalities and practices. Instead of assuming that the empirical varieties of risk are but instances of one type of instrumental rationality, it is possible to demonstrate that risk rationalities are not only multiple but heterogeneous and that practices for the government of risk are assembled from diverse elements and put together in different ways. There is a complex relation between Weber and critical theory (from Adorno to Habermas) and the Foucauldian analysis of rationality.[3] For present purposes one could note that in the former we witness the search for the normative content of reason, the tendency towards dialectical unification of processes of rationalization, and the privileging of the abstract and general. In the latter, by contrast, we find a resolutely substantive analysis of dispersed forms of reason, often taking a practical and technical form and found in multiple and intersecting genealogies. Finally, against the assumption of realism, it is easy to show the virtue of adopting a more nominalist position, i.e. one that analyses forms of risk as among the ways in which we are required to know and to act upon ourselves and others today in a range of moral and political programmes and social technologies (Dean, 1998b). All three assumptions are sustained, however, by a simple dichotomy, the identification of which allows us to specify a more fruitful way forward.

Drawing on the work of a contributor to the 'governmentality' literature, François Ewald, on the emergence of social insurance, Beck argues that private and public insurance practices were essential to the legitimation of the technical and economic development of industrial society and to the achievement of a consensus on progress (1992a: 100). Industrial society finds ways of calculating risks and a technology for creating present security in the face of the future hazards that are the result of that society. 'Modernity,' Beck claims, 'which brings uncertainty to every niche of existence, finds its counter-principle in a *social compact against industrially produced hazards and damages*, stitched together out of public and private insurance agreements' (1992a: 100, original emphasis). By contrast, a risk society becomes an uninsured society. It cannot insure against the 'worst imaginable accident' or the megahazards of nuclear power or the chemical industries because they abolish the 'four pillars of the calculus of risks' – compensation, limitation, security and calculation (1992a: 102). According to Beck, risks are now global in the sense that it is no longer possible to localize them spatially and temporally. The scenario of the 'worst imaginable accident', such as the Chernobyl meltdown, or the hazards attendant upon the destruction of the ozone layer, means that the 'accident becomes an event with beginning and no end; an "open-ended festival" of creeping, galloping and overlapping waves of destruction' (1992a: 102). Such events are not amenable to monetary compensation because damage can no longer be limited. There can be no security against risks because it is impossible to plan against the effects of the fatal hazards of the worst imaginable accident. Finally, there can be no standards of normality for measuring procedures against risk. Calculation, for Beck, becomes obsfucation.

We can note several things about this account. First, risk, which was once calculable, has become incalculable and it is this becoming incalculable that is at the heart of the transformation of society. Contrary to Beck's express intention to produce a positive account of the present that avoids what I have called 'post-ism', his risk society is perhaps more adequately characterized as a post-risk-calculation society. Second, this dichotomy rests on a double confusion. The first part of the confusion is the identification of risk with insurer's risks so that the possibility of events that can no longer be insured indicates the existence of incalculable risks. The other part of the confusion follows from this: risk is identified with quantitative forms of calculation. I shall address below both these aspects of confusion in the course of discussing the diversity of risk rationalities today. For now, I want to turn to François Ewald's account to exemplify an alternative and, in some ways, more satisfactory approach.

Insurance and government

In light of these comments, first consider Ewald's (1991) account of insurance and the emergence of social insurance. What is crucial is that he locates notions of risk in insurance with those of chance, probability, hazard and randomness rather than with notions of danger and peril (1991: 199). By this, I mean he locates risk as a form of calculation about reality rather than as a naturally occurring entity. If we make a distinction between modes of calculating and objective conditions, Beck's risk society is more properly conceived as one in which there is an increase in dangers arising from the development of the productive forces. For Ewald, by contrast, risk is a form of rationality, a way of thinking about and representing events. To say that risk is calculable is to say that it is a form of reasoning that allows us to make events calculable in a specific way. It is thus not possible to contrast calculable risks and incalculable risks. For insurance rationality, everything can be treated as a risk and the task of insurers has been both to 'produce' risks and to find ways of insuring what has previously been thought to be uninsurable. In insurance, risk is a form of calculation based on a statistical table that establishes the regularity of events and a calculus of probabilities in order to evaluate the chances of an event actually occurring (1991: 202). This account thus first contrasts with that of Beck in its preparedness to examine the particular form of *calculative rationality* in which notions of risk are found. Thus risk can give rise to or be a component in multiple forms of calculative rationality and should not be assigned to the calculable–incalculable dichotomy.

Insurance might be approached as an attempt to make the incalculable calculable. Ewald (1991: 204–5) argues that what is insured is not the actually lived and suffered injury itself but risk as a capital against whose loss the insurer offers a guarantee. The effects of the loss of a limb, or of a parent, are indeed incalculable. Nevertheless, viewed from the perspective of insurance, it is possible to compensate for such losses by assigning them a price based on the calculus of probabilities of such an event and the contractually agreed contribution of the insured. That this compensation can never truly compensate for the suffering is clear from the history of conflicts between insurers and the insured. Insurance risk does not mark the limited historical moment between premodern hazards and contemporary incalculable risk. Rather, it is an effort to render what is felt to be incalculable, what is understood to have no price, amenable to calculation and monetary compensation. The suffering of the injury can never be limited, only the indemnity for a loss of a specific form of capital.

Such forms of the rationality of risk do not exist as an ideal construct. This leads us to a second departure from Beck's approach: the requirement that we investigate *the technical and practical dimension of governing risk*. In Ewald's account risk is indissociable from the practices of insurance and from the techniques that allow us to intervene in a world rendered amenable to risk calculations. Indeed one might wish to say that the rationality of risk is bound up with a host of technical means for intervening in reality for the achievement of specific ends. Thus we have just noted that insurance risk depends upon particular calculative techniques such as the statistical table and the calculus of probabilities (1991: 204). Moreover, insurance itself can be regarded as technical in several different ways (1991: 206–8). First, it is an economic and financial technique to create a remuneration for risk. Second, it is a moral technology in that it is a means by which an individual can conduct his or her life in such a way as to maintain responsibility in the face of ill fortune. Third, it is a technique for the indemnification and reparation of damages. In this regard it is a mode of administering justice 'under which the damage suffered by one is borne by all, and individual responsibility is borne by all' (1991: 207). All of this makes insurance, finally, a political technology in that it is a way of combining and using social forces in a specific fashion, one in which the possibility of the optimization of individual responsibility is combined with a maximization of social solidarity. Insurance is thus a 'form of association which combines a maximum of socialization with a maximum of individualization' (1991: 204).

Ewald's account furthermore enables us to link the risk rationality of insurance to specific *forms of identity, agency and expertise* (1991: 201–2). Insurance practices displace the abstract, invariant norm of a responsible juridical subject with an individuality relative to other members of an insured population, an 'average sociological individuality'. In legal judgements concerning damages, the victim and the author of an accident are singularized and isolated and placed into an opposition. It is a matter of finding where, if any, fault lies. In insurance, risk is a characteristic of the population, a form of regularity that no one can escape but which each individual bears differently. Individuals are thus both members of the population and distinguished by the probability of risk that is their share. Insurance associations give rise to a kind of mutuality between members by which they benefit from association but which leaves each individual free. The movement then is from a notion of fault based on legal subjectivity to one of the socialization of risk.

Insurance risk is always collective. It implies a social rule of justice rather than a natural one. In legal judgements, the judge must apportion blame or responsibility for an accident to a particular party and fix damages according to a table which sets the rate for certain kinds of loss, e.g. of a hand, a leg, a life. The accident itself is to be regarded as a unique event that disturbs an otherwise harmonious order. Law seeks the restoration of that order by means of restitution to the victim. Insurance, in contrast, indemnifies the individual according to a contractually agreed tariff worked out in relation to the calculus of risk. The judge's position is taken over by the actuary who calculates tables or scales of compensation.

One can readily appreciate, then, why such a political technology would come to be taken up in the social legislation of many Western European nation-states at the end of the nineteenth century. In issues of workers' compensation against industrial accidents, insurance renders the relation between the employer and employee not as a class struggle between worker and boss, or as a matter of individual responsibility, but as a technical, calculable matter in which insurance experts assign a person an insurance identity and compensate accordingly. The struggle then becomes one of the worker seeking to receive as much as possible from the insuring association. Social insurance emerges and is deployed as a technology of solidarity that renders accidents, illness, unemployment and other ills associated with social life as insurable risks that are collectively borne and individually indemnified.

This rationality of risk, bound to a technology for creating solidarity out of individual contributions, is thus at the heart of the emergence of what we have called, after Rose (1993), 'social government', with its related notions of social justice. Several further points can be made about this insurance rationality of risk. First, insurance risk is a means of creating social right and social citizenship. It enables the construction of social rights – but in a way that undermines certain elements of the evolutionist story of citizenship put forward in T. H. Marshall's (1963) classic essay. Civil and political rights and liberties accrue to citizens as individuals, e.g. the right to enter into contracts, freedom of speech, religion and assembly, and the right to vote or participate in politics. Under social insurance, individuals are entitled to social provision in a quite different fashion – as a member of a collectivity defined by profession, age and so on. The political imaginary is of a contractual form of justice established no longer by a natural order of rights but by the conventions of society, and of an ideal of a society in which each member's burdens and shares are fixed by a social contract which is no longer a political myth but something made real by technical means. Risk and insurance technology become a social solution to the problems of capitalist industry, particularly of poverty and working class insecurity. If the emergence of social citizenship, according to Giovanna Procacci (1993; 1998), concerns the problem of inequality in a society of equals, then insurance surely is the most perfect technical realization of social rights. Each individual is a member of an association by which all agree to accept responsibility for each other's burdens. Yet because risk is distributed unequally the proportional share that each will receive varies according to the insurance calculus. This is why, at the end of the nineteenth century, particularly in the Third Republic in France, social insurance will emerge as the principal political technology of establishing social rights and providing solutions to the problems of poverty and inequality. The socialization of risk does not seek to undermine capitalist inequality. Precisely the opposite: it is a means of treating the effects of that inequality.

The success of social insurance as a political technology, however, was neither a feature of its efficiency as a political technology in its 'dedramatization of social conflicts' nor a matter of the teleology of citizenship. The success in France was only made possible by a process which Daniel Defert calls the 'demutualization of the workers' movement' – a dual process during the nineteenth century by which employers sought to take over the mutual benefit societies of the workers, which often doubled as a source of strike funds, and by which insurance companies started offering indemnification against risks in competition with employers' benevolent funds. The strategy of insurance rests upon a dissociation and reconstitution of the fabric of working class association (Defert, 1991: 213). It is for this reason that workers' organizations only gradually accepted the law on industrial accident compensation and embraced it only after it had been passed without their support (1991: 211). Social insurance may be a technical solution to the problems of inequality and poverty but it is a particular solution. Risk techniques are taken up under given historical conditions, in the service of particular political rationalities and by various social forces and agents in the course of historical struggles.

There is a last and important feature on the landscape of this genealogy of insurance risk that I can only briefly mention here. The socialization of risk is, as it were, welded onto general and abstract forms of political and social rationality that provide disciplines such as sociology and the 'new social economy' with an image of society, and politicians and jurists with a doctrine of state (Donzelot, 1988; 1991). It is in this sense that notions of 'society' can be viewed as much as an artefact of risk as vice versa. The Third Republic in France, which implements a programme of social insurance, is also the period of the invention of a notion of society as a reality *sui generis*. Emile Durkheim understands solidarity as a general social law of development. Society is characterized by a shift, never fully completed, from mechanical to organic solidarity, from a principle of sameness to a principle of the interdependence of different parties. Thus mechanical solidarity arises from the common feeling between members in a similar situation. This commonality is overlaid by another in which organic solidarity is forged through the interdependence of different and unequal members bound by the division of labour.

At a midway point between Durkheim's notion of society and the calculative rationality of insurance risk lies the progressive republican doctrine of state, Léon Bourgeois's *solidarisme*. The privileged technical form of intervention in the Third Republic is social insurance. Given their close historical proximity and their common linkage in the notion of solidarity, it is tempting to read the implementation of social insurance in Durkheimian terms. To do so, one would view social insurance as a technology of solidarity for all individuals in a society that renders accidents, illness, unemployment and other ills the result of the collective reality of the new division of labour. Social insurance thus expresses a form of organic solidarity and social legislation can be justified by this means. On the other hand, individuals receive entitlements not as individuals but as members of different collective bodies defined by profession, occupation or age. Thus social insurance also recognizes and reinforces the bonds between members of the same institutions and groups – their mechanical solidarity. Social insurance as a political technology can thus produce and reconcile two diverse images of society and forms of solidarity.

Insurance risk tells us a number of things about the nature of social government. It poses its technical character and the manner in which social government depends upon particular forms of calculative rationality. It illustrates the way social identities and social citizenship come to take a form that is irreducible to the civil, political and legal identities of the liberal subject. Moreover, it allows us to stress the way such identities are forged in relation to a particular set of relations among a collectivity: the relations of solidarity that exist among and go beyond the relations between the members of a population within the territorial borders of the sovereign nation-state. The story of social insurance and workers' compensation for industrial accidents shows how the social and the technical form it is given is the outcome of political struggles between diverse agents. Finally it demonstrates how these apparently minor and technical practices such as insurance exist in a complex fashion with not only practical forms of knowledge and calculation but often quite abstract forms of knowledge that address moral and political questions.

Social insurance is not the only technology of social government. Yet it is a particularly fecund one that had the virtue of encountering risk at the level of populations that both optimized solidarity and left the individual free. To the extent to which it avoids the eugenic approach to social problems that would lead to the path of the elimination of those who came to represent social dangers and a risk to the population, it is a decisive and exemplary illustration of the potential of liberal techniques of government. In the conclusion to this book, I shall return more specifically to this question of social government and its possible 'death'.

The way in which we seek to represent and address the risks to the security and welfare of populations is also a particularly illuminating way of thinking about forms of government. However, as we shall note below, insurance risk is not the only type of risk rationality we can identify. The above sketch might suggest why it is important to analyse the specific form of risk rationalities rather than immersing our analysis in a global narrative of risk society. It is important to analyse four dimensions of the government of risk. The first is how we come to know about and act upon different conceptions of risk; i.e. the different forms of risk rationality, or the *episteme* of risk. The second is how such conceptions are linked to particular practices and technologies, the *techne* of risk. The third is how such practices and technologies give rise to new forms of social and political identity. The fourth is how such rationalities, technologies and identities become latched onto different political programmes and social imaginaries that invest them with a specific ethos. The analysis of risk thus illustrates many of the features of the analytics of government discussed in Chapter 1 of this book. I shall now turn to the phenomenon of the proliferation of rationalities of risk today as illustrative of the way the bio-political government of processes is being recoded by a reflexive government of the mechanisms of government.

Reflexive government

Despite having concentrated on insurance risk in preceding sections of this chapter, I have already suggested that it is mistaken to identify risk rationality with any one of its forms and to identify risk with the quantitative calculation of probabilities of actuarial or insurance risk. The existing governmentality literature has already investigated a number of different forms of risk rationality. This is not to suggest that this literature enables us to constitute an exhaustive typology of risk. Rather, by identifying its different forms, we might begin to understand the diversity of understandings of risk, how risk can be linked to quite different programmes and technologies, and the way the vocabulary of risk can cross and bind together quite distinct sets of practices. We can also begin to delineate some of the moral, political and social significance of contemporary practices of risk.

The first, as we have just seen, might be called *insurance risk*. One can contrast this kind of risk with another long-standing and pervasive form of risk rationality, *epidemiological risk*. Epidemiological risk is concerned with the rates of morbidity and mortality among populations. It is similar to insurance risk in that the calculus of risk is undertaken on the basis of a range of abstract factors and their correlation within populations and, indeed, can be linked to insurance risk in public and private practices of health insurance. However, it has its own distinctive rationality and set of techniques and interventions. It is not the losses of capital but the health outcomes of populations that are subject to risk calculation. Its technical means are public health interventions such as sanitation, quarantine measures, inspection of food supply, inoculation programmes and so on. More recently, as Castel (1991) suggests, it has become linked to the 'screening' of populations as procedures for observing and monitoring populations in order to engage in a 'systematic pre-detection' that eliminates or minimizes future pathologies through interventions on 'modifiable risk factors'. Epidemiological risk therefore has a preventive ethos rather than the restitutive ethos characteristic of insurance risk.

In contrast to these two quantitative forms of risk rationality, it is possible to identify another form that is principally qualitative. I shall call this, for want of a better term, *case-management risk*. This kind of risk again has a long history. It is linked to a clinical practice in which certain symptoms lead to the imputation of dangerousness, e.g. of the likelihood of a mentally ill person committing a violent act (Castel, 1991). Here risk concerns the qualitative assessment of individuals and groups, especially families, as falling within 'at-risk' categories. Risk techniques are closely allied to the use of case management in social security, social work, policing and the sphere of criminal justice. Those judged 'at risk' of being a danger to the wider community are subject to a range of therapeutic (e.g. counselling, self-help groups, support groups), sovereign (prisons, detention centres) and disciplinary (training and retraining) practices in an effort either to eliminate them completely from communal spaces (e.g. by various forms of confinement) or to lower the dangers posed by their risk of alcoholism, drug dependency, sexual diseases, criminal behaviour, long-term unemployment and welfare dependency. Rather than their replacement by newer risk technologies, we have witnessed something of a proliferation of case-management approaches beyond the older delineation of social work and clinical medicine, e.g. as a response to structural unemployment in Australia and other OECD countries (Dean, 1995).

Case-management risk draws upon the techniques of the interview, the exercise of bureaucratic or clinical judgement, the case note and the file. These techniques might be supplemented by other, less observational modes that employ techniques that are derived from quantitative analysis. In the case of the unemployed in Australia, bureaucratic judgement about being at 'high risk of long-term unemployment' is aided by the development of such instruments as the Jobseeker Classification Index, based on questions about factors that increase the risk of long-term unemployment, including age, education, access to labour markets, disability, country of birth, language abilities, Aboriginal status, duration of unemployment, work experience and stability of residence (Dean, 1998a).

In its combination of the use of bureaucratic judgement and instruments to assess the existence of risk factors, case-management risk may perhaps be regarded as a variation on what Weir (1996) has called *clinical risk*. Clinical risk relies on epidemiological calculus of risk but combines techniques of risk screening with both diagnostics and therapeutics. Its procedures are those of the 'circumscription of individual pathology'. Mobilizing risk screening techniques, and combining them with more traditional modes of face-to-face diagnosis, clinical risk seeks to attach risk to the bodies of individuals so they might become objects of more intensive surveillance and treatment. The Ontario Antenatal Record analysed by Weir is used as a case record that summarizes clinical observation and test results and presents qualitative categories of risk for maternal and foetal health (1996: 380). What is interesting about clinical risk is that it involves both quantitative analysis of the calculus of probabilities across a population to distinguish risk factors and qualitative judgements based on the clinical judgement of doctors and midwives.

Of course even those already mentioned do not exhaust the forms of risk rationality. Pearce and Tombs (1996), for example, have examined changing forms of risk management in the United States' chemical industry. Such a case would appear to strongly resemble those envisaged by Beck's scenario of a festival of destruction. The hazards of that industry constitute an 'actuarial nightmare', 'involving mass victims, multiple injuries, fuzzy loss, multicollinearity (complex causal chains) and latency' (1996: 438). Indeed, liability under tort law, the unwillingness of insurance companies to provide comprehensive general liability without significant exemptions, disasters such as Bhopal, pressure from citizens' groups and so on suggest that risk has indeed become incalculable. However, it is clear that even here Beck's case is overstated. Rejecting techniques of risk assessment to deal with low-probability/high-consequence events, the chemical companies have turned to comprehensive risk-management strategies that recognize worst case scenarios. Such strategies encompass attention to training, managerial and organization systems, emergency procedures such as evacuation plans, risk education and other contingency measures. Crucially, strategies of risk management include the participation of those previously excluded by a scientific-technological rationality of risk assessment, such as workers and local communities. The point to be made here is that comprehensive risk-management techniques may fail – just as case-management techniques cannot prevent long-term unemployment – but that does not mean that we should regard them as merely obsfucating. One feature of governmental rationalities is that they might be regarded as 'congenitally failing' (Miller and Rose, 1990). Failure (itself judged through a particular epistemological framework) does not mean the abandonment of the attempt to construct coherent programmes of government. Rather, its discovery is an incitement to the problematization, reformation and replacement of such programmes.[4]

It is clear that the genealogy of risk is much more complex than the theory of risk society allows. Risk and its techniques are plural and heterogeneous and its significance cannot be exhausted by a narrative of a shift from a quantitative calculation of risk to the globalization of incalculable risks. Having made such a statement, however, can we find that the analysis of these rationalities of risk will permit of generalization? A fundamental tenet of the governmentality literature, though not always remembered, is that calculative rationalities such as those of risk have a certain political polyvalence, i.e. they can be invested with different sets of purposes depending on the political programmes and rationalities they come to be latched onto (O'Malley, 1996). A central significance of the rationalities of risk today is that they have been attached to a set of political programmes and formulas of rule that represent a major retraction of social rights and the ideal of a welfare state that drove social provision for much of the now receding century. At the end of the nineteenth century in France the socialization of risk was linked to the invention of social forms of government. In the twilight of the twentieth century, we might say that the individualization of risk is linked to new forms of liberal government.

In Chapter 8, we have discussed this individualization and dispersion of risk as the new prudentialism. Among the preferred models of the 'neo-liberal' prudential subject is the rational choice actor who calculates the benefits and costs or risks of acting in a certain way and then acts (1996: 197–8). As O'Malley points out, the prudential subject of neo-liberal programmes faced with health and crime risks overlays the responsible and the rational, the moral and the calculating (1996: 200–1). The rational subject, located within a governmentally contrived set of arrangements (e.g. the rules governing private and public health insurance), calculates the best means of providing security against risks. The responsible subject seeks to optimize his or her independence from others and from the state, e.g. by employing epidemiological data of health risks, and undertaking diet, lifestyle and exercise regimes recommended by private health and fitness professionals or publicly funded health promotion. The types of attitudes and behaviours these various authorities urge us to adopt means that risk management becomes what Foucault called 'practices of the self'. As O'Malley has pointed out, it is not only unhealthy but, some would suggest, 'immoral' to engage in risky behaviour such as smoking or lack of exercise, and even for 'high-income earners' to depend on indexed public health insurance.

Risk has been to some extent desocialized, privatized and individualized. One might want to argue that a new terrain for politics is associated with this process. This politics invokes a plurality of the different forms of association from the household to the neighbourhood to the region but, as Rose (1996a) suggests, perhaps is best captured as the 'birth of community'. In Chapter 8 I called this politics a 'contemporary pluralism'. Looked at from 'top down', those identified as 'at risk' or at 'high risk' – those who compose the 'targeted populations' – are to be empowered or entered into partnership with professionals, bureaucrats, activists and service providers. With the help of markets – often governmentally contrived – in services and expertise, these targeted populations are enjoined to recognize the seemingly natural bonds of affinity and identity that link them with others and to engage in their own self-management and political mobilization. These bonds of affinity and identity might be forged around the household, neighbourhood, workplace or region, through symbolic, cultural or lifestyle identities, or through political identifications and social movement associations. From below, these aggregations appear as consumer organizations, citizens' initiatives, social movements, cultures and sub-cultures, and, perhaps above all, as communities, resisting and opposing the decisions of authorities, claiming rights, contesting the claims of expert knowledge, and demanding consultation over planning and services tailored to their needs.

If this is something like the sub-politics of Beck's risk society it is important to recognize that these aggregations form not simply around the risks engendered by techno-economic systems, but in a complex reciprocity with diverse forms of political authority deploying the rationalities and technologies of government described in Chapter 8. For Beck, sub-politics emerges in the space between what has conventionally been understood as political and what has been understood as non-political in a growing awareness of the risks generated by a techno-economic domain previously defined as non-political. This may well be the case. But surely this is only one manifestation of a politics that operationalizes the local solidarities of diverse aggregations rather than the attributes of the socially identified citizen, i.e. the individual whose first responsibility is to the national society and state. If we are witnessing the 'birth of community' in a new form, it is not as the traditional bonds and hierarchies of small-scale human association such as the village but as the transitory, overlapping, multiple relations of affinity and identifications felt by self-responsible subjects. It is important to realize that this politics is not simply about the growing appreciation of risks among certain sectors of a national population but also about the way in which groups of various kinds have come to understand themselves, their futures and their needs in terms of risks, with the assistance of a range of specialists and tutors in the identification and management of risk.

It may be that this proliferation of risk rationalities and reliance on the prudential individual means that authorities of all sorts – including national governments – have found a way of governing without governing society. Yet I think we must realize that there are limits to the 'solutions' that have been generated out of the diverse problematizations of the welfare state. If, in the nineteenth century, the development of social citizenship, the emergence of social government, and the socialization of risk correspond to the solution of an enduring problem of liberal-capitalist societies, i.e. the existence of inequality and poverty in a society of equals, then such a problem cannot be simply wished away by those who would retract the welfare state, individualize responsibility for the ills of the social system, and disperse risks onto the multiple communities and bodies which are to be made to bear them. From a Durkheimian perspective, the problem of organic solidarity, of the interdependence of all these 'differents', has been left unresolved. One does not have to appeal to foundational normative morality to assert the necessity of 'the social'.

That, however, is not the only reason why we should remain circumspect about posing the question of the 'death of the social' to transformations in contemporary government (Rose, 1996a). This seems to me inadequate in at least two further ways. First, the genealogy of the social shows the necessity of a sphere of practices and rationalities that address such questions of poverty, inequality and need within a liberal political community of equal and autonomous individuals. Second, to talk of a transition to a new form of governing in which citizens are regarded and enjoined to regard themselves as members of multiple and heterogeneous aggregations is to miss the sense in which these new forms of governing seek both to provide solutions to social problems and to effect a reformation of society through cultural means, as we saw in the previous chapter. Rather than the 'death of the social' it is more appropriate to discuss its 'metamorphoses' (Castel, 1995); what is problematized and transformed by contemporary liberalism is not the social itself, but its welfarist form. The social will no longer be inscribed within a centralized and coordinating state; it will be reconfigured as a set of constructed markets in service provision and expertise, made operable through heterogeneous technologies of agency, and rendered calculable by technologies of performance that govern at a distance.

Foucault suggested that liberal and social forms of government be understood as features on the trajectory of the 'governmentalization of the state'. One way of giving coherence and intelligibility to the new regimes of government – and the new post-welfarist regime of the social – in advanced liberal democracies is to locate them on a different trajectory, the 'governmentalization of government'. The hypothesis is that the governmentalization of the state – by which the state came to take on the function of the care of populations and individuals – is today meeting, being partially displaced by, reinscribed and recoded within another trajectory whereby the mechanisms of government themselves are subject to problematization, scrutiny and reformation. This turning of the government of the state upon itself can be described as the governmentalization of government. What results might be called 'reflexive government'. The imperative of reflexive government is to render governmental institutions and mechanisms, including those of the social itself, efficient, accountable, transparent and democratic by the employment of technologies of performance such as the various forms of auditing and the financial instruments of accounting, by the devolution of budgets, and by the establishment of calculating individuals and calculable spaces, as Peter Miller (1992) put it so aptly.

Classical liberal and social forms of government were the outcome of the governmentalization of the state. This is to say that the government of the state was conceived as acting on processes that are external to the state and independent of its existence. These included industrial, economic, social, biological and psychological processes. In order to govern on behalf of the welfare of the governed populations and individuals that make up the citizenry found within the limits of the sovereign state, it became necessary to rely on new forms of knowledge of such processes and techniques of intervention. Sociology (and other social sciences) and social insurance could be viewed as important instances of this. The first analyses the hazards produced by industrial societies and their social and economic processes. The latter provides security against such hazards by relying on a knowledge of processes immanent to the population – of the number of accidents, of birth and death rates, of cyclical and structural unemployment, etc. The question of security is central here. Social and liberal forms of government are correlates of a liberal problematic of security in which the welfare of each citizen and the population as a whole is dependent on the security of social and economic processes.

Much of what has been under discussion concerning new ways of governing suggests that this problematic of security is itself undergoing a process of transformation. What is at issue is no longer the security of processes considered external to the formal apparatuses of government but the security of governmental mechanisms themselves. One could begin to elucidate this transformation by examining the shift in the government of national economies and the governmental perception that we have entered into a new type of economic globalization (Hindess, 1998b). As Hindess has argued, the notion of 'the economy' as a self-regulating system and part of a system of national economies engaging in mutually advantageous international trade has been largely displaced by the less benign governmental perception of a global economic system that distributes countries and regions into winners and losers in a new 'zero-sum' competitive game. The task of national government is no longer to engage in the prudential management of self-regulating national economies so as to secure benefits to 'society' conceived as the totality of the members of a national population. Rather, the task is to reform those kinds of individual and institutional conduct that are considered likely to affect economic performance compared with that of the members of other national and even regional populations. A corollary of this view is that this is often best achieved by contriving and constructing market systems of allocation in domains where they had not previously been in operation. One of the conditions of such a transformation, Hindess argues, is that the technology of national accounting has led government and corporations to be more, rather than less, informed about the relative performance of their own and other national economies.

There are several effects of this transformation. In the absence of a theoretically mandated set of technical means for conducting 'macro-economic' policy, national governments can only hope to improve their performance relative to other countries. Levels of public and private indebtedness, the condition of national and state budgets, and a raft of policies that go under the heading of 'micro-economic reform' – from reforming uncompetitive public sectors, 'corporatizing' and 'privatizing' public utilities, breaking union monopolies and 'deregulating' labour markets – become the stuff of national economic governance. Rather than seeking to 'pull the levers' of macro-economic policy, national economic governance is increasingly concerned to reform the conduct of individuals and institutions in all sectors to make them more competitive and efficient. In this sphere, at least, a government of economic processes is being displaced by a government of governmental mechanisms. Economic security is now less a matter of the security of economic processes and more about the security of tax-raising measures, of national budgets, of systems and styles of public management, of privatization plans, and of the implementation of micro-economic reform. Indeed, national and state governments who fail to secure these governmental mechanisms can themselves be subject to forms of direct and indirect government by private corporations (e.g. credit rating downgrades, capital flights), international non-government agencies such as the World Bank and the International Monetary Fund (as in contemporary East Asia), and international associations (e.g. conditions of entry into the European Union). In the economic sphere at least, the presence of a reflexive government is clear.

Reflexive government is not, however, limited to the economic sphere. Ashenden (1996) has shown that public inquiries could be regarded as forms of 'reflexive government' in that they seek to arbitrate between different and competing forms of government, such as legal versus human science knowledge in the case of child protection. One could also argue that managerial doctrines, such as total quality management or customer-focused service provision, concern themselves with the forms of self-government of companies and other organizations. More significantly, there is a kind of elective affinity between reflexive government and the types of technology discussed in Chapter 8. Cost or management accounting, the devolution of financial responsibility onto budget units or cost centres, the establishment of quasi-markets, or the various uses of audit are all forms of indirect regulation of other regimes of regulation, whether they be of the school, the hospital, the university, the delivery of home care or child care services, as well as of the corporation. What I have called 'technologies of performance' thus clearly indicate a contemporary form of reflexive government that is concerned to govern the risks to taxpayers, shareholders and governments of the activities of public servants, state professionals, community organizations and their workers, state-owned enterprises, and private companies and their management.

What may not be so clear is how what I have called 'technologies of agency' also indicate the governmentalization of government. The pervasiveness of the notion of consultation indicates a form of government that can only govern through existing or potential 'indigenous' mechanisms of government, whether these be of communities, cultural groups, neighbour-hoods and so on (O'Malley, 1998). More generally, technologies of citizenship that foster the capacities for active participation might be viewed as constructing the conditions of reflexive government by establishing local sites of self-government that can be indirectly managed by the new tech-nologies of performance. If classical liberal forms of economic government sought to foster economic liberty, this is because the security of economic processes is linked to the natural freedom of economic actors to pursue their own interests. Today the appeal to freedom is made because security depends on the constitution of individuals, professionals, communities, orga-nizations and institutions as sites for the exercise of a 'responsible autonomy' that can be indirectly regulated by the technologies of perfor-mance. In this sense one might say that freedom, agency and choice become artefacts of particular governmental practices, including those that seek to elicit the enterprise of individuals and populations within contrived market regimes, e.g. the reconstitution of the unemployed as an active job seeker and customer within a market in 'employment placement services' (Dean, 1998a).

The pervasiveness and diversity of risk rationalities and techniques appear to be linked to this governing of government. Thus we have seen that risk-management strategies are forms of evaluation of the internal government of chemical companies and nuclear power plants and that risk screening can be mobilized as a way of regulating the doctor–patient relation and so ulti-mately increase the efficiency of the use of clinical techniques. The explosion of audit now means that auditing is concerned not only with the management of financial risks of companies for shareholders but with the risks that all types of governmental institutions – whether public, newly privatized, or contractualized – pose to both taxpayers and customers.

My final hypothesis is then about this idea of the 'death of the social'. I would suggest that social government is not so much dispensed with, as a victim of its own success. On the one hand, the welfarist regime of the social is first subject to a crisis of governability – encapsulated by the almost end-less identification of crises from the 1970s (crisis of capitalism, crisis of the state, fiscal crisis, crisis of democracy, legitimation crisis) – and then enclosed in new regulatory regimes and calculative practices. On the other, it is the success of liberal and social forms of governing in forming populations with the capacities of responsibility and autonomy that today makes it possible to govern through the aspirations and choices of individuals and groups.[5] Hence, there is some validity in the proposition that reflexive government no longer seeks to govern through society. This does not mean, however, that reflexive government no longer seeks to transform society. Societal trans-formation is at the heart of reflexive government. However it seeks to achieve this transformation no longer through the government of processes but through the government of the mechanisms, techniques and agencies of government themselves. The liberal problematic of security, in which security depends on the processes of economy and society, is displaced by a new problematic of security which concerns the securing of the mechanisms of government. Society itself can be changed, according to this view, but this will be no longer through conscious design based on the rational knowledge of social processes but through the transformation of the mechanisms through which it had previously been governed.

Society perhaps is as much an artefact of risk as the other way around. The proliferation and individualization of risk today are not so much components of the death of the social as transformations of the liberal and social problematic of security. The many kinds of risk rationality are central to the forms of calculative rationality that seek to secure governmental mechanisms. They are components of what I have termed 'reflexive government'. Today it is possible to change society – perhaps even revolutionize it – by acting upon the mechanisms through which it is governed. If the discovery of risk was a component of the governmentalization of the state, a knowledge of social and economic processes, and the emergence of a social form of citizenship, then its contemporary diversification and proliferation are linked to the governmentalization of government, a knowledge and indirect regulation of the conduct of individuals and institutions, and new forms of economic citizenship from the customer to the enterprise.

Notes

1 My argument here is not inconsistent with that of Nikolas Rose. I would emphasize the question mark in the title of his paper, 'The death of the social? Re-figuring the territory of government' (1996a). On close inspection, I think Rose's argument entails a mutation in social government, not a death, and that his account of this mutation is not unlike that charted here.
2 See Wynne (1996) for a related and much more extensive criticism. On the way in which a critical history of truth and rationality can suspend the assumption of realism without falling prey to the social constructionism of either Berger and Luckmann or Bruno Latour, see Dean (1998b).
3 I have made some attempt at beginning this task in my *Critical and Effective Histories* (1994a) and in the article, 'Foucault and Habermas on law, liberalism and democracy' (Dean, 1999).
4 Conversely, 'success' does not mean the continuation of a programme. See, for example, Barbara Cruikshank's (1994) analysis of the success of empowerment strategies in anti-poverty programmes in the US in the 1960s as a reason for their winding back.
5 A point made by Hindess (1993). Beck (1995: 74) argues the parallel position that a new modernity is a result of the successes as much as the failures of the old.

CONCLUSION: 'NOT BAD . . . BUT DANGEROUS'

> The state is become, under ancient and known forms, a new and undefinable monster. (Bolingbroke, c. 1736)[1]

We have followed Foucault in defining government very broadly as the 'conduct of conduct' – the more or less deliberate attempt to shape the actions of others or of oneself. By studying government in this sense as an assemblage of practices, techniques and rationalities for the shaping of the behaviour of others and of oneself, we are contributing to a critique of political reason, if that means that we are investigating the surfaces of emergence of political discourse and action. We cannot claim, however, to have completed the study of politics and of power relations. Alongside the techniques and rationalities of government stand what Foucault termed 'strategic games between liberties' or what Weber called 'politically oriented action' (Foucault, 1988a: 19; Weber, 1968: 55). Both these ideas stress the nature of politics as a struggle or competition between competing forces, groups or individuals attempting to influence, appropriate or otherwise control the exercise of authority. Thus while government, in our sense, is a condition of political action and rationality, it does not exhaust it. As Hindess (1997) has shown, political reason is not equivalent to governmental rationality, and it is misleading to use the terms interchangeably. It follows that governmental rationality might try to regulate politics, and that this is particularly the case where government seeks to operate through free individuals – as it does in the case of liberal forms of rule. Thus many of the institutional and constitutional arrangements of liberal democracies – from doctrines of the separation of powers to the representative institutions themselves – are precisely attempts to do that. Further, many of the techniques of 'advanced' liberal government are also attempts to govern political actors such as government departments, public servants and politicians by promoting quasi-market relations between them, and between them and their clients, or by removing the provision of public services from the sphere of political decision altogether (1997: 265).

Thus our study of government does not amount to a study of politics or power relations in general; it is a study only of the attempts to (more or less) rationally affect the conduct of others and ourselves. Thus an analytics of government approaches the study of politics from a single, and in that sense narrow, viewpoint, that of how the political conduct of collectives and individuals is governed. There is, however, a sense in which the study of government is broader than the study of politics conceived as a study of the competing forces and actors in struggles over the exercise of power and authority. It examines the ways in which those political actors and forces are already to some extent the result of various kinds of governmental action – whether disciplinary, bio-political or 'ethical' in the sense of an action on oneself – that have tried to give them a certain shape as citizens or consumers, as communities or societies. By stressing that governmental activity is heterogeneous, pervasive and multiple, the tendency of *liberal* political rationalities to regard government as a unitary activity limited by rights and liberties of individuals is called into question. An analytics of government thus links the study of politics to the study of how we conduct ourselves and others in all spheres of our lives. On one reading of Weber, for example (Hennis, 1988), we might say that an analytics of government provides a bridge between the comprehension of our social existence (or 'life conduct') and of our political conduct.

Returning to our particular focus on government as the shaping of the conduct of others or of oneself, we find that the attempts to do this are framed within quite different general matrices. Thus the government of conduct involves the government of acts and things, of processes and conditions, and of existing forms of government and self-government. An elementary example would concern the way in which we dress. Various regulations have required certain groups to wear particular items of clothing on special occasions, e.g. until recently, the wearing of hats by women in church, for the simple reason that this is how things should be done. In late medieval times, these were called sumptuary regulations. They bear a similarity with the regulations we have discussed that were made under the rubric of police in continental Europe, particularly in Germany. In more recent times, the wearing of hats might be recommended as a part of public health campaigns to protect individuals from levels of exposure to the sun that risk skin cancer and melanoma. Here the wearing of hats is a component of an attempt to govern the rate of particular kinds of morbidity and mortality within populations. Finally, the wearing of hardhats for certain types of workers might be recommended to protect against undue levels of insurance or workers' compensation claims, and so minimize the costs of such insurance. Of course, the wearing of hardhats can answer both to the protection of individual workers against known risks within building sites and also to the objective of the financial security of the company or government agency by limiting workers' compensation claims. A conduct as apparently mundane as hat-wearing can thus appear within the government of acts and things, the government of processes, or the government of government, or some combination of these.

We could thus summarize what we have been saying about acts and things, processes, and existing or potential forms of government, in the following way. In the various forms of householding and dispositional government, it is the detailed regulation of acts and things that is stressed, although processes might be recognized (such as the circulation between trading households and countries in mercantilism) and forms of self-government invoked (the training of the prince, the discipline of the army, etc.). In the case of liberal and social forms of government, it is processes that are stressed, such as those found in the tendencies of populations or even in the interior life of individuals. The 'homosexual', for example, can be known both in relation to norms of sexual orientation within populations and as the outcome of specific psychological processes. Acts and deeds are not important except as they exhibit such processes or deviate from them. Self-government becomes extremely important as the mechanism through which individuals can be normalized and through which their identities are formed and stabilized. Finally, in the case of reflexive forms of government, processes might be invoked (e.g. those of economic globalization), acts may need to be reformed (such as uncompetitive individual and institutional conduct), but what is stressed is the need to secure existing mechanisms of government and to mobilize and work through the capacities of all sorts of self-governing agencies (risk-taking and risk-managing individuals, communities, institutions, etc.). Identities are invoked now less because they represent a norm or a deviation and more because it is through identifications that various self-governing agencies are formed.

These three frames (the dispositional, the processual, the reflexive) within which governing occurs offer us a way of making sense of our present, of the formulas and programmes of rule and the exercise of authority which we participate in today. All three are extant today. And all three have long histories. Thus these frames within which governing occurs do not amount to a periodization of forms of government. However, they enable us to distinguish two trajectories and sets of processes that lend intelligibility to present forms of rule and authority. These are the governmentalization of the state, and the governmentalization of government.

The governmentalization of the state is the trajectory on which the dispositional and householding conception of government meets with a bio-political government through processes immanent within populations. The governmentalization of government is the trajectory on which this government through social, economic and vital processes meets with a government of government. Both of these trajectories are relatively recent in the sense that they have emerged since the end of the eighteenth century. The governmentalization of the state is the trajectory by which the government of the state came to be conceived as operating through processes found in a reality external to the formal apparatuses of political rule and encapsulated in divisions between state and civil society. The government of the state would no longer be conceived solely or principally as the 'right disposition of things'.

Practices and rationalities of rule such as sovereignty, reason of state, police, cameralism and mercantilism belong to the latter in that they conceive the task of the government of the state to be the direct regulating, ordering, marking, collecting together, distributing and deducting of things, and of the relationships between 'humans and things'. 'Things' here can be quite heterogeneous and include humans' relations with the soil, rivers and land, with territory, its roads, squares and settlements, with the state itself, with customs, habits and occupations, with property, goods and trading, with labour, bodies, blood and life itself. This 'right disposition of things arranged to a convenient end' presupposes a transparency of the objects of government and the transcendence of the agents of government – governors – in relation to such objects.

A paradigmatic example of the dispositional government is the notion of rule as rule over a household. The household – the *oikos* – is the framework in which forms of patriarchal rule occur over members of the household, including wives, children, servants and animals, and over property. Notions of economy such as Aristotle's *œconomia* are derived from this to refer to the wise management and organization of the household. The understanding of economy as the sovereign's stewardship of his kingdom can be found in texts of 'political œconomy' until the middle of the eighteenth century. Here political economy is modelled on the management of the 'œconomy' of the household. The kingdom is thought to be an extension of the royal household and also composed of many households.

Particularly clear illustrations of rationalities of government of this kind are provided by 'reason of state' and 'police'. While reason of state doctrine departs from accounts of sovereignty that refer to the wisdom of God or the strategies of the prince, it still conceives of government as an instrumental activity. To govern here means to take account of a particular object, the state, and the internal and external means through which states form, strengthen themselves, endure and grow. And, while it deploys forms of political expertise in its objectification of the state, such as political arithmetic and statistics, this is a form of knowledge that renders the state directly amenable and transparent to the exercise of sovereign authority. Reason of state exemplifies a distinctively modern conception of the state as something which is separate from both the rulers and the ruled, from the sovereign and his subjects, and from any particular set of institutions of government (Skinner, 1989).

Among the external techniques of reason of state are the standing army, and the arts of war and diplomacy. Among its internal techniques are police. Regulations of police have the character of issuing specific sets of orders concerning a range of heterogeneous things and activities within a particular jurisdiction, whether that be a municipality, a principality, an ecclesiastical authority, a guild or a kingdom.

Both police and reason of state, and the models of 'political œconomy' founded on the household, all presume the existence of a sovereign authority that makes treaties, issues regulations, and benefits from the circulation of wealth among productive households. This sovereignty itself has a long and complex history. However, it assumes the transcendence of the sovereign with regard to a transparent object to be governed, the kingdom or principality. Sovereignty is exercised over the acts, things and subjects within a particular territory. It marks bodies and it commands the labour, products, blood and ultimately life of its subjects. It too is thus a kind of rule over 'things', and assumes that 'things' can be ruled in accordance with the will of the sovereign.

We have just grouped together sovereignty with police and reason of state as rationalities of *rule* concerned with disposing things in La Perrière's sense. It should be noted, however, that sovereignty is not a rationality of *government* in at least two of the senses in which reason of state, police, mercantilism and related doctrines are. First, the notion of sovereignty differs from rationalities of government proper in that the latter are concerned with a fostering of the *living* and augmentation of *life*. In contrast, sovereignty operates by deduction, as a right of death rather than a power over life. Second, the right of sovereignty remains transcendent within a territory rather than a way of thinking and acting that is immanent either to its objects or to a set of institutions. Thus Foucault notes that the arts of government emerge in relation to such objects as a family, a child, a soul, a territory or a population. Skinner (1989: 121–5) proposes another sense in which the theory of sovereignty is 'transcendent', especially in theorists like Hobbes and Bodin: it presupposes a 'state' with sovereignty which is separate from both those whose agreements are supposed to ground the rights of sovereignty and from those who exercise sovereignty. For Hobbes, and for those who desire to legitimize the developing absolutist forms of government, the 'state' is inherent in but greater than any particular institutions that comprise civil government. It is in this sense that Lord Bolingbroke, anticipating Nietzsche's *monstre froid* by 150 years, called the state an 'undefinable monster'.

By contrast with those forms of government that seek to govern the 'imbrication of men and things', as Foucault (1991a: 93) put its, most nineteenth- and twentieth-century forms of rule such as liberalism and social government can be characterized as government through processes. They presuppose the existence of realities that are formally separate from the state and which the exercise of authority must take into account if it is to be effective. The exemplar of this matrix of government is most clearly the economy, conceived as an autonomous and largely self-regulating system external to the state. In optimistic versions, like that of Adam Smith, the motor of the processes that constitute the economy is the pursuit by rational individuals in a commercial society of 'bettering their own condition'. A commercial society is thus a 'system of natural liberty'. In less optimistic versions, the motor of these economic processes is a kind of scarcity inscribed in humankind's relation with nature, manifest in the Malthusian principles of population, the differential theory of rent or the tendency of the rate of profit to fall.

There are, however, other no less important processes of the population, of life and of society. Indeed the notion of population binds the discovery of the economy as a separate reality with what we have called a bio-politics, i.e. a set of knowledges, practices and interventions rationalized by the norm of the optimization of the life of each individual and the population as a whole. The discovery of the notion of population as a dynamic entity points in two quite different directions: on the one hand, towards the limiting of state interventions and assistance so as not to encourage the unwarranted increase in population beyond the means of its subsistence; and, on the other, to the investigation of the processes of the life of the population and the fostering of that life.

Social forms of government lie within this general matrix of the government of processes. Their necessary but not sufficient condition is the existence of a liberal critique of too much government that presupposes, first, the existence of a sphere outside the state, and second, the constitution of this sphere by processes that are independent of sovereign will and somewhat opaque to it. However, the spheres which are constituted by these dense, opaque processes do not necessarily sum into a society, that is a totality of the relations coincident with the existence of a national territory. The notion of society is a particular way of rendering reality amenable to government that is linked to the diverse problematizations of the liberal economy of government and its effects. The problem addressed by society is how solidarity is possible given the fragmenting and dissolving effects of the liberal economic regime. Society is thus a 'self-rending unity', a sphere separate from and including the state, constituted by diverse and conflicting processes, a broader reality in which economic and demographic processes can be observed and exist, and which is a condition of their effective functioning. The social is an 'artefact' of the institutions that are consequent upon these problematizations of a liberal economy. The figure that emerges might be considered as an attempt to invent and install a form of citizenship that is compatible with the existence of inequality and poverty in a community of equals.

Even though we have conceived of the governmentalization of the state as a movement from the government of a complex of humans and things to a government through definite processes, there is a sense in which a rule over things remains a condition of the government of processes. The emergence of forms of governmental rationality from reason of state to social democracy can all be understood as a separation of an art of government from the state. However, the existence of a sovereign authority exercised over a territory 'forces open' the spaces in which government can operate and command, collect together and distribute the resources that it will use. In this way, modern forms of government cannot do without sovereign authority and without instruments such as law and taxation systems. Their historic relations with liberal, social and bio-political government no doubt transform sovereignty and the law. Law becomes part of normalizing institutions and acts more like a norm. Sovereignty becomes democratized and linked to the juridical and political rights of the citizen. All modern forms of rule must articulate the elements of sovereignty with those of bio-politics. As we have seen, this is as true for state socialism as for liberalism, for National Socialism as for social democracy. National Socialism is a particularly instructive example: here we see the sovereign elements of blood, lineage and fatherland rearticulated with the bio-political administration of the processes of life and death in a murderous, suicidal and genocidal manner.

Social government, in the form of 'Keynesian' techniques of the welfare state and mechanisms of social insurance, develops as a form of the government of the state in which a feedback loop is established between social processes (meeting the needs and managing the risks of citizens within industrial society) and economic processes (levels of aggregate demand affecting the inverse variations of unemployment and inflation). The social articulates the elements of sovereignty and government by trying to constitute a form of citizenship that is adequate to a democratized sovereignty and a state pastorate that governs the risks of an industrial market economy – of unemployment, of poverty and of inequality.

We might regard the ideal of the welfare state that would act on the social conditions of the population, and the ideal of a perfect race that would act on the processes of heredity within populations, as two ways of articulating forms of sovereignty with the imperatives of bio-politics. They can also be viewed as two responses to the question of how it is possible to provide security and colonize the future in the face of the risks of an industrial capitalist economy, its struggles and forces of consolidation and dissolution.

It would be a mistake to think that liberal forms of rule are succeeded in the twentieth century by social forms on the one hand, and authoritarian governmentality on the other. Since the liberal art of government concerns the constant struggle to achieve an equilibrium between economic government and a government of the processes of life, between a political economy and a bio-politics of the population, it must situate itself in relation to knowledges of the social, biological, economic and cultural processes found within populations. As a critique of 'too much government' which is at the same time compelled to govern on behalf of the welfare of the population, liberalism's processes of self-review invariably entail a dialogical relation with a knowledge of life, of health and of the relations between humans as individuals and groups. The social may not be reducible to liberal arts of government, but is one possible structure in which the liberal ethos of review can be brought into a dialogue with the various forms of knowledge of those processes that are external and necessary to the exercise of formal political authority. Moreover, the development of the social as a domain of struggle and contestation is fostered by the emergence of liberal democratic forms of sovereignty with their civil and political freedoms and representative institutions.[2]

The relation between liberalism and authoritarian types of rule in the twentieth century is also complex. As a review of excessive government that draws upon the language of rights, liberalism would appear to be in a position to check authoritarian governmentality. Yet it is precisely because liberalism appeals to and tries to work through the capacities and freedom of the judicial, political and economic subject of rights that it contains the possibility of *illiberal* practices and rationalities of government. This is because liberalism as an art of government constantly produces a division between those populations who are capable of exercising such capacities and those who are not, whether because they are perpetually incompetent or because they are yet to be improved or trained to the point where they are competent.[3]

For the yet to be improved populations, or those permanently unimprovable, liberalism necessarily produces forms of despotic rule. This applies to colonialized and indigenous peoples as much as to specific populations within liberal democracies. Moreover, because liberalism depends on the exercise of a kind of responsible autonomy on the part of its subjects, it seeks to form such subjects and their capacities through a range of often despotically employed disciplinary practices. If the liberal art of government can be viewed as being extremely inventive, one part of what it invents will prove essential to the constitution of what we might call authoritarian governmentality. As a political philosophy that offers guarantees to legitimate the operation of governmental practices, moreover, it may be the case that the democratized sovereignty on which liberalism relies is simply too heterogeneous with the bio-political imperative it seeks to check. Notions of rights, of choice and of consumer sovereignty might transform the nature of the application of contemporary genetic screening, for example, but that might not protect us from a programme that promises a *de facto* realization of the eugenic dream.

At the end of the twentieth century, the social and racial strategies of the management of risk are widely perceived as failures: one because they led to the greatest catastrophe of the century; the other because the risks of the strategy to the security of the fiscal processes of the state itself were held to outweigh the risks that the strategy had sought to prevent. Various versions of neo-liberalism emerged in Europe and the USA that took different targets of critique: in one case, national and state socialism, and war planning; in another, the New Deal, Keynesianism and the Great Society; and, in a third, the 'counter-culture', multiculturalism and the decline of moral responsibility. The outcome of these critiques of too much government was the downloading of the responsibility for risk aversion and management onto individuals and communities. The 'social' services previously offered by the welfare state are increasingly being reconfigured as markets in which individuals as consumers will make choices, and in which – so the story goes – provision is tailored to their needs. If classical liberalism could be considered as a system of natural liberty in that the freedom of interested individuals was necessary to the security of economic processes, advanced liberal rule makes freedom into a technical means of government and contrives the conditions under which such freedom can be exercised as a form of 'responsible autonomy' or rational choice.

This freedom is no longer thought of principally as being necessary to the operation of economic processes. Its rationale is rather its necessity for the security of the governmental mechanisms themselves. It is by deploying the freedom of individuals as consumers and members of communities that it is possible to address the complaints made about the welfare state from the 'bottom' – its rigidity, the uniformity of provision, the lack of flexibility of services – while, at the same time, deploying the choices of consumers as a means of making the allocation of resources more efficient and the activities of professionals, bureaucrats and service providers more accountable.

Moreover, these neo-liberal approaches to government constitute new types of freedom of professionals and service providers by devolving authority onto local units, departments and centres, making them both self-managing and responsible for their own budgets. By establishing such units as centres of authority and calculation, it is possible to reform them by indirect measures such as the audit and cost accounting. Risk is thereby devolved onto individuals, communities and workplaces, and managed by mechanisms that endeavour to provide transparency and accountability.

If freedom is no longer the quasi-natural freedom to pursue one's own interest on the market, as it is in classical liberalism and social forms of government, security is no longer principally the security of the economic and social processes that exist outside the state. Security has come to entail the security of the governmental mechanisms – whether these are through private for-profit, public, or community or third-sector organizations. To provide against risk is now to set in place the systems (of accounting, auditing, training, planning) that will ensure that these diverse agencies are customer-focused, goal-directed, accountable to taxpayers, governments and shareholders, and transparent to the technologies of performance. These new forms of government imagine, in a sense, a government without a centre, a form of administration in which there is no longer a centrally directing intelligence.

Neo-liberal philosophies of government and advanced liberal forms of government are events within an emerging series on a trajectory that is somewhat different from that of the governmentalization of the state. They are but the first instances of another trajectory in which the government of processes is being displaced by and reinscribed within the government of government itself. The lament over the lack of economic sovereignty consequent upon 'globalization' will perhaps be one day viewed as merely the strange and somewhat limited perception that our priorities have changed with the shift of the liberal problematic of security. Rather than viewing the debate over globalization as a debate over the reality of economic transformation, it will be understood as a debate about the frame in which national economic governance occurs.

Just as classical liberalism stood as a kind of signal that the older frame of governing was being displaced and recoded within a new bio-political field of the processes of population and economy, the 1980s might one day be viewed as making the same somewhat naïve discovery that the frame in which governing is to be conceived has once again, after two centuries, changed. The naïveté of classical liberalism was manifest in the belief that the naturalistically conceived processes of the economy could be left alone. The naïveté of neo-liberalism is that the boundary between the public sector and the market economy can be dissolved and that government can occur without a centre or that the centre can be reduced to a set of indirect measures of surveillance. The danger of both is that they make room for the return of what is their condition, the use of sovereign authority, in a brutal rule of things – of bodies and labour. It is not without note that both classical liberalism and neo-liberalism share a fondness for forced labour for those who will not work. Nor is it without note that neo-liberalism fosters a new kind of dialogical space with paternalism and neo-conservatism. One danger of neo-liberalism is that it believes all activities can be made operable by using consumer choice. Another is that it cedes responsibility to paternalism for those who, for whatever reason, cannot or do not exercise responsible choices. This might include pregnant teenagers, 'dead-beat dads' who fail to provide child support, 'fragile families', the homeless, drug addicts, truants, the unemployed, the mentally ill, and, quite simply, the poor, to list the contents of a recent volume on the topic (Mead, 1997).

Neo-liberalism is naïve because it imagines that it is no longer necessary to provide solutions to social questions, that they too will be dissolved as well as the division between the private spheres of the market and the sphere of public authority. Advanced liberal democracies will have to face up to the problems of the forms of inequality and poverty generated by these contrived markets and the absence of those capacities required to exercise choice within these markets by certain sectors of the population. But just as it is naïve to accede to the proposition of the death of the social, so too would it be naïve to imagine that the social will remain the same. The social is undergoing a 'metamorphosis' rather than a death. The social will be reconfigured within the frame of reflexive government. Provision will be made through diverse agencies, community groups and associations, coordinated by market rather than bureaucratic means. It will emphasize the self-management and the self-expressed needs of the consumers of expertise and services. We have thus spoken of a 'post-welfarist regime of the social'. The retraction of the welfare state, and of welfarist modes of provision, may mean less state intervention, but not necessarily less government (not least in Foucault's sense of the word). By these emphases the social will be open to dialogue and participation with communities, social groups and movements and the needs definition of consumers and users of specialist expertise and services.

A post-welfarist regime of the social, however, will also emphasize the responsibilities of those who receive social support, who have children, who consume educational services, and so on. In this respect, the social will take on a more sovereign character such as in 'workfare' and 'work-for-dole' schemes and in the promulgation of charters of social and family responsibility (Larner, 1998). It will also emphasize the mutual obligations between individuals and between the individuals and the communities who are charged with their support. In the name of such obligations the social takes on a paternalistic and coercive character. In these dual, and sometimes contradictory trajectories, we might note, a line of contestation, transformation and invention opens up.

Reflexive government means that the task for the twenty-first century is the reinvention of the social in a manner which operationalizes the capacities of diverse associations, movements and groups (cf. Hirst, 1993). If we fail in the latter task, or allow ourselves to be distracted by nostalgia for forms of government that have now passed, we might find that alternative forms of social government and, even less benignly, alternatives to social government re-emerge and proliferate. If this occurs, it might not be simply the death of the social that we shall be lamenting.

Notes

1 Lord Bolingbroke's (1678–1751) phrase is found at the end of his eighth letter 'on the study and use of history' (1967: 173–334). The first letter is dated 6 November 1735.
2 See Stenson (1998) for a recent discussion of the under-theorized notion of sovereignty among governmentality writers and its relation to liberalism.
3 In this respect it is interesting to see the return of paternalism in governmental discourse in a manner that recalls J. S. Mill's attitude toward colonized peoples and illiterates (Mead, 1997).

GLOSSARY

Advanced liberalism   A number of different types of government that are assembled from similar elements and resources. These include the contrivance of markets in areas of formerly public provision, the employment of indirect means of regulation such as the calculative technologies of auditing and accounting, the dispersion and individualization of the management of risk, and the construction of multiple forms of agency through which rule is accomplished. Key forms of agency of advanced liberal rule include the consumer and the community. Advanced liberal forms of government can also include paternalistic and coercive measures for those deemed not to display the capacities of responsible and prudential autonomy.

Authoritarian governmentality   Like liberalism, an articulation of elements of sovereignty and bio-politics. Authoritarian governmentality can be a component of liberalism to the extent that the latter requires despotic practices for those populations who do not have, or do not yet possess, the capacities and attributes of responsibility and freedom. As a mode of government proper, authoritarian governmentality differs from liberalism in that it regards its subjects' capacity for action as subordinate to the expectation of obedience. It typically makes the neutralization and even elimination of opposition and resistance a central governmental objective. Authoritarian governmentality operates through a more intensive and generalized use of sovereign instruments of repression. Many of the twentieth-century forms of authoritarian governmentality rely on a bio-political racism that makes the fostering of the life of some dependent upon disallowing the life of others.

Bio-politics   Term for a form of politics, conducted largely since the eighteenth century, concerned with the administration of the conditions of life of the population. The concept of the population as a living entity composed of vital processes is essential to bio-politics. Bio-political interventions are made into the health, habitation, urban environment, working conditions and education of various populations.

Government   The 'conduct of conduct'. Any more or less calculated and rational activity, undertaken by a multiplicity of authorities and agencies, employing a variety of techniques and forms of knowledge, that seeks to shape our conduct by working through our desires, aspirations, interests and beliefs, for definite but shifting ends and with a diverse set of relatively unpredictable consequences, effects and outcomes. Agencies of government, in this sense, can be local, regional, national, international or global; they can be philanthropic, for profit or public.

Governmentality   How we think about governing others and ourselves in a wide variety of contexts. In a more limited sense, the different ways governing is thought about in the contemporary world and which can in large part be traced to Western Europe from the sixteenth century. Such forms of thought have been exported to large parts of the globe owing to colonial expansion and the post-colonial set of international arrangements of a system of sovereign states.

Governmentalization of government The trajectory by which government through processes comes to be displaced by a government of governmental mechanisms themselves. An example would be the shift of economic government from a government of economic processes of the production and distribution of wealth to one concerned to secure the governmental mechanisms of national budgets, interest rates, money supply, and the international competitiveness and efficiency of individual and institutional conduct.

Governmentalization of the state The long-term trajectory by which the exercise of sovereignty comes to be articulated through the regulation of populations and individuals and the psychological, biological, sociological and economic processes that constitute them.

Liberalism The critique of excessive government. An approach to government that recommends mechanisms of regular review and rationalization. Can be approached as a form of political philosophy or as a practical art of government. As the former, it usually refers to a philosophy of limited government that respects the rights and liberties of citizens and employs the rule of law. As the latter, it uses the capacities of free subjects as among the means of achieving its purposes and goals. As an art of government, liberalism thus seeks to shape the capacities of individuals and collectivities through disciplinary and bio-political means. Liberalism can also be understood more broadly as a way of articulating a democratized form of sovereignty, and its notion of the rights of responsible and autonomous juridical and political subjects, with a bio-politics.

Neo-liberalism Several different governmental rationalities might be described as variants of neo-liberalism. They are modes of problematization of the welfare state and its features such as bureaucracy, rigidity and dependency formation. They recommend the reform of individual and institutional conduct so that it becomes more competitive and efficient. They seek to effect this reform by the extension of market rationality to all spheres, by the focus on choices of individuals and collectives, and by the establishment of a culture of enterprise and responsible autonomy.

Political rationality Any form of calculation about political activity, i.e. about any activity which has as its objective the influence, appropriation, redistribution, allocation or maintenance of powers of the government of the state or other organizations. Political rationality is a species of governmental rationality in so far as it entails thinking about directing the conduct of others or ourselves. To the extent that its objective is to influence the way governmental organizations exercise their powers, its concerns are quite distinct.

Problematization One of the forms of rationality that are constitutive of regimes of practices. Each regime is associated with a way of questioning and interrogating past, present and potential alternatives and may itself be subject to such questioning and interrogating. Problematization includes modes of evaluation of success or failure.

Programmes   One aspect of governmental rationality. These are explicit, planned attempts to reform or transform regimes of practices by reorienting them to specific ends or investing them with particular purposes. Programmes often take the form of a link between theoretical knowledge and practical concerns and objectives.

Rationality of government; mentality of government   Any relatively systematic way of thinking about government. This can include the form of representation of the field to be governed, the agencies to be considered and enrolled in governing, the techniques to be employed, and the ends to be achieved. Rationalities of government can be theoretical knowledges, particular programmes, forms of practical know-how, or strategies.

Reflexive government   A government of government and governmental mechanisms. Does not necessarily entail a greater degree of reflection in the sense of deliberation or thought than other forms. It is simply when government begins to conceive its task as operating upon existing forms of government rather than governing either things or processes.

Regimes of practices; regimes of government   These terms refer to the relatively organized and systematized ways of doing things, such as curing, caring, punishing, assisting, educating and so on. Regimes of government are the subset of regimes of practices concerned with ways of directing the conduct of self and others. These regimes can be known along four independently varying but related axes: fields of visibility; forms of rationality; techniques and technologies; and identities and agencies. It is these regimes which constitute the object of an analytics of government.

Risk   A powerful way of understanding transformations in forms of government in the twentieth century. Social government and state racism can be viewed as the two great strategies for the management of risk in the twentieth century consequent upon the separation of environment and heredity at the end of the nineteenth century. Social government emerges from a series of measures for managing the risk to the various populations in a liberal economy, e.g. workers' compensation, social insurance, unemployment, sickness and aged pensions, etc. Bio-political state racism addresses these risks through a racialized social policy that seeks to eliminate the populations identified as likely to bear such risks. Neo-liberalism problematizes both of these forms of centralized risk management and advanced liberal government seeks to disperse risk onto individuals and collectives, largely conceived as consumers and communities.

Sovereignty. Form of rule modelled on the relation between the sovereign and its subjects. Usually presupposes the transcendence of the sovereign over its subjects within a given territory. Its principal institutions are law and juridical systems; its means are deductive, of goods, labour, time and life; and its symbols are those of the sword and of blood. Sovereignty is expressed as a right of death. Sovereignty has as its external conditions a set of international governmental arrangements that recognizes the existence of a system of states but is itself the condition of the emergence of government because it forces open the spaces upon which the latter will operate.

Strategy   The intentional but non-subjective logic or form of intelligibility of regimes of practices that can only be known through the realm of its effects. The critical nature of an analytics of government can often take the form of noting the disjunction between the explicit, programmatic rationality that invests regimes of practices and their strategy which can be known and codified through the field of effects. Strategy is the medium in which government exists rather than its instrument.

Techniques and technologies of government   The diverse and heterogenous means, mechanisms and instruments through which governing is accomplished. These concepts emphasize the practical features of government which might include forms of notation, ways of collecting, representing, storing and transporting information, forms of architecture and the division of space, kinds of quantitative and qualitative calculation, types of training and so on. Technologies of government are typically assembled from diverse elements, take part in techno-economic systems, constitute logistical and infrastructural powers, and subsume the moral and political shaping of conduct by performance criteria.

The social   The plural and heterogenous forms of interventions that cross and connect various formally separate public and private spheres in response to and sometimes in opposition to the effects of a liberal governmental economy and a depoliticized sphere of the family. May be viewed as an attempt to install a form of social citizenship compatible with a liberal-democratic-capitalist form of government, i.e. one that can address the questions of poverty and inequality in a society of equals. Gives rise in the nineteenth century to technologies and programmes of the government of the state such as social insurance and *solidarisme*, and to a theoretical knowledge of society as a form of social solidarity. In the twentieth century, the ethical ideal of a welfare state is elaborated on the basis of diverse social interventions and practices, and on the project of establishing a mutually reinforcing circularity between the social and the economic. 'Keynesian' techniques of national economic management are often viewed as a condition of the latter project.

REFERENCES

APA (1994) *Diagnostic and Statistical Manual of Mental Disorders: DSM-IV*. Washington, DC: American Psychiatric Association.

Arendt, H. (1958) *The Origins of Totalitarianism*, 2nd edn. London: Allen and Unwin.

Ashenden, S. (1996) 'Reflexive governance and child sexual abuse: liberal welfare rationality and the Cleveland Inquiry', *Economy and Society* 25 (1): 64–88.

Ashenden, S. and Owen, D. (eds) (1999) *Foucault Contra Habermas: Recasting the Dialogue between Genealogy and Critical Theory*. London: Sage.

Bachrach, P. and Baratz, M.S. (1962) 'Two faces of power', *American Political Science Review* 56: 947-52.

Bachrach, P. and Baratz, M.S. (1970) *Power and Poverty: Theory and Practice*. Oxford: Oxford University Press.

Ballard, J. (1998) 'The constitution of AIDS in Australia: taking government at a distance seriously', in M. Dean and B. Hindess (eds), *Governing Australia: Studies in Rationalities of Government*. Melbourne: Cambridge University Press, pp. 125–38.

Barry, A., Osborne, T. and Rose, N. (eds) (1996) *Foucault and Political Reason: Liberalism, Neo-Liberalism and Rationalities of Government*. London: UCL Press.

Bartos, M. (1994) 'Community vs. population; the case of men who have sex with men', in P. Aggleton, P. Davies and G. Hart (eds), *AIDS: Foundations for the Future*. London: Taylor and Francis.

Baudrillard, J. (1983) *In the Shadow of the Silent Majorities . . . or the End of the Social*. New York: Semiotext(e).

Bauman, Z. (1989) *Modernity and the Holocaust*. Ithaca, NY: Cornell University Press.

Beck, U. (1988) 'On the way to the industrial risk-society? Outline of an argument', *Thesis Eleven* 23: 86–103.

Beck, U. (1992a) 'From industrial society to risk society', *Theory, Culture and Society* 9: 97–123.

Beck, U. (1992b) *Risk Society: Towards a New Modernity*. London: Sage.

Beck, U. (1994) 'The reinvention of politics: towards a theory of reflexive modernization', in U. Beck, A. Giddens and S. Lash (eds), *Reflexive Modernization: Politics, Tradition and Aesthetics in the Modern Social Order*. Cambridge: Polity Press, pp. 1–55.

Beck, U. (1995) *Ecological Politics in the Age of Risk*. Cambridge: Polity Press.

Beck, U. (1996) 'The provident state', in S. Lash, B. Szersznski and B. Wynne (eds), *Risk Environment and Modernity: Towards a New Ecology*. Sage: London, pp. 27–43.

Becker, G. S. (1964) *Human Capital*. New York: National Bureau of Economic Research.

Bell, D. (1979) *The Cultural Contradictions of Capitalism*. London: Heinemann.

Bell, V. (1993) 'Governing childhood: neo-liberalism and the law', *Economy and Society* 22 (3): 390–405.

Bentham, J. (1843) *Works*, vol. 8 (ed. J. Bowring). Edinburgh: William Tait.
Bentham, J. (1950) *The Theory of Legislation*. London: Routledge and Kegan Paul.
Bernstein, R. (1994) 'Foucault: critique as a philosophic ethos', in M. Kelly (ed.), *Critique and Power: Recasting the Foucault/Habermas Debate*. Cambridge, MA: MIT Press, pp. 211–41.
Blackstone, W (1830) *Commentaries on the Laws of England*, vol. 4, 17th edn (ed. E. Christian). London: Dawsons of Pall Mall.
Bolingbroke, Lord (1967) *Works*, vol. 2. London: Frank Cass.
Booth, C. (1889–1897) *Life and Labour of the People in London*, 9 vols. London: Macmillan.
Bourdieu, P. (1990) *The Logic of Practice*. Cambridge: Polity Press.
Braudel, F. (1980) *On History*. Chicago: University of Chicago Press.
Brown, P. (1987) 'Late Antiquity', in P. Veyne (ed.), *A History of Private Life*, vol. 1. *From Pagan Rome to Byzantium*. Cambridge, MA: Belknap Press, pp. 235–312.
Brown, P. (1992) *Power and Persuasion in Late Antiquity: Towards a Christian Empire*. Madison: University of Wisconsin Press.
Brown, P. (1995) *Authority and the Sacred: Aspects of the Christianisation of the Roman World*. Cambridge: Cambridge University Press.
Burchell, D. (1994) 'The curious career of economic rationalism: government and economy in current policy debate', *Australian and New Zealand Journal of Sociology* 30 (3): 322–33.
Burchell, D. (1998) '"The mutable minds of particular men": the emergence of "economic science" and contemporary economic policy', in M. Dean and B. Hindess (eds), *Governing Australia: Studies in Contemporary Rationalities of Government*. Melbourne: Cambridge University Press, pp. 194–209.
Burchell, G. (1991) 'Peculiar interests: civil society and the "the system of natural liberty"', in G. Burchell, C. Gordon and P. Miller (eds), *The Foucault Effect: Studies in Governmental Rationality*. London: Harvester Wheatsheaf, pp. 119–50.
Burchell, G. (1996) 'Liberal government and techniques of the self', in A. Barry, T. Osborne and N. Rose (eds), *Foucault and Political Reason: Liberalism, Neo-Liberalism and Rationalities of Government*. London: UCL Press, pp. 19–36.
Burchell, G., Gordon, C. and Miller, P. (eds) (1991) *The Foucault Effect: Studies in Governmentality*. London: Harvester Wheatsheaf.
Burke, P. (1990) *The French Historical Revolution: the Annales School 1929–1989*. Cambridge: Polity Press.
Callon, M. (1986) 'Some elements of a sociology of translation: domestication of the scallops and the fishermen of St Brieuc Bay', in J. Law (ed.), *Power, Action and Belief: a New Sociology of Knowledge*. London: Routledge and Kegan Paul, pp. 196–233.
Castel, R. (1989) *The Psychiatric Order*. Cambridge: Polity Press.
Castel, R. (1991) 'From dangerousness to risk', in G. Burchell, C. Gordon and P. Miller (eds), *The Foucault Effect: Studies in Governmentality*. London: Harvester Wheatsheaf, pp. 281–98.
Castel, R. (1995) *Les Métamophoses de la question sociale*. Paris: Fayard.
Castel, R., Castel, F. and Lovell, A. (1982) *The Psychiatric Society*. New York: Columbia University Press.
Chadwick, E. (1965) *A Report on the Sanitary Conditions of the Labouring Population of Great Britain of 1842* (ed. M. Flinn). Edinburgh: Edinburgh University Press.
Checkland, S.G. and Checkland, E.O. (eds) (1974) *The Poor Law Report of 1834*. Harmondsworth: Penguin.
Colquhoun, P. (1806) *A Treatise on Indigence*. London: J. Mawman.
Corrigan, P. and Sayer, D. (1985) *The Great Arch: English State Formation as Cultural Revolution*. Oxford: Basil Blackwell.
Cruikshank, B. (1993) 'Revolutions within: self-government and self-esteem', *Economy and Society* 22 (3): 327–44.

Cruikshank, B. (1994) 'The will to empower: technologies of citizenship and the war on poverty', *Socialist Review* 23 (4): 29–55.

Cruikshank, B. (1998) 'Moral entitlement: personal autonomy and political reproduction', in S. Hänninen (ed.), *The Displacement of Social Policies*. Jväskylä: SoPhi, pp. 145–72.

Cruikshank, B. (1999) *The Will to Empower: Democratic Citizens and other Subjects*. Ithaca, NY: Cornell University Press.

Dean, M. (1991) *The Constitution of Poverty: Toward a Genealogy of Liberal Governance*. London: Routledge.

Dean, M. (1992) 'A genealogy of the government of poverty', *Economy and Society* 21 (3): 215–51.

Dean, M. (1994a) *Critical and Effective Histories: Foucault's Methods and Historical Sociology*. London: Routledge.

Dean, M. (1994b) 'The genealogy of the gift in Antiquity', *Australian Journal of Anthropology* 5 (3): 320–9.

Dean, M. (1994c) '"A social structure of many souls": moral regulation, government and self–formation', *Canadian Journal of Sociology* 19 (2): 145–68.

Dean, M. (1995) 'Governing the unemployed self in an active society', *Economy and Society* 24 (4): 559–83.

Dean, M. (1996a) 'Foucault, government and the enfolding of authority', in A. Barry, T. Osborne and N. Rose (eds), *Foucault and Political Reason: Liberalism, Neo-Liberalism and Rationalities of Government*. London: UCL Press, pp. 209–29.

Dean, M. (1996b) 'Putting the technological into government', *History of the Human Sciences* 9 (3): 47–68.

Dean, M. (1997) 'Sociology after society', in D. Owen (ed.), *Sociology after Postmodernism*. London: Sage, pp. 205–28.

Dean, M. (1998a) 'Administering asceticism: re–working the ethical life of the unemployed citizen', in M. Dean and B. Hindess (eds), *Governing Australia: Studies in Contemporary Rationalities of Government*. Melbourne: Cambridge University Press, pp. 87–107.

Dean, M. (1998b) 'Questions of method', in R. Williams and I. Velody (eds), *The Politics of Constructionism*. London: Sage, pp. 182–99.

Dean, M. (1999) 'Normalizing democracy: Foucault and Habermas on law, liberalism and democracy', in S. Ashenden and D. Owen (eds), *Foucault contra Habermas*. London: Sage.

Dean, M. and Hindess, B. (eds) (1998) *Governing Australia: Studies in Contemporary Rationalities of Government*. Melbourne: Cambridge University Press.

Defert, Daniel (1991) '"Popular life" and insurantial technology', in G. Burchell, C. Gordon and P. Miller (eds), *The Foucault Effect: Studies in Governmentality*. London: Harvester Wheatsheaf, pp. 211–33.

Deleuze, G. (1979) 'Foreword: the rise of the social', to J. Donzelot, *The Policing of Families*. New York: Pantheon, pp. ix–xvii.

Deleuze, G. (1988) *Foucault*. Minneapolis: University of Minnesota Press.

Deleuze, G. (1991) 'What is a dispositif?', in T. J. Armstrong (ed.), *Michel Foucault: Philosopher*. New York: Harvester Wheatsheaf, pp. 159–68.

Deleuze, G. and Guattari, F. (1981) 'Rhizome', *Ideology and Consciousness* 6: 49–71.

Dicey, A. V. (1914) *Lectures on the Relation between Law and Public Opinion in England during the Nineteenth Century*, 2nd edn. London: Macmillan.

Dillon, M. (1995) 'Sovereignty and governmentality: from the problematics of the "New World Order" to the ethical problematic of the world order", *Alternatives* 20: 323–68.

Donzelot, J. (1979) *The Policing of Families*. New York: Pantheon.

Donzelot, J. (1984) *L'Invention du social*. Paris: Fayard.

Donzelot, J. (1988) 'The promotion of the social', *Economy and Society* 17 (3): 395–427.

Donzelot, J. (1991) 'The mobilisation of society', in G. Burchell, C. Gordon and P. Miller (eds), *The Foucault Effect: Studies in Governmentality*. London: Harvester Wheatsheaf, pp. 169–79.

Durkheim, E. (1992) *Professional Ethics and Civic Morals*. London: Routledge.

Ehrenreich, B. and English, D. (1979) *For Her Own Good: 150 Years of the Experts' Advice to Women*. London: Pluto Press.

Elias, N. (1978) *The Civilizing Process*, vol. 1. *The History of Manners*. New York: Urizen.

Elias, N. (1982) *The Civilizing Process*, vol. 2. *State Formation and Civilization*. Oxford: Basil Blackwell.

Elias, N. (1983) *The Court Society*. Oxford: Basil Blackwell.

Etzioni, A. (1995) *The Spirit of Community: Rights, Responsibilities and the Communitarian Agenda*. London: Fontana Press.

Etzioni, A. (1996) *The New Golden Rule: Community and Morality in a Democratic Society*. New York: Basic Books.

Ewald, F. (1986) *L'Etat–Providence*. Paris: Grasset.

Ewald, F. (1990) 'Norms, discipline and the law', *Representations* 30: 138–61.

Ewald, F. (1991) 'Insurance and risk', in G. Burchell, C. Gordon and P. Miller (eds), *The Foucault Effect: Studies in Governmentality*. London: Harvester Wheatsheaf, pp. 197–210.

Foucault, M. (1970) *The Order of Things: an Archaeology of the Human Sciences*. London: Tavistock.

Foucault, M. (1977) *Discipline and Punish: the Birth of the Prison*. London: Allen Lane.

Foucault, M. (1979) *The History of Sexuality*, vol. 1. *An Introduction*. London: Allen Lane.

Foucault, M. (1980) *Power/Knowledge: Selected Interviews and Other Writings 1972–1977* (ed. C. Gordon). Brighton: Harvester.

Foucault, M. (1981) 'Omnes et singulatim: towards a criticism of "political reason"', in S. McMurrin (ed.), *The Tanner Lectures on Human Values*, vol. 2. Salt Lake City: University of Utah Press, pp. 223–54.

Foucault, M. (1982) 'The subject and power', in H. Dreyfus and P. Rabinow (eds), *Michel Foucault: Beyond Structuralism and Hermeneutics*. Brighton: Harvester, pp. 208–26.

Foucault, M. (1985) *The Use of Pleasure*. New York: Pantheon.

Foucault, M. (1986a) *The Care of the Self*. New York: Pantheon.

Foucault, M. (1986b) *The Foucault Reader* (ed. P. Rabinow). Harmondsworth: Penguin.

Foucault, M. (1988a) 'The ethic of the care of the self as a practice of freedom', in J. Bernauer and D. Rasmussen (eds), *The Final Foucault*. Cambridge, MA: MIT Press, pp. 1–20.

Foucault, M. (1988b) 'The political technology of individuals', in L.H. Martin, H. Gutman and P.H. Hutton (eds), *Technologies of the Self: a Seminar with Michel Foucault*. London: Tavistock, pp. 145–62.

Foucault, M. (1988c) 'Politics and reason', in *Politics, Philosophy, Culture: Interviews and Other Writings 1977–1984* (ed. L.D. Kritzman). Routledge: New York, pp. 57–85.

Foucault, M. (1988d) 'Practising criticism', in *Politics, Philosophy, Culture: Interviews and Other Writings 1977–1984* (ed. L.D. Kritzman). Routledge: New York, pp. 152–6.

Foucault, M. (1988e) 'Technologies of the self', in L.H. Martin, H. Gutman and P.H. Hutton (eds), *Technologies of the Self: a Seminar with Michel Foucault*. London: Tavistock, pp. 16–49.

Foucault, M. (1989a) *Foucault Live* (ed. S. Lotringer). New York: Semiotext(e).

Foucault, M. (1989b) *Resumé des cours 1970–1982*. Paris: Juilliard.

Foucault, M. (1991a) 'Governmentality', in G. Burchell, C. Gordon and P. Miller (eds), *The Foucault Effect: Studies in Governmentality*. London: Harvester Wheatsheaf, pp. 87–104.

Foucault, M. (1991b) 'Questions of method', in G. Burchell, C. Gordon and P. Miller (eds), *The Foucault Effect: Studies in Governmentality*. London: Harvester Wheatsheaf, pp. 73–86.

Foucault, M. (1993) 'About the beginnings of the hermeneutics of the self', *Political Theory* 21 (2): 198–227.

Foucault, M. (1994) 'Critical theory/intellectual history', in M. Kelly (ed.), *Critique and Power: Recasting the Foucault/Habermas Debate*. Cambridge, MA: MIT Press, pp. 109–38.

Foucault, M. (1996) 'What is critique?', in J. Schmidt (ed.), *What is Enlightenment? Eighteenth-Century Answers and Twentieth-Century Questions*. Berkeley, CA: University of California Press, pp. 382–98.

Foucault, M. (1997a) *The Essential Works 1954–1984*, vol. 1. *Ethics, Subjectivity and Truth* (ed. Paul Rabinow). New York: The New Press.

Foucault, M. (1997b) *'Il faut défendre la société'*. Paris: Gallimard/Seuil.

Fraser, N. and Gordon, L. (1994) 'A genealogy of dependency: tracing a keyword of the US welfare state', *Signs* 19 (2): 309–36.

Furniss, E.S. (1957) *The Position of the Laborer in a System of Nationalism: a Study of the Labor Theories of the Late English Mercantilists*. New York: Kelley and Millman.

Gane, M. and Johnson, T. (1993) 'Introduction', in *Foucault's New Domains*. London: Routledge.

Giddens, A. (1985) *The Nation-State and Violence*. Cambridge: Polity Press.

Giddens, A. (1991) *Modernity and Self-Identity*. Cambridge: Polity Press.

Glass, D.V. (1973) *Numbering the People: the Eighteenth-Century Population Controversy and the Development of Census and Vital Statistics in Britain*. Farnborough: D.C. Heath.

Gordon, C. (1980) 'Afterword', to M. Foucault, *Power/Knowledge*. Brighton: Harvester, pp. 229–59.

Gordon, C. (1986) 'Question, ethos, event', *Economy and Society* 15 (1): 73–87.

Gordon, C. (1991) 'Introduction', in G. Burchell, C. Gordon and P. Miller (eds), *The Foucault Effect: Studies in Governmentality*. London: Harvester Wheatsheaf, pp. 1–51.

Gough, I. (1979) *The Political Economy of the Welfare State*. London: Macmillan.

Gupta, A. (1998) *Postcolonial Developments: Agriculture in the Making of Modern India*. Durham, NC: Duke University Press.

Habermas, J. (1987) *The Theory of Communicative Action*, vol. 2. *Lifeworld and System: a Critique of Functionalist Reason*. Boston: Beacon Press.

Hacking, I. (1982) 'Biopower and the avalanche of printed numbers', *Humanities in Society* 5: 279–95.

Hacking, I. (1986) *The Taming of Chance*. Cambridge: Cambridge University Press.

Hacking, I. (1991) 'How should we do a history of statistics?', in G. Burchell, C. Gordon and P. Miller (eds), *The Foucault Effect: Studies in Governmentality*. London: Harvester Wheatsheaf, pp. 181–5.

Hacking, I. (1994) 'Memoro-politics, trauma and the soul', *History of the Human Sciences* 7 (2): 29–52.

Hadot, P. (1995) *Philosophy as a Way of Life*. Oxford: Basil Blackwell.

Hale, M. (1683) *A Discourse Touching Provision for the Poor*. London: William Shrowsbery.

Halévy, E. (1928) *The Growth of Philosophic Radicalism*. London: Faber.

Hänninen, S. (ed.) (1998) *The Displacement of Social Policies*. Jväskylä: SoPhi.

Hänninen, S. and Karjalainen, J. (eds) (1997) *Biovallan Kysymyksiä: Kirjoituksia Köyhyyden ja Sosiaalisten uhkien Hallinnoimisesta (Questions of Biopower: Governing Poverty and Social Risks)*. Helsinki: Gaudeamus.

Harrington, M. (1963) *The Other America: Poverty in the United States* New York: Penguin.

Hayek, F.A. (1976) *Law, Legislation and Liberty*, vol. 2. *The Mirage of Social Justice.* London: Routledge and Kegan Paul.

Hayek, F.A. (1979) *Law, Legislation and Liberty*, vol. 3. *The Political Order of a Free People.* London: Routledge and Kegan Paul.

Heelas, P. and Morris, P. (eds) (1992) *The Values of the Enterprise Culture: the Moral Debate.* London: Routledge.

Hennis, W. (1988) *Max Weber: Essays in Reconstruction.* London: Allen and Unwin.

Hill, L. (1996) 'Anticipations of nineteenth and twentieth century social thought in the work of Adam Ferguson', *Archives of European Sociology* 37 (1): 203–88.

Hindess, B. (1987) *Freedom, Equality and the Market.* London: Tavistock.

Hindess, B. (1993) 'Liberalism, socialism and democracy: variations on a governmental theme', *Economy and Society* 22 (3): 300–13.

Hindess, B. (1996) *Discourses of Power: from Hobbes to Foucault.* Oxford: Blackwell.

Hindess, B. (1997) 'Politics and governmentality', *Economy and Society* 26 (2): 257–72.

Hindess, B. (1998a) '"Divide and rule": the international character of modern citizenship', *European Journal of Social Theory* 1 (1): 57–70.

Hindess, B. (1998b) 'Neo-liberalism and the national economy', in M. Dean and B. Hindess (eds), *Governing Australia: Studies in Contemporary Rationalities of Government.* Melbourne: Cambridge University Press, pp. 210–26.

Hirst, P. (1981) 'The genesis of the social', *Politics and Power* 3: 67–82.

Hirst, P. (1993) *Associative Democracy; New Forms of Economic and Social Governance.* Cambridge: Polity Press.

Hobbes, T. (1983) *De Cive: the English Version.* Oxford: Clarendon.

Hopwood, A. and Miller, P. (eds) (1994) *Accounting as Social and Institutional Practice.* Cambridge: Cambridge University Press.

Hume, L.J. (1981) *Bentham and Bureaucracy.* Cambridge: Cambridge University Press.

Hunt, A. and Wickham, G. (1994) *Foucault and Law: Towards a Sociology of Law as Governance.* London: Pluto Press.

Hunter, I. (1988) *Culture and Government.* London: Macmillan.

Hunter, I. (1994) *Rethinking the School: Subjectivity, Bureaucracy, Criticism.* Sydney: Allen and Unwin.

Hunter, I. (1998) 'Uncivil society: liberal government and the deconfessionalisation of politics', in M. Dean and B. Hindess (eds), *Governing Australia: Studies in Contemporary Rationalities of Government.* Melbourne: Cambridge University Press, pp. 242–64.

Illich, I., Zola, I.K., McKnight, J., Caplan, J. and Shaiken, H. (1977) *Disabling Professions.* London : Marion Boyars.

Kelly, M. (ed.) (1994) *Critique and Power: Recasting the Foucault/Habermas Debate.* Cambridge, MA: MIT Press.

Knemeyer, F.-L. (1980) 'Polizei', *Economy and Society* 9 (2): 172–96.

Kosellek, R. (1989) *Critique and Crisis: Enlightenment and the Pathogenesis of Modern Society.* Oxford: Berg.

Krinks, K. (1998) 'Government as a practice of freedom'. PhD dissertation, Australian National University.

Larner, W. (1998) 'Post-welfare-state governance: the code of social and family responsibility', in M. Alexander, S. Harding, P. Harrison, G. Kendall, Z. Skrbis and J. Western (eds), *Refashioning Sociology: Responses to a New World Order*, The Australian Sociological Association Conference Proceedings. Brisbane: Queensland University of Technology, pp. 293–98.

Latour, B. (1986a) 'The powers of association', in J. Law (ed.), *Power, Action and Belief: a New Sociology of Knowledge?* London: Routledge and Kegan Paul, pp. 264–80.

Latour, B. (1986b) 'Visualisation and cognition: thinking with eyes and hands', *Knowledge and Society* 6: 1–40.

Lui-Bright, R. (1997) 'International/national: sovereignty, governmentality and international relations', *Australasian Political Studies* 2: 581–97.

McCarthy, T. (1994) 'The critique of impure reason: Foucault and the Frankfurt School', in M. Kelly (ed.), *Critique and Power: Recasting the Foucault/Habermas Debate*. Cambridge, MA: MIT Press, pp. 243–82.

Macey, D. (1993) *The Lives of Michel Foucault*. London: Hutchinson.

Maffesoli, M. (1990) 'Post-modern sociality', *Telos* 85: 89–92.

Maffesoli, M. (1991) 'The ethics of aesthetics', *Theory, Culture and Society* 8: 7–20.

Mann, M. (1988) *States, War and Capitalism*. Oxford: Basil Blackwell.

Marshall, T.H. (1963) 'Citizenship and social class', in *Sociology at the Crossroads and Other Essays*. London: Heinemann, pp. 67–127.

Mauss, M. (1978) *Sociology and Psychology*. London: Routledge and Kegan Paul.

Mead, L. (ed.) (1997) *The New Paternalism: Supervisory Approaches to Poverty*. Washington, DC: Brookings Institution Press.

Meuret, D. (1988) 'A political genealogy of political economy', *Economy and Society* 17 (2): 225–50.

Miller, P. (1992) 'Accounting and objectivity: the invention of calculating selves and calculable spaces', *Annals of Scholarship* 9 (1/2): 61–86.

Miller, P. and O'Leary, T. (1993) 'Accounting expertise and the politics of the product: economic citizenship and modes of corporate governance', *Accounting, Organisations and Society* 18 (2/3): 187–206.

Miller, P. and Rose, N. (1990) 'Governing economic life', *Economy and Society* 19 (1): 1–31.

Minson, J. (1985) *Genealogies of Morals: Nietzsche, Foucault, Donzelot and the Eccentricity of Ethics*, London: Macmillan.

Minson, J. (1993) *Questions of Conduct: Sexual Harassment, Citizenship and Government*. London: Macmillan.

Nelson, S. (1996) 'Care of the sick: nursing, holism and pious practice'. PhD dissertation, Griffith University.

OECD (1988) *The Future of Social Protection*. OECD Social Policy Studies no. 6. Paris: Organization for Economic Co-operation and Development

Oestreich, G. (1982) *Neostoicism and the Early Modern State*. Cambridge: Cambridge University Press.

O'Farrell, C. (ed.) (1997) *Foucault the Legacy*. Brisbane: Queensland University of Technology.

O'Malley, P. (1992) 'Risk, power and crime prevention', *Economy and Society* 21(2): 252–75.

O'Malley, P. (1996) 'Risk and responsibility', in A. Barry, T. Osborne and N. Rose (eds), *Foucault and Political Reason: Liberalism, neo-Liberalism and Rationalities of Government*. London: UCL Press, pp. 189–207.

O'Malley, P. (1998) 'Indigenous governance', in M. Dean and B. Hindess (eds), *Governing Australia: Studies in Contemporary Rationalities of Government*. Melbourne: Cambridge University Press, pp. 156–72.

O'Malley, P., Weir, L. and Shearing, C. (1997) 'Governmentality, criticism, politics', *Economy and Society* 26 (4): 501–17.

Osborne, D. and Gaebler, T. (1993) *Reinventing Government: How the Entrepreneurial Spirit Is Transforming the Public Sector*. New York: Plume Books.

Osborne, T. (1993) 'On liberalism, neo-liberalism and the "liberal profession" of medicine', *Economy and Society* 22 (3): 345–56.

Owen, D. (1995) 'Genealogy as exemplary critique', *Economy and Society* 24 (4): 489–506.

Owen, D. (1996) 'Foucault, Habermas and the claims of reason', *History of the Human Sciences* 9 (2): 119–38.

Owen, D. (1999) 'Orientation and enlightenment: an essay on critique and genealogy', in S. Ashenden and D. Owen (eds), *Foucault contra Habermas*. London:
Sage.

Pasquino, P. (1978) *'Theatricum politicum*. The genealogy of capital: police and the
state of prosperity', *Ideology and Consciousness* 4: 41–54.

Pasquino, P. (1980) 'Criminology: the birth of a special *savoir*', *Ideology and
Consciousness* 7: 17–32.

Pasquino, P. (1993) 'The political theory of war and peace: Foucault and the history
of modern political theory', *Economy and Society* 22 (1): 77–88.

Patton, P. (1998) 'Foucault's subject of power', in J. Moss (ed.), *The Later Foucault*.
London: Sage, pp. 64–77.

Pearce, F. and Tombs, S. (1996) 'Hegemony, risk and governance: "social regulation"
and the American chemical industry', *Economy and Society* 25 (3): 428–54.

Peters, M. (1995) '"After Auschwitz": ethics and educational policy', *Discourse* 16 (2):
237–51.

Peukert, D. (1989) *Inside Nazi Germany*. Harmondsworth: Penguin.

Peukert, D. (1993) 'The genesis of the "Final Solution" from the spirit of science', in
T. Childers and J. Caplan (eds), *Reevaluating the Third Reich*. New York: Holmes
and Meier, pp. 234–52.

Philpott, S. (1997) 'Knowing Indonesia: orientalism and the discourse of Indonesian
politics'. PhD dissertation, Australian National University.

Poggi, G. (1978) *The Development of the Modern State*. London: Hutchinson.

Polanyi, K. (1957) *The Great Transformation*. Boston: Beacon Press.

Power, M. (1994) 'The audit society', in A. Hopwood and P. Miller (eds), *Accounting
as Social and Institutional Practice*. Cambridge: Cambridge University Press, pp.
219–316.

Procacci, G. (1978) 'Social economy and the government of poverty', *Ideology and
Consciousness* 4: 55–72.

Procacci, G. (1993) *Gouverner la misère: la question sociale en France (1789–1848)*.
Paris: Seuil.

Procacci, G. (1998) 'Poor citizens: social citizenship and the crisis of the welfare
state', in S. Hänninen (ed.), *The Displacement of Social Policies*. Jväskylä: SoPhi,
pp. 7–30.

Putnam, Robert D. (1996) 'The strange disappearance of civic America', *American
Prospect* 24: 34–48.

Rabinow, P. (1989) *French Modern: Norms and Forms of the Social Environment*.
Cambridge, MA: MIT Press.

Radzinowicz, L. (1956) *A History of English Criminal Law and its Administration
from 1750*, vol. 3. *The Reform of the Police*. London: Steven and Sons.

Rejali, D. (1994) *Torture and Modernity: Self, Society and State in Modern Iran*.
Boulder, CO: Westview Press.

Rose, N. (1985) *The Psychological Complex: Politics, Psychology and Society in
England 1869–1939*. London: Routledge and Kegan Paul.

Rose, N. (1989) *Governing the Soul: the Shaping of the Private Self*. London:
Routledge.

Rose, N. (1992) 'Governing the enterprising self', in P. Heelas and P. Morris (eds), *The
Values of the Enterprise Culture: the Moral Debate*. London: Routledge, pp.
141–64.

Rose, N. (1993) 'Government, authority and expertise in advanced liberalism',
Economy and Society 22 (3): 283–99.

Rose, N. (1995) 'Authority and the genealogy of subjectivity', in P. Heelas, P. Morris
and S. Lash (eds), *De-Traditionalization: Authority and Self in an Age of Cultural
Uncertainty*. Oxford: Basil Blackwell, pp. 294–327.

Rose, N. (1996a) 'The death of the social? Re-figuring the territory of government',
Economy and Society 25 (3): 327–56.

Rose, N. (1996b) 'Governing "advanced" liberal democracies', in A. Barry, T. Osborne and N. Rose (eds), *Foucault and Political Reason: Liberalism, Neo-Liberalism and Rationalities of Government*. London: UCL Press, pp. 37–64.

Rose, N. (1996c) *Inventing Our Selves: Psychology, Power and Personhood*. Cambridge: Cambridge University Press.

Rose, N. (1998) 'The crisis of welfare states', in S. Hänninen (ed.), *The Displacement of Social Policies*. Jväskylä: SoPhi, pp. 54–87.

Rose, N. (1999) *Powers of Liberty*. Cambridge: Cambridge University Press.

Rose, N. and Miller, P. (1992) 'Political power beyond the state: problematics of government', *British Journal of Sociology* 43 (2): 173–205.

Sigley, G. (1996) '"Governing Chinese bodies": the significance of studies in the concept of governmentality for the analysis of government in China', *Economy and Society* 25 (4): 457–82.

Skinner, Q. (1978) *The Foundations of Modern Political Thought*, 2 vols. Cambridge: Cambridge University Press.

Skinner, Q. (1988) 'A reply to my critics', in *Meaning and Context: Quentin Skinner and his Critics*. Oxford: Polity Press, pp. 231–88.

Skinner, Q. (1989) 'The state', in T. Ball, J. Farr and R.L. Hanson (eds), *Political Innovation and Conceptual Change*. Cambridge: Cambridge University Press, pp. 90–131.

Skinner, Q. (1998) *Liberty before Liberalism*. Cambridge: Cambridge University Press.

Skocpol, T. (1979) *States and Social Revolutions: a Comparative Study of France, Russia and China*. Cambridge: Cambridge University Press.

Small, A.W. (1909) *The Cameralists*. Chicago: University of Chicago Press.

Smith, A. (1956) *Lectures on Justice, Police, Revenue and Arms* (ed. E. Cannan). New York: Kelley and Millan. Reprint of 1896 edn.

Smith, A. (1976) *An Inquiry into the Nature and Causes of the Wealth of Nations*, 2 vols (eds R.H. Campbell and A.S. Skinner). London: Oxford University Press.

Smith, A. (1998) 'Bad habits or bad conscience? Sexual harassment in the Australian Defence Force', in M. Dean and B. Hindess (eds), *Governing Australia: Studies in Contemporary Rationalities of Government*. Melbourne: Cambridge University Press, pp. 70–86.

Stenson, K. (1993) 'Community policing as governmental technology', *Economy and Society* 22 (3): 373–89.

Stenson, K. (1998) 'Beyond histories of the present', *Economy and Society* 27 (4): 333–52.

Steuart, Sir J. (1966) *An Inquiry into the Principles of Political Œconomy (1767)*, 2 vols (ed. A.S. Skinner). Edinburgh: Oliver and Boyd.

Stoler, A.L. (1995) *Race and the Education of Desire*. Durham, NC: Duke University Press.

Thatcher, M. (1985) 'Facing the new challenge', in C. Ungerson (ed.), *Women and Social Policy*. London: Macmillan, pp. 213–17.

Thatcher, M. (1987) 'Interview', *Women's Own*, October: 8–10.

Thatcher, M. (1993) *The Downing Street Years*. London: HarperCollins.

Tilly, C. (ed.) (1975) *The Formation of National States in Western Europe*. Princeton, NJ: Princeton University Press.

Tribe, K. (1978) *Land, Labour and Economic Discourse*. London: Routledge and Kegan Paul.

Tribe, K. (1981) *Genealogies of Capitalism*. London: Macmillan.

Tribe, K. (1987) *Governing Economy: the Reformation of German Economic Discourse, 1750–1840*. Cambridge: Cambridge University Press.

Tribe, K. (1995) *Strategies of Economic Order: German Economic Discourse 1750–1950*. Cambridge: Cambridge University Press.

Tully, J. (1988) 'The pen is a mighty sword', in J. Tully (ed.), *Meaning and Context: Quentin Skinner and his Critics*. Cambridge: Polity Press, pp. 7–25.

Tully, J. (1993) 'Governing conduct', in *An Approach to Political Philosophy: Locke in Contexts*. Cambridge: Cambridge University Press.

Tully, J. (1995) *Strange Multiplicity: Constitutionalism in an Age of Diversity*. Cambridge: Cambridge University Press.

Valverde, M. (1996) '"Despotism" and ethical governance', *Economy and Society* 25 (3): 357–72.

Valverde, M. (1998a) *Diseases of the Will: Alcohol and the Dilemmas of Freedom*. Melbourne: Cambridge University Press.

Valverde, M. (1998b) 'Governing out of habit', *Studies in Law, Politics and Society* 18: 217–42.

Veyne, P. (1982) 'The inventory of differences', *Economy and Society* 11 (2): 173–98

Veyne, P. (1987) 'The Roman Empire', in P. Veyne (ed.), *A History of Private Life,* vol. 1. *From Pagan Rome to Byzantium*. Cambridge, MA: Belknap Press, pp. 5–234.

Veyne, P. (1990) *Bread and Circuses: Historical Sociology and Political Pluralism*. London: Allen Lane.

Veyne, P. (1992) 'Foucault and going beyond (or the fulfilment of) nihilism', in T.J. Armstrong (ed.), *Michel Foucault: Philosopher*. New York: Harvester Wheatsheaf, pp. 340–3.

Veyne, P. (1997) 'Foucault revolutionizes history', in A. I. Davidson (ed.), *Foucault and his Interlocutors*. Chicago: University of Chicago Press, pp. 146–82.

Weber, M. (1927) *General Economic History*. London: Allen and Unwin.

Weber, M. (1948) *The Methodology of the Social Sciences* (ed. and trans. E.A. Shils and H.A. Finch). New York: Free Press.

Weber, M. (1968) *Economy and Society: an Outline of Interpretive Sociology*, 3 vols (eds G. Roth and C. Wittich). New York: Bedminster Press.

Weber, M. (1972) *From Max Weber: Essays in Sociology* (ed. and trans. H.H. Gerth and C.W. Mills). London: Routledge and Kegan Paul.

Weber, M. (1985) *The Protestant Ethic and the Spirit of Capitalism*. London: Unwin.

Weir, Lorna (1996) 'Recent developments in the government of pregnancy', *Economy and Society* 25 (3): 372–92.

Wilson, E. (1977) *Women and the Welfare State*. London: Tavistock.

Wynne, Brian (1996) 'May the sheep safely graze? A reflexive view of the expert–lay knowledge divide', in S. Lash, B. Szersznski and B. Wynne (eds), *Risk Environment and Modernity: Towards a New Ecology*. Sage: London, pp. 44–83.

Yeatman, Anna (1994) *Postmodern Revisionings of the Political*. New York: Routledge.

Yeatman, Anna (1998) 'Interpreting contemporary contractualism', in M. Dean and B. Hindess (eds), *Governing Australia: Studies in Contemporary Rationalities of Government*. Melbourne: Cambridge University Press, pp. 227–41.

Young of Graffam, Lord (1992) 'Enterprise regained', in P. Heelas and P. Morris (eds), *The Values of the Enterprise Culture: the Moral Debate*. London: Routledge, pp. 29–35.

INDEX

Adenauer, Konrad, 56
Adorno, Theodor, 42, 46, 182
advanced liberal government, 164–74; and auditing and accounting, 169; and consumers, 169–70; and contemporary pluralism, 170–1; defined, 149–50; origins of term, 174n; and performance government, 173; and practices of liberty, 165–6; regulation of professionals, 169–70; and risk, 166–7; and social, 173; and technologies of government, 167–70, 173; and victims, 170–1; *see also* neo-liberalism
agape, 79
Aid to Families with Dependent Children (ADFC), 61, 63
American Federalists, 118, 121
analytics of government, 20–27; and criticism, 36–8; ethos of, 34–8, four dimensions of analysis, 30–3; and global or radical positions, 34–36; and 'how' questions, 28–9; how to do, 27–38; and problematizations, 27–8; and regimes of government, 29–30; role of values in, 34; and study of politics, 98–9; *see also* genealogy
Annales School, 16; on *longue durée*, 74
anti-Machiavellian literature, 85, 104, 106
Arendt, Hannah, 15, 148n
Aristotle, 201
Ashenden, Samantha, 3, 6, 176, 195
Aut...aut (journal), 8n
authoritarian governmentality, 131–48, 148n; compared to police, 147–8; general meaning, 131; and National Socialism, 145; within liberal government, 131–8, 146–7; *see also* bio-politics

Bachrach, Peter, and Baratz, Morton S., 68
Ballard, John, 169
Barry, Andrew, 3, 4, 41, 51
Bartos, Michael, 169

Baudrillard, Jean, 152
Bauman, Zygmunt, 148n
Beck, Ulrich, 6, 166, 177, 178–83, 197n; on sub-politics, 181, 192
Becker, Gary S., 57
Bell, Daniel, 43, 155
Bell, Vikki, 3
Bentham, Jeremy, 116–7, 134–5, 136–7, 147, 157, 174n
Berger, Peter, and Luckmann, Thomas, 197n
Beveridge, William, 135–6
bio-politics, 20, 94, 98–102, 202; and Chinese one-child policy, 144–5; and classical political economy, 115; dark side of, 139; defined, 98, 99; and Foucault's work, 111–12n; and genocide, 132, 139–40; international, 99–100; and liberalism, 99, 101, 113; and National Socialism, 140–2, 145; and population, 107–8; and power over life, 139–40; and race and racism, 100, 140–5; and right of death, 139; and social, 112n; and society, 101; and sovereignty, 100–1, 109, 145, 147; and state socialism, 144; and torture, 139
Blackstone, William, 89
Bodin, Jean, 202
Bolingbroke, Lord, 198, 202, 208n
Bolshevism, 148
Booth, Charles, 135–6
Botero, Giovanni, 84, 86
Bourdieu, Pierre, 78
Bourgeois, Léon, 187
Braidotti, Rosi, 8n
Braudel, Fernand, 74
Bread and Circuses, 77
Brown, Peter, 5, 38n, 76, 78–9, 80
Budé, Guillaume, 87
Burchell, David, 45, 172
Burchell, Graham, 1, 3, 4, 8n, 49, 124, 155
Burke, Peter, 16

Callon, Michel, 168

cameralism, 92–3
Cassian, John, 45
Cassirer, Ernst, 41
Castel, Robert, 3, 174, 189, 193
Catherine the Great (Catherine II, Empress of Russia), 89, 91
Chadwick, Edwin, 126, 136
Chernobyl, 183
Chicago School of Economics, 57–8, 158–9
Child, Josiah, 94
China, one-child policy, 144–5
Chirac, President Jacques, 87
Chrysostom, St. John, 80
citizenship, active, 161, 167; in Antiquity, 76–82; social, 126, 147, 186–7, 197, 203–4; technology of, 168, 196; and welfare-state problem, 82–3
city-citizen game, 76–9
civil prudence (*prudentia civilis*), 84–5, 87–8.
Clausewitz, Carl von, 25
Colquhoun, Patrick, 126
Commentaries on the Laws of England, 89
communitarianism, 152, 174n
community, 68; alien (*Gemeinschaftsfremde*), 143; and Antiquity, 76, 81–2; Christian, 79–80; and contemporary pluralism, 170–1, 192; and empowerment, 68–9; and police science, 90; political, 76, 83; and technology of citizenship, 154; and risk, 192
Community Action Programs (USA), 67–72
Congress of Vienna (1815), 106
Contract with America, 33, 162
Corrigan, Philip, 38n
critique and criticism; and analytics of government, 36–8, 69–70; exemplary, 38; of ideology, 63–6; liberalism as, 49–51
Cruikshank, Barbara, 3, 8n, 67–72, 154, 162, 168, 174n, 197n

De Cive, 109
de Lamare, N., 91
Dean, Mitchell, 3, 4, 5, 11, 17, 31, 33, 38n, 44, 45, 47, 159, 173, 182; and eighteenth and nineteenth-century government, 93, 106, 115; on poverty and population, 64, 84, 95, 107, 116, 126, 134, 137, 166; on unemployment in Australia, 160, 168, 189–90, 196,
Defert, Daniel, 129, 186
Deleuze, Gilles, 3, 5, 151
dependency, 60–7; and industrialization, 61–2; language of, 63–5; meaning of, 60–1; and post-industrial society, 62; range of types, 62; welfare, 62–3

Dillon, Michael, 5, 106
Discipline and Punish, 111n
discipline, disciplinary power, 19–20, 25, 88, 92, 96, 102, 109–10, 113, 116, 118, 122, 171; and Hayek's concept of freedom, 155–7; and National Socialism, 141
Donzelot, Jacques, 3, 54, 129, 150, 163, 187; on liberal definition of the state, 127–8
Durkheim, Emile, 16, 38n, 124–5, 163; on solidarity, 187

East Timor, 87
economic government, *see* economy
economy, 16, 17, 19, 45, 49, 52, 54, 59n, 114–5, 127–8, 203–4; Aristole's concept of, 201; and bio-politics, 115, 202; and Chicago School of Economics, 57–8; and classical political economy, 115; and globalization, 194–5; and Keynesian techniques, 150; and liberal interventions, 127–8; and ordoliberals, 56–7, 58; and Physiocrats, 114; and population, 115
Economy and Society (journal), 4
Education of the Prince, The, 87
Ehrenreich, Barbara, 154
Elias, Norbert, 38n, 88, 91, 92
empowerment, 67–72
English, Deirdre, 154
Enlightenment, 42–3, 180, 182; blackmail of, 42; Scottish, 49,124, 155, 159
Erhard, Ludwig, 56
ethics, analysis of, 17; and practices of the self, 12–13
ethos, of analytics of government, 34–38; of genealogy, 41–8; of review in liberalism, 51–52
Etzioni, Amitai, 152, 174–5n
euergesia, 76–8
eugenics, 134, 136–8
European Union, 195
Ewald, François, 3, 110, 119–120, 129, 177, 182, 183–5
expertise, 17, 22, 23, 65–6; and Community Action Programs, 68; and pastoral power, 75–6; regulation of, 169–70; and social questions, 128

Fabian socialism, 134
family, the, and conceptions of government, 93–4, 107–8, 111; and liberal interventions, 127–8
Ferguson, Adam, 49, 124
Final Solution, the,141–2, 143
Foucault Effect, The, 8n

Foucault, Michel, 10, 17, 18, 19, 21, 22, 24, 30, 40, 45, 72n, 88, 89, 129, 131, 164, 198, 202; on anti-Machiavellian literature, 85–7, 97n; on avoidance of global or radical positions, 34–5; on bio-politics, 99–102, 139–41; and concept of society, 110–11; and concepts of economy, 93, 114–5; and concepts of power, 25–6, 35, 46, 47, 111n; and criticism and critique, 36–8, 39n, 47; on cultural critique, 42; and democracy, 120–1; on demonic character of states, 96–7, 132; and dividing practices, 132–4; on dual character of liberal government, 132; and Enlightenment, 37, 42; on freedom and security, 117; and identity, 45; on *laissez-faire*, 117; on law, 110, 118–19; 120–21, 130n; lecture on 'Governmentality', 103–11; lectures, 25, 92, 112n, 117; and liberalism, 51, 54, 58, 101, 111n; and Machiavelli, 85, 104; on National socialism, 141–5; and neo-liberalism, 55–8; and pastoral power, 74–6, 81–2; and political action, 198; and present, 43; and reason of state, 84–6; and sovereignty, 103–6, 109–10, 141; and state rationality, 92; on state socialism, 144; and states of domination, 35; on suicide, 125; on welfare state problem, 82–3

Foucault–Habermas debate, 3

Foundations of Modern Political Thought, The, 97

Frankfurt School, 41, 144, 181–2; and Freiburg School, 56

Franklin, Benjamin, 56, 99

freedom, as artefact, 155–6; and choice and interests, 158–9; and constructivism, 157; and emancipation, 154–5; and free subject in advanced liberalism, 164–5; and free subject and illiberality, 132–3; and government, 13–15; Hayek's concept of, 155–8; and *Homo œconomicus*, 155–6; and ordoliberals, 56–7; responsible and disciplined, 153–9; and security, 116–7; as technical instrument, 155, 205–6

Fraser, Nancy, 61–7, 71

Freiburg School, 56

Furniss, E.S., 94–5

Gaebler, Ted, 28, 68, 163

Galton, Francis, 136–7

Gane, Mike, 2

genealogy, 40–8; as anti-anachronistic, 44–5; and concepts of power, 46–7; of

dependency, 61; as diagnostic, 44; ethical-political orientation of, 43–4; and government, 41–8; and liberalism, 46; and Marxism, 47–8; types of, 41–3; and welfare-state problem, 48, 82, 96

Giddens, Anthony, 38n, 45

gift-giving in Antiquity, 77–9, 80–2

Gingrich, Newt, 33

Glass, D.V., 93

Gordon, Colin, 10, 22, 51, 52, 56, 57, 72, 84, 85, 88, 117, 125; and emergence of the economy, 114–15; and ethos of genealogy, 41–3; and post-war liberalism, 156–9

Gordon, Linda, 61–7, 71

Gough, Ian, 154

government, 10–16; advanced liberal, 164–71; analysing regimes of, 27–38; analytics of, 20–7; as 'conduct of conduct', 2, 10, 198–9; contrasted with sovereignty, 106–7; defined, 10–11; early modern, 93–5; economic, 19, 100; and genealogy, 46–8; householding conception of, 93–6; 199–201; international, 88–9, 99–100, 106; matrices of, 199; as moral, 12–13; and population, 107–8; of processes, 200; and self-government, 12; separation from sovereignty, 103–5; *telos* of, 33; *see also* reflexive government

governmentality, 16–20; defined, 2; feminist studies of, 3; as field of study, 2–3; general meaning of, 16–17; historically specific meaning of, 19–20; influence of studies of, 1, 3–4; relation to sovereignty and discipline, 19–20 *see also* authoritarian governmentality

governmentalization of government, 6, 176, 193–200

governmentalization of the state, 6, 20, 26, 98, 102–11, 194, 195, 200, 203

Great Society, the, 163, 205

Great Transformation, The, 157

Grotius, Hugo, 104

Groupe d'Information de Prisons, 42

Guattari, Felix, 3

Gupta, Akhil, 5

Habermas, Jürgen, 41, 43, 96–7, 182

habitus, 78

Hacking, Ian, 3, 8n

Hadot, Pierre, 17, 38n, 45

Hale, Sir Matthew, 73, 94

Halévy, Elie, 157

Hänninen, Sakari, 3

Harrington, Michael, 68

Hayek, Friedrich von, 15, 41, 155–8, 172; on
    rule of law, 157–8; on sociology, 163
Heelas, Paul, 33, 162
Helliwell, Christine, 112n
Hennis, Wilhelm, 199
Hill, Lisa, 124
Hindess, Barry, 3, 4, 5, 36, 38n, 47, 105, 109,
    112n, 128, 159, 197n, 198; on economic
    globalization, 194; on international
    government, 106; and liberalism, 51; and
    political action, 72n, 117; and theory of
    representation, 121
Hirst, Paul Q., 151, 207
History of Sexuality, The, 107, 118, 139
Hitler, Adolph, 15
HIV/AIDS, 170, 171
Hobbes, Thomas, 104, 109, 202
Hobbesian problem of order, 125
Homo œconomicus, 15, 57, 117, 125
Hopwood, Anthony, 3
Horkheimer, Max, 42, 46, 182
householding conception of government,
    93–6, 199–201 *see also* family
Hume, David, 118
Hume, L.J., 89, 91
Hunt, Alan, 3
Hunter, Ian, 3, 104
Husserl, Edmund, 56

Ideology and Consciousness (journal), 1, 8n
'Il faut défendre la société', 25
Illich, Ivan, 154
Inside Nazi Germany, 143
International Monetary Fund (IMF), 195
insurance, 182–5; social, 185–8

Johnson, Terry, 2
Judaism, ancient, 74, 79
Justi, Johann Heinrich Gottlieb von, 92

Karjalainen, Jouko, 3
Kelly, Michael, 3
Keynesianism, 56, 150, 203–4, 205
King, Gregory, 93
Knemeyer, F.-L., 90, 91, 92
knowledge, 16–17, 18, 31–2; and bio-politics,
    99–100; economy, 114–15; and liberalism,
    51–2; and pastoral power, 75–6; and
    reason of state, 86; of risk, 188–91; of
    society, 127–8, 163 *see also* expertise
Kossellek, Reinhardt, 5
Krinks, Kate, 13

La Perrière, Guillaume de, 6, 73, 85–6, 97n,
    104, 111, 202

Larner, Wendy, 207
Latour, Bruno, 26, 197
law, 118–23; Bentham's theory of ends of
    legislation, 116; and liberalism and
    democracy, 113, 120–3; and norm,
    118–19; and normalizing practices, 120;
    and social, 127–8; and sovereignty and
    discipline, 25–6, 109–110; *see also*
    sovereignty
liberal government, and despotism, 133–4,
    146; distinguished from non-liberal, 147;
    and exclusions from liberal subject, 155;
    and freedom, 15, 155; illiberality of,
    132–8; *see also* liberalism
liberalism, 48–55, 113–30; ambivalence of
    subject of, 165; approach to, 49; as art,
    50–1; as articulation of sovereignty and
    bio-politics, 132, 137–8, 147; and bio-
    politics, 101, 113; and colonialism, 133,
    147; as critique, 50–2; and definition of
    the state, 127; and economy, 114–15; and
    law and democracy, 120–3, 129–30; and
    non-political, 51; and norm, 121–2; and
    reason of state and police, 49–50; and
    rights and liberties, 50; and security,
    116–18; and social government, 113,
    126–30; and society, 123–6; *see also*
    liberal government
Life and Labour of the People of London, 135
Lipsius, Justus, 84, 87, 88
Lui-Bright, Robyn, 5, 99, 105

Macey, David, 42
Machiavelli, Niccolo, 85, 86
Malthus, Thomas, 100, 107, 115, 136–7
Malthusianism, 94–5, 136, 145, 166, 202
Maffesoli, Michel, 32
Mann, Michael, 38n
Marcuse, Herbert, 43
Marshall, Alfred, 137
Marshall, T.H., 126, 186
Marx, Karl, 179
Mauss, Marcel, 16, 38n,
Mead, Lawrence, 207, 208n
mentality, mentalities, 16; utopian aspect of,
    33 *see also* rationality, rationalities
mercantilism, 94–5, 106–7
methodology *see* analytics of government
Meuret, Denis, 45
Mill, John Stuart, 133–4, 208n
Millar, John, 124
Miller, Peter, 3, 169, 190–1,193
Minson, Jeffrey, 3, 92
Mirabeau, Victor de Riquetti, marquis de, 98,
    111n, 114

Miroir politique, 85
modernist social theory, 42–3, 46
modernization, classical, 180; reflexive, 180–1;
    and social compact, 182–3
monetarist arguments, 150
Morel, B.A.,136
Morris, Paul, 33, 162

National Socialism, 138, 140–4, 148n, 203;
    and human sciences, 141–3; and social-
    welfare education, 142–3
National Welfare Rights Organization, 66
Nelson, Sioban, 79
neo-conservatism, 162–3, 174n
neo-liberalism, 150–64, 205–7; and active
    citizenship, 161; and concepts of
    freedom, 155–9; and Conservative
    parties, 160; and critique of welfare state,
    155, 171–2; and cultural reform, 162–3,
    172; distinguished from advanced liberal
    government, 149; and economic
    globalization, 161; and emancipatory
    movements, 155; and enterprise culture,
    161–2; Foucault on, 55–8; and markets,
    157–8, 159–60; naïveté of, 206–7; and
    neo-conservatism, 153, 162–3; and
    society, 151–3; types of, 56–8, 159–64;
    and unemployment in Australia, 160–1;
    see also advanced liberal government
New Deal, 33, 57, 205
New Labour (UK), 64–5
new contractualism, 167–8
new paternalism, 207, 208n
new prudentialism, 166–7, 191
Nietzsche, Friedrich, 42
norms, and eugenics, 136–7; of government,
    100–2, 147; relation to law, 118–19,
    120–3; technical, 119

Oestreich, Gerhard, 5, 38n, 84, 85, 87–8, 90–1
O'Farrell, Clare, 4
O'Leary, Ted, 3
O'Malley, Pat, 3, 39n, 48, 72n, 149, 166, 191
Ontario Antenatal Record, 190
Ordoliberalen, ordoliberals, 15, 59n;
    Foucault's discussion of, 56–7; and
    freedom, 157; market constructivism, 56,
    160–1
Organization for Economic Co-operation and
    Development (OECD), 60
Origins of Totalitarianism, The, 148n
Osborne, David, 28, 68, 163
Osborne, Thomas, 8n
Osse, Melchior von, 90, 92
Other America, The, 68

Owen, David, 3, 39n; on exemplary criticism,
    38

paideia, 78
pastoral power, 74–83; and ancient Greece,
    75; and Christianity, 74–6; and expertise,
    75–6; Hebraic conceptions of, 75;
    relation to poor, 79–81; and shepherd-
    flock game, 75–6, 79–82
Pasquino, Pasquale, 25, 36, 46, 54, 94, 128,
    129, 170
Patton, Paul, 13
Pearce, Frank, and Tombs, Steve, 190
Peters, Michael, 141
Petty, Sir William, 94
Peukert, Detlev, 131, 141–4
philanthropy, and Christian almsgiving,
    79–80; and *euergetism*, 76–9; and liberal
    state, 128; and poor in Antiquity, 79–82
Philosophie rurale, 111n
Philpott, Simon, 5, 148n
Physiocrats, 114
Poggi, Gianfranco, 38n
Polanyi, Karl, 38n, 41, 157
police, 89–96; and cameralism, 92–3;
    evolution of, 91–2; liberal critique of,
    49–50; moral dimension, 91; range of
    ordinances, 90–1; science of
    (*Polizeiwissenschaft*), 90, 92–3; in
    Strasbourg, 90–1
political action, 117–18, 198
Political Arithmetick, 94
political economy, classical, 100, 115
Political Œconomy, 93, 201
Poor Laws, 64, 136
Poor Law Report (1834), 126, 134
population, 202–3; and arts of government,
    107–8; and bio-politics, 99–101, 139–41;
    and Chinese one-child policy, 144–5; and
    concept of society, 124–5; and
    epidemiology, 189; nineteenth-century
    conceptions of, 135–8; targeted, 167–8,
    192
postmodernism, and cultural critique, 42–3,
    46
poverty and pauperism, 126–7
power, concepts of, 46–7; and discourse of
    war, 46; extremist view of, 25; juridical
    conception of, 46
Power, Michael, 21, 169
practices of the self, 12–13, 191; ancient, 45,
    75
present, the, characterization of, 1–2;
    Foucault's attitude towards, 43
Prince, The, 85, 87, 97n

problematizations, 21–2; identification of, 27–8
Procacci, Giovanna, 3, 54, 126, 128, 129, 186
programmes of government, 22, 32, 33, 34; and strategy, 22, 69–70, 72
Pufendorf, Samuel von, 104
punishment, capital, 14–15; contemporary, 170–1
Putnam, Robert D., 152, 174n

Quesnay, François, 114
Quételet, Adolphe, 119

Rabinow, Paul, 3
race, racism, and bio-politics, 100, 140, 145–6; and Darwinian categories of species, 136; degeneration of, 136; and management of risk, 146–7; and National Socialism, 140–4; and population, 136–7
Radzinowicz, Leon, 89
rationality, rationalities, analysis of, 31–2; calculative, 184: different approaches to, 182; meaning, 11; of risk, 189–90
Realpolitik, 89
reason of state, 84–9, 201; central features of, 86; and Christian and juridical traditions, 87–8; and civil prudence, 84, 87; contemporary examples of, 87; liberal critique of, 49–50; relation to police, 88–9
Reason of State, 86–7
reflexive government, 6, 172, 176–7, 179, 193–7, 200; and economic globalization, 194–5; examples, 195; and social, 196–7; and technologies of agency, 195–6; and technologies of performance, 195
Reformation (and Counter-Reformation), 74, 88
regimes of practices, regimes of government, 18–19, 21–23, 26–7; analysis of, 27–38; and fields of visibility, 30–1; and identity formation, 32–3; and rational aspect, 31–2; and technical aspect, 31; and utopian dimension, 33
Rejali, Darius, 14–15, 139–40
Report on the Sanitary Conditions of the Labouring Population (1842), 126
Ricardo, David, 115
risk, 176–97; and agency, 185; approaches to, 177–9; Beck's assumptions about, 181–2; and calculative rationality, 183–4; and dangerousness, 166–7; Ewald's account of, 183–5; and insurance, 183–8; and justice, 185; and new prudentialism,

166–7, 191–2; and racial hygeine, 146; and retraction of social rights, 191; strategies of management of, 146–8, 174, 176, 204; technical dimension of, 184–5; and theory of reflexive modernization, 179–83; types of, 189–91
Risk Society, 180
Roosevelt, Franklin Delano, 33
Rose, Nikolas, 3, 8n, 33, 54, 127, 134, 167, 186, 190–1, 193; and 'advanced liberalism', 174n; on contemporary government at a distance, 169; on death of the social, 178, 193, 197n; on eugenic social policies, 135–7; on liberalism and limits to action of state, 50
Rouseau, Jean-Jacques, 109
Rüstow, Alexander von, 41, 158; and vital policy (*Vitalpolitik*), 56–7, 156

Sayer, Derek, 38n
Schumpeter, Joseph, 41
Second Coming, the, 87
security, 116–18, 205–6; apparatuses of, 20; and Bentham, 116; and economic globalization, 194–5; and *laissez–faire*, 117; and liberty, 116–17, 205; mechanisms of, 52; and neo-liberalism, 172, 196–7; and political action, 117–8
Seneca, 45, 88
shepherd-flock game, 74–6, 79–82; *see also* pastoral power
Sigley, Gary, 144–5
Skinner, Quentin, 5, 38n, 84; and Machiavellian literature, 87, 97n; modern concept of the state, 38n, 103–4, 201–2; on reason of state, 86–7; relation to the present, 97; on sovereignty, 10, 202
Skocpol, Theda, 38n
Small, Albion, 90, 92–3, 94
Smith, Adam 107, 202; and 'invisible hand', 114; lectures of, 89, 91; and system of natural liberty, 15, 155, 202
Smith, Alison, 3
social, 53–5, 126–30, 203–5; and aspirations, 53; and citizenship, 53–4, 126; 'death'of, 152, 192, 196–7; different themes of, 129; as hybrid and artefact, 151; metamorphosis of, 193–8; necessity of, 183; and philanthropy, 127; post-welfarist regime of, 65, 171–4, 193, 207; and problematization, 53; and society, 54, 128; and solidarity, 187–8; and sovereign interventions, 207; *see also* society
Social Contract, The, 109

society, 123–6, 150–3; bypassing, 153, 164–6, 170; civil, 124; as external to government, 101; and knowledge of, 163; and liberal government, 124; and loss of identity, 150; as non-political sphere, 110–11; as problem-space of government, 123–4; and risk, 187, 197; and security, 125; and Thatcher, 151–3; as totality, 124–5; *see also* social

solidarisme, 163, 187

solidarity, sociological account of , 125

Sombart, Werner, 43

sovereignty, 24, 102–11; 201–2; and analysis of power, 25–6; democratization of, 101; functions of, 109; and government, 19–20, 103–6, 203; and law and right, 109–10; meaning of, 104; and National Socialism, 142; relation to discipline and government, 102–3; and right to kill, 139–40; and symbolics of blood, 140–1; transformation of, 108–10

Stanford University, 92

state, the, conventional approaches to, 9; demonic character of, 84, 96–7, 132; racism of, 140–1, 144–5, 148n; and risk strategies, 146–7; theories of, 23–4

state socialism, 138, 144

Stenson, Kevin, 3, 208

Steuart, Sir James, 93, 104

Stoicism, revival of, 84, 85–6, 87–8

Strasbourg, 90–1

strategy, 22, and programmes, 69–70, 72

Stoler, Ann Laura, 140, 144

Suarez, Fransesco, 104

Tableau économique, 114

Tacitus, 88

targeted populations, 142

technologies (of government), 23, 31, 173; of agency, 167–9; 195–6; of citizenship, 67–9, 168; of performance, 168–9, 195

Thatcher, Lady Margaret, 151–3, 162, 163, 172, 174–5n

Theory of Legislation, The, 116

Third Republic (France), 187

Thirty Years War, 89, 110

Tilly, Charles, 38n

torture, 14–15, 139–40

Treaty of Westphalia, 89, 106, 110

Tully, James, 3, 8n, 97n, 104

Tribe, Keith, 5, 45, 59n, 93, 107, 111n, 114, 115

unemployment policies (Australia), 160–1, 175n; and Labor government, 160; under Liberal–National government, 160–1

Valverde, Mariana, 8n, 133–4; on habit, 133

Veyne, Paul, 5, 38n, 76, 77–8, 105

victim, 66, 170–1

vocabulary, of rule, 63–5; of social government, 129

Volk, 142, 148n

war, and bio-politics, 139; language of, 25; religious and civil, 88

War on Poverty, 68, 69

Wealth of Nations, 114–15

Weber, Max, 11, 36–7, 38n, 41, 71, 72n, 83, 179, 181, 198, 199; definition of politically oriented action, 117, 198; definition of the state, 83; influence on ordoliberals, 56; and law, 130n; on serving moral forces, 36–7; and value relevance, 44

Weimar Republic, 142

Weir, Lorna, 3, 52, 128, 190

welfare state, 150–1; and Antiquity, 82–3; critique of, 153–4; and democracy, 121, 129–30; ethos and ideal of, 55; and genealogy, 74; limits to solutions to the crisis of, 192; problems of, 82–3, 96;

welfarism, 54–5, 196

Wickham, Gary, 3

Wilson, Elizabeth, 154

Wittgenstein, Ludwig, 8n

World Bank, 195

Wynne, Brian, 197

Yeatman, Anna, 154, 168, 169

Young, Lord, 162